Civilization in Crisis

Civilization in Crisis
A Christian Response to Homosexuality, Feminism, Euthanasia, and Abortion
Second Edition

Richard A. Fowler
and
H. Wayne House

BAKER BOOK HOUSE

Grand Rapids, Michigan 49516

To
our godly wives . . .
our helpmates on this earth

Contents

Preface   ix

Part 1   Feminism   1

1. The Roots of the Feminist Movement in America   3
2. In the Beginning . . .   9
3. The Woman and the Family   19
4. And the Two Shall Become One   33
5. Confronting the Problem and Its Solution   49

Part 2   Abortion and Euthanasia   57

6. The Respect for Life in a Permissive Society   59
7. The Slaughter of the Innocents   67
8. When Do We Pull the Plug?   101

Part 3   Homosexuality   109

9. Homosexuality: A Contagious Epidemic   111
10. Two Halves Do Not Necessarily Make a Whole   125
11. A Look from the Other Side of the Fence   137

Part 4   A Christian Response   149

12. Putting Your Own House in Order   153
13. Taking a Stand   161
14. Restructuring Priorities at Home   169
15. Restoring Dignity to Human Life   175
16. Reaching Out to the Homosexual   191

Appendixes

1. Structural Development of Genesis 1:26-28   197
2. Ephesians 5:21-33   199
   Selected Bibliography   201
   Scripture Index   203
   Subject Index   207

Preface

America in the 1980s is a civilization in crisis. The rampant immorality in all levels of society can no longer be hidden or denied. The women's movement has left the family unit adrift and unstable. The slaughter of unborn children is so common that our hearts have become calloused to the travesty. And controlling the AIDS epidemic has eluded our most diligent research efforts.

Perhaps even the word *crisis* is too soft to describe the headlong fall toward disaster that seems to await us. Our only hope as a civilization is to somehow reverse this fast-moving trend. *Civilization in Crisis* gives wise and timely advice for those who are seeking Christian answers to these problems.

God has called us not to the status quo, to personal pleasure and affluence, but to confronting this crisis in our society. We cannot accomplish this, however, through our own efforts; the power of the Holy Spirit, working in our lives, is necessary.

In choosing the least-walked path, the mountain trail of moral values and actions, one should recognize that a price must be paid. A Christian who is willing to confront the crisis of his civilization, instead of passively pretending it doesn't exist, becomes a marginal person in his culture, a person on the rim who in many ways no longer fits, especially in a culture that has reverted to pagan thought. And yet, in Scripture this is the position to which God has called us:

> If the world hate you, you know that it hated me before it hated you. If you were of the world, the world would love its own; but because you are not of the world, but I have chosen you out of the world, therefore the world hates you. [John 15:18-19, NASB*]

Also, in 1 Peter the apostle makes it plain that Christians should not consider themselves permanent members of society; they have their citizenship in heaven. Nevertheless, they are to have an impact for the King while they are in this life. This state of nonpermanence (1 Pet. 1:17) is brought to mind by the words of the psalmist, "Lord, . . . let me know how transient I am" (Ps. 39:4). Thus the essence of marginalization is not being unusual, but rather not being too comfortable with this world. Confronting the elements of our culture keeps our perspective in tune with our heavenly home rather than our earthly home.

In analyzing areas of our culture that clearly challenge the Christian value system, three categories emerge. They are:

1. The issue of women in our culture; their status, their roles, and their affect on the emerging family unit.
2. The right to life issue, especially in relation to abortion and mercy killing.
3. The homosexual issue in regard to its cause — hereditary or voluntary — and its short-and long-term affects on our culture.

Not only are the various arguments on each of the above issues presented in the book, but the fourth section is devoted exclusively to the practical aspects of those problems. Strategies, counseling tips, and case studies are presented in each of those areas to aid the Christian in applying the material in a helpful manner. Questions such as, What should the church's position be on those issues? are tackled in this unit.

Yes, we as Christians are called to a life on the margin of culture as we confront those values that oppose the cause of Jesus Christ. This book is intended to help us become more aware of those pertinent areas upon which we *must* take a stand.

* *New American Standard Bible.*

Part One _____

Feminism

In America today, the woman is caught in a quandary. In generations past she was often content (more often expected) to assume the pinnacle role as wife and mother, the heart of the home in every sense. A little girl was encouraged to find fulfillment in emulating her mother; now she is urged to seek her freedom from "domestic slavery."

Indeed, women, regardless of their decision to remain single, marry later, or become wives, are losing their identity with the traditional, established role. Increasingly more appealing is the openness and opportunity for women to be career builders outside the home. In *The Subtle Revolution: Women at Work*, edited by Ralph E. Smith, the authors estimated that of the approximately eleven million women who will probably enter the job market by the end of the 1980s, almost eight million will be married women with children. The stereotype of the wife who stays home to care for children will fit only about one-fourth of all American wives.

On the surface, the American family appears to be adapting to the evolution of the woman's role and seems to have adopted the idea that the wife's earning power is a more important asset than her abilities as a full-time home manager, mother, and wife. That idea, whether born of financial pressure or role awareness, has added earning power and brought radical change to the family's economic structure and expectations. However, it has also brought about an enormous change in domestic relationships and a total restructuring of the traditional American home. Many believe that this phenomenon will dissolve the home as we now know it. That belief carries even more validity as we watch the

1

alarming divorce statistics continue to rise and permeate the church itself.

The intention of this section is to examine the evolution of the feminist role in American life today in view of the changes of the past two hundred years, and to determine the impact of those developments on the Christian life-style. In addition, we desire to consider what biblical principles may be applied to help Christians successfully cope with this onslaught against the family.

1

The Roots of the Feminist Movement in America

Coming out from the shadow of the man in the search of a unique and independent identity has been the goal of many women in American history. The American feminist movement is not simply a present-day phenomenon; its roots can be traced back to the post-Revolutionary War era. Thomas Paine, a spokesman for the Revolution, was one of the first to challenge the position of women in early American society. His assessment was that women "were constrained in their desires, constrained in the disposal of their goods, robbed of freedom and will by laws, and were slaves of opinion."[1] The right to life, liberty, and the pursuit of happiness fought for in the Revolutionary War inspired the same spirit in the cause for women's rights. New Jersey, for example, gave women the right to vote during that time, but revoked the privilege in 1807.

New conditions in the 1830s caused women to unite in an effort to obtain their rights. As early as 1831 Anne Royall, a journalist, published a newspaper in Washington that addressed itself to such issues as the antislavery cause and the right to vote for women.[2] Men who were fighting for temperance reform, education, and the abolition of slavery recognized that they needed the help of women to get their message across to the people of America. In return they gave the women's rights issues help and credence before the public.

Philosophically, the antislavery movement tended to provide impetus for the feminist movement in America. Many parallels existed between

1. Betty Friedan, *The Feminine Mystique* (New York: Dell, 1963), 77.
2. Beverly J. Hawkins, "Women, Work, and the Law: A Legislative Review" (Springfield, Va.: National Technical Information Service, February 1974), 3-8.

the two movements. Both blacks and women, for example, were "under bondage" in a legal and social sense and dependent on the white male for their survival. Thus it was natural and timely for women leaders such as Sarah and Angelina Grimké to denounce not only slavery of the black American, but also the "slavery" of the American woman as well.[3]

The feminist movement reached a peak in 1920 with the ratification of Amendment Nineteen to the Constitution, which gave women the right to vote. That amendment resulted in part from the crusade efforts of such aggressive female reformers as Susan B. Anthony and Elizabeth Cady Stanton, who founded the radical National Woman Suffrage Association.[4]

The movement went into a state of limbo following that historic accomplishment and would stay there for the next three decades, largely as a result of two world wars that threatened national security and the American way of life.

In recent times, the woman's cause has resurfaced to become a highly debated issue. Its impact, however, extends far beyond agreement or disagreement with the goals of the movement. The real heart of the movement today concerns itself with the issue of sexism, which refers to "all those attitudes and actions which relegate women to a secondary and inferior status in society."[5]

It is on the foundation of inferior status that some in our government sponsored legislation (i.e., the Equal Rights Amendment) to promote women's rights. It is exactly at this point that Christian men and women need to examine society's definitions and biases in the light of God's Word. How valid is the premise that declares the female role synonymous with "inferior status"? We will attempt to answer that question as we deal with the concepts of the role of the woman.

THE EFFECTS OF THE FEMINIST MOVEMENT IN AMERICA

Keeping in mind that the discipline of sociology focuses its attention on how mankind operates in a group setting, we will analyze the effects of the feminist movement on our American culture.

As mentioned in the introduction, the working woman has affected our economic base and technological fervor. A new value system is emerging that permeates both the working world and the family system.

---

3. Sheila Rowbotham, *Women, Resistance & Revolution* (New York: Vintage Books, 1974), 107.
4. Gerda Lerner, *The Woman in American History* (Menlo Park, Calif.: Addison-Wesley, 1971), 108.
5. "Guidelines for Improving the Image of Women in Text Books" (Bloomington, Ind.: Phi Delta Kappa, October 1973), 103.

We find reflections of those values in the media. Magazines perpetuate the new, liberated working woman with her designer clothes, male secretaries, and even her very own brand of cigarettes. Newspaper employment ads are careful to include the statement, "This firm is an equal opportunity employer." The television networks air situation comedies and dramas that feature struggling working women or powerful executive women.

The change in values has also affected our educational system. For example, federal regulation Title Nine guarantees equal opportunity, facilities, and faculty for female students to participate in all the areas of education, including intercollegiate athletic competition. Agricultural sciences, automotive, carpentry, and welding classes have been opened to female students. Even the English language is being reconstructed by some educators to eliminate the sexist use of masculine pronouns that refer to both male and female.

ECONOMIC IMPLICATIONS

There has always been a percentage of women in the labor force. What is unique to the twentieth century, however, is the ever-increasing proportion of women in the work force. According to the Bureau of the Census, in 1920, 20 percent of all women sixteen years of age and over were in the work force. By the end of 1976, nearly half of all women were working or looking for work, constituting approximately 41 percent of the labor force.

What then are the characteristics of the working woman in America today? In contrast to earlier times, 58 percent of these women are married, living with their husbands, and likely to have school-aged children. That dramatic increase may be the result of an emerging concept of the family that emphasizes individual independence of its members rather than the corporate dependence of all members. The remaining category of female workers (42 percent) is composed of individuals who are single, divorced, separated, or widowed.[6]

According to a UNESCO report, this unmarried category will supersede the married category in the near future because people now enter marriage assuming, in light of current statistics and trends, that their marriage has a one-in-three chance of surviving at best. The acceptance of that kind of thinking mandates the need for a woman to develop transferable skills that can be used in the labor market.

6. Alan Pifer, *Women Working Toward a New Society* (New York: Carnegie Corporation of New York, 1976), 4-12.

Those statistics should begin to flash a warning signal for the Christian, especially since the following observations have been reported:

1. "The housewife will be a rare breed by 1990 . . . the work place is no longer a man's world."[7]
2. "A fat paycheck and divorce go together for a lot of top female executives, a recent study showed."[8]
3. "At least two million children in America between ages of three and thirteen must care for themselves while their mothers work!"[9]

The church must begin to question those trends and face the issues with a willingness to take a firm biblical stand. The value structure that reflects the mind and person of our Lord must be upheld.

SHIFTING VALUES

Anything a society values tends to influence and dictate other values within that society. That was true in America after the Depression of the 1930s. Those who had lived in a hand-to-mouth existence for years began reaching for material security. They became engrossed with the newest, the most luxurious, the most laborsaving, and the biggest of everything. We are just now beginning to realize the disadvantages and problems resulting from such ideals. Our gas-guzzling cars squander our financial and mineral resources. Food from the convenient can, in many cases, may rob us of essential vitamins. Our prepackaged cuisine, while reducing preparation time, may be contributing to an increase of cancer cases.

It is encouraging that many thoughtful people have begun to rethink and redirect their goals and values. Unfortunately, too many of us, while aware of the inherent dangers, have succumbed to the lethal mind-set that insinuates that most is best, easiest is happiest, and success is measured only by material standards. Rita Carver hints at that as she discusses the enticement of what the world terms *fulfilling employment.* She writes: "In today's world one wonders if mother is not headed for extinction. . . . Some of our feminist sisters have declared that as nonworking mothers we are only maids doing the job any eight-year-old could accomplish."[10]

7. Ralph E. Smith, "Authors Say Job Lure Changing Wives' Image," *Longview* (Tex.) *Daily News,* 24 September 1979.
8. Patricia McCormach, "Happy Marriages and Fat Pay Checks Don't Always Mix for Female Executives," *Longview* (Tex.) *Daily News,* 30 September 1979.
9. *The Church Around the World,* November 1978, vol. 8, no. 12.
10. Rita Carver, "The Myths of Motherhood," *Kindred Spirit,* vol. 3, no. 4 (December 1979), 8-10.

Mrs. Carver goes on to show that even with increased technology, which results in making housework easier in some instances, no substitute can successfully accomplish the tasks and fulfill the role God ordained for wife and mother. It is important to realize also that although our age has amply supplied us with laborsaving services, it has to the same degree given the wife and mother more responsibilities and abilities for service.[11]

An interesting point to ponder at this juncture is the about-face by women's movement leader Betty Friedan. Twenty years ago she urged wives to shake off the drudgery of housework and find fulfillment in the labor force of America. Today she has openly declared that such a philosophy caused frustration and disillusionment. It seems the home is the right place for the woman after all!

While the media and our educational system have been a reflector of the new values, they have also been a catalyst for ever-increasing support of this new role for women. Books and magazines, television programs, and advertisements tend to place a high value on total freedom and self-dependence for the woman in every area of her life.

There almost seems to be a current media and educational campaign promoting the ideas that for a woman to be fulfilled she must have a sense of control over her destiny, and for American freedom to survive we need to see the pragmatic basis of individual independence, including the woman's from the man.[12]

What appears at first to be a comfortable adaptation to the restructuring of family and labor is being shown to be both a strain and a weakening force on the individuals who make up our new liberated mind-set.

For instance, many women are finding it emotionally difficult to cope with the new demands placed on them as a result of their dual-role function of working in and outside the home. Studies now reveal that the stress and tension levels in women have drastically increased as a result of this cultural shift.[13]

Evidence is beginning to reveal the consequences of this new life-style for children. Although many declare that there is no detrimental effect on a working mother's children, studies by some scientists have found that it is much more difficult for a surrogate or stand-in mother to meet all the needs of a child. This may result in a wide range of maladies including insecurity, frustration, and disciplinary problems. That is

11. Ibid.
12. Pifer, 5-9.
13. Patricia McCormach, "The 'Everything Woman' — Newest Victim of Stress," *Longview* (Tex.) *Daily News*, 14 October 1979.

nowhere more evident than in our deteriorating school system.[14] Such results require Christians to evaluate seriously their participation in the growing consequences, both for themselves and their children.

We need to take a long, hard look at the foundations of our family structures and follow up by making decisions and commitments appropriate for restoring and maintaining the emotional security and spiritual health designed by God for the family.

QUESTIONS TO PONDER

1. After the passage of the Nineteenth Amendment, the feminist movement went into a state of limbo. Why?
2. Define the concept of *inferior status* as proposed by the feminist movement. How does that differ from the biblical concept of *roles*?
3. How has technology affected the role of the wife?
4. How have the media and our educational system been a catalyst in changing the traditional cultural values concerning woman's independence?
5. Analyze some of the possible consequences a mother might face by putting her children in a day-care center while she works.

14. Clifford T. Morgan and Richard A. King, *Introduction to Psychology*, 5th ed. (New York: McGraw-Hill, 1975), 82-84.

2

In the Beginning . . .

The narratives of Genesis 1-3 give us foundational data from which we can develop a biblical view of the sexes. Here male and female receive their orientation from the creative hand of God, and God's intention for them becomes clear. These chapters concern the creation of man in the image of God; they reveal that man is male and female, discuss the role of man, and provide the understanding of man's fall. These passages have received considerable attention through the centuries, and recently, in view of a new feminine consciousness, a renewed interest in explaining them has developed. Our objective is to give direction to the Christian who desires to regulate his life in view of God's purposes for man and woman established from creation.

MALE AND FEMALE AS EQUAL IMAGE-BEARERS

Genesis 1:26-28 reveals mankind to be the crown of God's creation (see Appendix 1). The author constructs these three verses into a pyramid, which we will demonstrate shortly, with verses 26 and 28 giving the proposal and commission of man, and verse 27 being the emphasized verse, defining who man really is.

Three emphases are found in verses 26-28: (1) man is seen as created in the image of God; (2) man is expected to procreate; and (3) man is to be master over all of God's other created beings on the earth. The image of God is not clearly defined in these verses; other passages of Scripture must be consulted for a fuller understanding of the *imago Dei*.[1] Neverthe-

---

1. Theologians differ about the nature of the image of God. Some believe it is man's moral righteousness, some his personality; still others believe it refers to his ability to relate to

less, we may safely say that it enables one to communicate and to subdue the earth because God mandated the communion with Him and with creation. That ability requires the capacity for intelligence, feeling, and choice. God also expected man to populate the earth. In addition, he is to be the ruler over all of God's creation, and harness the powers of nature for the glory of God. The creation may be used by man to accomplish whatever tasks will complete the purposes of God. Whether an individual plows a field or types on a typewriter, he is fulfilling that mandate because he is using the resources of creation to express dominion.

We need to consider briefly the purpose of God for man and the rest of the creation in general. In short, that purpose is to bring glory to God. By fulfilling the various acts commissioned by God; each level of His creation proclaims the greatness of God (Pss. 8, 19) and declares His character, but only man does so in a personal manner. C. S. Lewis, an Oxford medieval scholar and Christian apologist, saw the relationship of male and female as a symbolic one. Margaret Howe, a professor of religion, says of Lewis:

> [He] suggests that the male-female distinction may be intended to reflect the distinction between God (the most masculine thing in the universe) and his creation (we are all feminine with respect to God). The male-female distinction in the human realm need not reflect any difference in spirituality, intelligence, or general ability. It may be intended merely as a sort of allegory which strikes deep emotional chords in the human subconscious, and which accounts for God's picturing himself as our father rather than our mother. Such an allegory is built into the very structure of the universe.[2]

God and other persons. Several Scriptures refer to that image: Gen. 9:6; 1 Cor. 11:7; Eph. 4:21-24; Col. 3:10; James 3:9. See the various discussions on the *imago Dei:*

James Oliver Buswell, *A Systematic Theology of the Christian Religion* (Grand Rapids: Zondervan, 1962), 231-43.
Umberto Cassuto, *A Commentary on the Book of Genesis,* trans. Israel Abrahams (Jerusalem: Magnes Press, Hebrew U., 1961), 56.
Walter Eichrodt, *Theology of the Old Testament,* vol. 2, trans. J. A. Baker (Philadelphia: Westminster, 1967), 122-28.
Edmond Jacob, *Theology of the Old Testament,* trans. Arthur W. Heathcoate and Philip J. Allcock (New York: Harper & Row, 1958), 166-72.
H. C. Leupold, *Exposition of Genesis* (Columbus, Ohio: Wartburg, 1942), 89-92.
John Theodore Mueller, *Christian Dogmatics* (St. Louis: Concordia, 1955), 205ff.
A. H. Strong, *Systematic Theology* (Westwood, N.J.: Revell, 1907), 514-32.
Gerhard von Rad, *Old Testament Theology,* vol. 1, trans. D. M. G. Stalker (New York: Harper & Brothers, 1962), 1:144ff.
Theodorus C. Vriezen, *An Outline of Old Testament Theology* (Oxford: Basil Blackwell, 1958), 145ff, 208.

2. E. Margaret Howe, "Women and Church Leadership," *The Evangelical Quarterly* (April-June 1979, 100. Compare C. S. Lewis, *God in the Dock: Essays on Theology and Ethics,* ed. Walter Hooper (Grand Rapids: Eerdmans, 1970), 236-38.

Thus, male and female mirrored God's involvement with the world. As they faithfully related to each other and the world, they reflected the character of God and His relationship as Creator with His creation.

Verse 27 defines more exactly the nature of this man who has been given the mandate by God in verse 28 (which in turn was based on God's intentions stated in v. 26). Whereas verses 26 and 28 are written in prose, verse 27 is clearly a poetic passage in the Hebrew text. Umberto Cassuto, the eminent Hebrew scholar, said, "At this point the text assumes a more exalted tone and becomes poetic. The verse consists of three lines, each of which has four stresses and contains the verb *bara'* — 'create' — the repetition being for emphasis."[3] This verse, then, serves as a pinnacle or peak in the argument, given the preeminent place by the author by means of the poetic style. Thus the idea of a pyramid with verses 26 and 28 bolstering and focusing on verse 27.

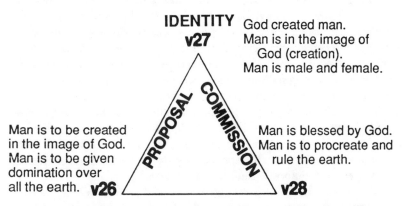

IDENTITY
v27
God created man.
Man is in the image of God (creation).
Man is male and female.

Man is to be created in the image of God. Man is to be given domination over all the earth. **v26**

PROPOSAL COMMISSION

Man is blessed by God. Man is to procreate and rule the earth.
v28

The emphasis of these 3 verses is the creation in vs. 27.

Figure 2.1

The emphases of verse 27 are discerned from the Hebrew text by noting those words that appear at the beginning of the clauses. The italicized words in the following clauses will reveal the emphases of the verse: "God *created* man in His own image, in the *image* of God He created him; *male and female* He created them" (emphasis added).

Those three clauses give us a full-orbed understanding of God's creation called *man*. The first one clearly identifies the proper perspective of man: he is God's creation. Man is not viewed as the result of chance

---

3. Umberto Cassuto, *A Commentary on the Book of Genesis*, trans. Israel Abrahams (Jerusalem: Magnes Press, Hebrew U., 1961), 57.

forces at play in the universe (i.e, evolution); he is a deliberative and purposive act of the Creator (see Ps. 8 for a "commentary" on creation). The second clause portrays man as created in the image of God, bearing indelibly the character of the divine Being, and thus he can fulfill the work assigned to him.[4] The third clause is of primary importance for the biblical view of the sexes, for we see that the man is created male and female.

It is the clear intent of verses 26-28 that male and female are equal, both bearing the Divine image and having the responsibility that that image entails. Male and female are to be jointly concerned about procreation.[5] The woman is not merely a vessel for the man's child, but neither is the child the sole concern and responsibility of the woman. As a unit they are to populate the earth to fulfill the purpose of God and show His glory on the earth (Ps. 8).

Man's dominion over God's creation has been the source of much confusion. Often women have been relegated a small part of God's creation; namely, the dishes, floors, and the like. Certainly the primary domain of the woman is domestic (Titus 2:5), but it is not her *total* domain. It has been assumed that men alone are to occupy the world outside the house. However, God originally intended that men and women work together in agriculture, education, the arts, commerce — even the housework! Women have the ability to function in other capacities besides housework. Deborah was a great leader. Ruth was a prime example of dedication to family. Mary, mother of Jesus, composed a beautiful hymn. Women were the first to announce the resurrection. Women were of great help to the apostle Paul in his ministry.

The woman of Proverbs 31 deserves special notice. Here is a woman who has proper priorities in caring for her family (certainly the major function for her in the Genesis 1 mandate), but she also is capable of functioning in a nondomestic environment. She has the full confidence of her husband. She provides for the needs of her family — food, clothing — but still works outside the home in business and charity. She has an agile and industrious mind. If a woman can meet the needs of her family properly (the God-given maternal responsibilities to children must be carefully considered), she may broaden her domain in outside employment or in other interests (see chap. 5 for a greater development of this idea).

---

4. Derek Kidner, *Genesis, The Tyndale Old Testament Commentaries* (London: Tyndale, 1967), 52.
5. H. Wayne House, "Paul, Women, and Contemporary Evangelical Feminism," *Bibliotheca Sacra*, vol. 136, no. 541 (January-March 1979), 40-53.

FUNCTIONAL RELATIONSHIP OF MALE AND FEMALE

Genesis 2:18 begins with the statement, "And Yahweh God said, 'It is not good for the man to be alone. I will make a helper suitable for him.' " Man by himself is not the ideal; a helper corresponding to him is needed.

God declared that because of the intrinsic inappropriateness of man being alone, He would make a complement for him. Although wrongly interpreted as "help mate," the "help meet" of the King James Version conveys the meaning of the Hebrew text ("a helper suitable") quite nicely. Unfortunately, time has obscured the sense. The Hebrew literally reads, "a helper corresponding to him." The word *helper* carries the meaning of a "counterpart" or "opposite,"[6] and in Genesis 2:18 it signifies a "help *corresponding* to him, i.e. equal and adequate to himself."[7] Because God appoints the celibate life for only a few, we can assume that the term *helpmeet* refers to a wife—a helper suitable to a husband. The wife is equal with the husband in every way and can relate to him at every level of his being.[8]

> Eve was not given to Adam only to bear his children, but to be his companion. "As if," he objects, "she had been given to him only to sleep with him, and not to be the inseparable companion of his life." Her purpose, which she is to learn from the account of her creation, is to "help him live more comfortably." Eve is created from Adam in order to teach Adam to recognize himself in her "as in a mirror," and to teach Eve "to be willingly subject to her husband." Indeed, "mankind, which was like a partially built edifice, has been perfected and finished in the person of the woman." Until then, "the male was only half the man"; once Eve had been created, Adam "saw himself complete in his wife, where he was only one half formerly . . . . Through their legitimate union, man and woman are united in one body and one soul."[9]

Only woman was truly like man in the parade of Genesis 2, for she was taken from his very being, her bone from his, and her flesh from his.[10] Notice Adam's perspective of God's creation as it is portrayed from the Hebrew text:

6. William L. Holladay, *A Concise Hebrew and Aramaic Lexicon of the Old Testament* (Grand Rapids: Eerdmans, 1971), 226.
7. Francis Brown, S. R. Driver, and Charles Briggs, *A Hebrew and English Lexicon of the Old Testament* (Oxford: Clarendon, 1907), 617.
8. Helmut Thielicke, *The Ethics of Sex*, trans. John W. Doverstein (New York: Harper & Row, 1964), 4.
9. George Tavard, *Woman in Christian Tradition*, 176, cited by Duane A. Dunham, "Women in the Ministry." Paper presented at the Seminar on Women in the Ministry, Western Conservative Baptist Seminary, November 1976.
10. Cassuto, 134.

> This one! This time!
> Bone—from my bones!
> And flesh—from my flesh!
> For from man this one was taken![11]

There is no indication that Adam perceived the woman to be inferior to him or that she was made to be a slave for him. When God brought the animals before Adam he readily recognized that they did not share the Divine image with him and could not be addressed as equals. However, the woman was one who could function with him to procreate and dominate the earth. She was his counterpart, a suitable helper to do God's work!

We must in no way diminish the equality of essence shared by male and female, but at the same time we must recognize that Genesis 2 also presents the man as having a *functional* headship over the woman. The male's role in fulfilling the mandate in Genesis 1:26-28 is not independent from the female's; however, neither are they egalitarian as many feminists have argued. By chronological order of creation, she is a vice-regent with him. Although there is no *explicit* statement in the text that indicates the male is to have authority over the female, a subtle argument is seen in Adam's naming the animals and the woman. In Hebrew society the prerogative of naming is a sign of a superiority (although here in Genesis it is not essence we are speaking of, only position).[12] When Adam named the animals, he did so by discerning their natures.[13] When he came to the woman he immediately knew that she was unlike the animals; she instead was one "like him." Cassuto speaks to the significance of naming:

> She is worthy of being called by the same name as myself . . . that is to say: I have given names to all living, but I have not succeeded in finding one among them fit to be called by a name resembling mine, thus indicating its kinship with me. She, at last, deserves to be given a name corresponding to my own.[14]

When we say she is a helper, we are not suggesting that she is to be under her husband as a child or slave. She is to be respected as an equal,

---

11. We adopted this from Ronald B. Allen, "Male and Female: the View from Genesis." Paper presented at the Seminar on Women in the Ministry, Western Conservative Baptist Seminary, November 1976.
12. J. A. Motyer, "Name," *New Bible Dictionary*, ed. J. D. Douglas (Grand Rapids: Eerdmans, 1962), 862; Cassuto, 130; Fritz Maass, *Theological Dictionary of the Old Testament*, ed. G. Johannes Botterweck and Helmer Ringgren, trans. John T. Willis (Grand Rapids: Eerdmans, 1974), 1:84.
13. Kidner, 65.
14. Cassuto, 136.

one in God's image, who with her husband and under his loving direction fulfills God's task of ruling the earth.

THE BATTLE OF THE SEXES BEGINS

As God originally planned it, man and woman as a team would explore and control the world, and in so doing manifest the character of a benevolent and beneficent Creator. That perfect plan was ruined by the Fall of Adam and Eve into sin (Gen. 3), and the effects of the curse from that Fall have been evident in the history of the world and are present in our own lives. Let us first look at the Fall and then observe its impact on our world.

When Eve succumbed to the temptation of the devil recorded in Genesis 3:1-7 she was seeking to act independently of Adam, with whom she was to make decisions. That may have been the cause for her sin. She manifested clearly her understanding of God's commands but was deceived into sinning. As well, Adam failed in his responsibility to provide proper leadership for Eve by quickly yielding to her request to eat also of the fruit. Both woman and man received a curse from God for sin; both incurred the penalty of death and received appropriate and separate punishment.

Genesis 3:16 gives the curse on the woman. The words read in the KJV*: "Unto the woman he said, I will greatly multiply thy sorrow and thy conception; in sorrow thou shalt bring forth children, and thy desire shall be to thy husband, and he shall rule over thee."

There are two effects of the Fall in this verse: the pain of woman in childbirth, and tension between husband and wife. The latter is our concern in this chapter.

Before the Fall, Adam and Eve had a totally harmonious relationship. They respected each other, worked together to fulfill God's commission to rule the earth, and no doubt would have begun to populate the earth. Each operated within the authority structure God intended in creation. When the pair sinned, a distortion of that relationship occurred.

The foretelling of that distortion is found in Genesis 3:16: "Your desire shall be for your husband." Some have considered this desire to be sexual desire for the husband[15] but because that would have been part of the makeup of the male and female as sexual beings that could not be true. That sexual desire is somehow perverted or improper is a total misreading of the Old and New Testament concepts of the sexuality of man and

---

* King James Version
15. *Midrash Rabbah, Bereshith*, ed. Harry Freedman and Maurice Simon (London: Soncino, 1939), chapter 20:7, 1:166.

woman. Within the marriage union sexuality is properly and beautifully expressed. We must remember that part of the original intention of God for Adam and Eve was to bear children and fill the earth.

If the desire was not sexual, what was it? It may be understood best in conjunction with the remainder of the verse, "And he shall rule over you." Some have said that the husband's authority over his wife did not begin until the curse; if Eve had not sinned, she would not have been subject to her husband.[16] Rather than the rule being an intention of creation, it disturbed the original peace of creation.[17]

Others, stressing the desire of the woman and taking this clause as coordinate with the statement on the rule of the man have considered it to mean the desire to be ruled by man. She is instinctively dependent on him[18] and recognizes a need for his protection.[19] Scanzoni and Hardesty, popular Christian feminist authors, primarily see this passage as a description of how man, "degenerated by sin, would take advantage of his headship as a husband to dominate, lord it over, his wife."[20]

We consider all of those interpretations to be inadequate explanations of the passage at hand.

The major difficulty we encounter in developing a proper understanding of Genesis 3:16b is the translation of the two clauses as synonymous. Rather than the two clauses presenting two thoughts they are made to present only one effect from the Fall. The source of the confusion in translation comes from rendering the Hebrew conjunction as "and" (a coordinating idea), rather than "but" (an antithetical concept). The translation should be: "And your desire shall be for your husband, *but* he shall rule over you."

Susan Foh, writing in the *Westminster Theological Journal,* has suggested that the grammar of 3:16b should be understood in light of an identical Hebrew construction in Genesis 4:7b. Both passages include the word *desire* and a comparison of the two passages gives us an understanding of what the woman's desire is.[21] Notice the parallels:

> Genesis *3:16b:* "And your desire shall be for your husband, But he shall rule over you."

16. Martin Luther, *Lectures on Genesis, Luther's Works,* ed. Jaroslav Pelikan (St. Louis: Concordia, 1958), 1:203.
17. Thielicke, 8.
18. John Skinner, *A Critical and Exegetical Commentary on Genesis,* International Critical Commentary (Edinburgh: T & T Clark, 1930), 82.
19. Clarence J. Vos, *Woman in Old Testament Worship* (Delft, D.V.: Vereinigde Drukkerijen Judels and Brinkman, n.d.), 24.
20. Letha Scanzoni and Nancy Hardesty, *All We're Meant to Be* (Waco, Tex.: Word, 1974), 35.
21. Susan Foh, "What Is the Woman's Desire?" *Westminster Theological Journal,* vol. 37, no. 3 (Spring 1975), 377-78.

Genesis *4:7b*: "Its [sin's] desire shall be for you, but you must master it."

Genesis 4:7*b* portrays sin as a power that desired to rule. A struggle is implied. That is, if Cain wanted to control sin he had to exert himself.

In a similar fashion, because of the Fall, woman now desired to occupy the place of authority that God gave to man, as we have examined in Genesis 2. Contrary to the harmony expressed in the pre-Fall world, a battle of the sexes began. If man was to exercise dominion over the woman, he would do so with great struggle. Foh gives clear expression to the significance of the curse:

> These words mark the beginning of the battle of the sexes. As a result of the fall, man no longer rules easily; he must fight for the headship. Sin has corrupted both the willing submission of the wife and the loving headship of the husband. The woman's desire is to control her husband (to usurp his divinely appointed headship [sic]) and he must master her, if he can. So the rule of love founded in paradise is replaced by struggle, tyranny and domination.[22]

The curse on Adam has also had a disastrous impact on the relationship of husbands and wives in properly carrying out God's desire for them. Rather than his work being easy, it would be very difficult. Rather than nature cooperating with him, it would fight against him. The fruit of a man's labor would not be commensurate with the amount of energy he expends. Because of the sin of Adam, the ground is cursed and will remain so until the consummation of all things in Christ (cf. Rom. 8).

How would the curse adversely affect man and woman in their association? The agony of "toiling out a living" would no doubt cause psychological stress on the man, which would be carried over into his marriage. Also, it might affect the amount of time he would spend away from home since he would need to work more to make an adequate living. The negative effects of husbands trying to make ends meet are with us today. The jealously of some husbands over their hard-earned paychecks (as though marriage were not a joint endeavor) also helps to spotlight the problem.

CONCLUSION

We have seen that God created man as male and female, equal bearers of the Divine image. We understand He intended for them to procre-

---

22. Foh, 382. Irvin A. Busenitz recently gave an alternative to Foh's views in "Woman's Desire for Man: Genesis 3:16 Reconsidered," *Grace Theological Journal*, vol. 7 (1986): 203-12. I find Busenitz's arguments unpersuasive. See my review of his article in *Bibliotheca Sacra*, vol. 144 (1987): 462-63.

ate and dominate the earth. By so doing, man and woman manifest God's character and become partakers in His creative activity. Their equality is expressed by their joint creation in His image; the man is the head because he was created first and the woman was derived from him. That original unity was destroyed in the Fall. Woman would desire to usurp man's rule, and man, if he was to rule, would not do so easily. Man would become absorbed in his work and bring many pressures to the marriage. The history of man and woman in society has demonstrated the impact of the curse. Fortunately, the situation may be rectified in Christ's work for and in His people (Eph. 5:21-33), with the original intention of God for male and female made possible once again.

Questions to Ponder

1. Give examples in present-day society of persons who are equally in the image of God but function differently.
2. Are there other components of the image of God that may be discerned from reading the creation narratives?
3. Give ways in which men and women could fulfill jointly the responsibility to dominate creation.
4. What are characteristics of God that men and women express differently that give a more complete view of God? Does the Bible portray God at times in distinctly masculine or feminine terms? Why is that so?
5. Although man and woman equally have responsibility to rule over the earth, do they have primary and secondary responsibilities?
6. Should men and women seek the celibate life?
7. Would Adam and Eve have had children if they had not sinned?
8. Why does priority of creation result in man's leadership of woman but not in the animals' leadership of man?

3

The Woman and the Family

The problems created for the Christian in regard to working wives comes both from the historical feminist movement and the distortion of God's original intention for husband and wife (Gen. 1-2). The root misconception is not the equality of creation of male and female, but the created function of husbands and wives.

In general, secular society (including evangelicals) has defined the traditional family structure and assumed the husband to be the superior ruler and the wife to be the inferior servant. That concept lies far to the right of what God ordained. On the other hand, the feminist movement has swung the pendulum far to the left, largely refusing the family structure and roles God has given.

Exactly what is God's ideal here? This part will discuss these three major positions using the accompanying chart as a basis: (1) the *ideal position*—a biblical portrait; (2) the *traditional distortion*—generally adhered to until about 1960; and (3) the *emerging distortion*—representing present trends and practices.

From a sociological standpoint we must note that this model represents a collective feeling by a particular group. There will be those who are exceptions to the rule in any category.

ISSUE: PHILOSOPHICAL BASIS

IDEAL POSITION: BIBLICAL PRINCIPLES

The basic presupposition of the ideal view of philosophy has the Word

of God as its foundation. Biblical principles present the framework for all
thought and action.

THE FAMILY: GOD'S INTENTION; SOCIETY'S DISTORTION

Issue	Ideal Position	Traditional Distortion (1776-1960)	Emerging Distortion (1960-Present)
Philosophical	Biblical	The Bible distorted for man's exploitation	Humanistic principles
Values	Subject to all of God's absolutes	Arbitrary selection of absolutes	No absolutes; Existentialism
Interpersonal Relationships	Concept of unity (Unselfish dependence)	Concept of cohesion (Role dependence)	Concept of pluralism; Selfish independence
Basic Unit of Society	Family	Family	Individual
Authority	Patriarchal	Patriarchal	Dual-Archal that may lead to anarchy)
Roles	1. Naturally and positionally equal in God's eyes	1. Naturally and positionally unequal	1. Naturally and positionally equal
	2. Role differentiation	2. Role differentiation	2. No role differentiation
Love	What can I give to a relationship?	What do I need to sustain this relationship?	What can I get from this relationship?

TRADITIONAL DISTORTION: THE BIBLE DISTORTED FOR MAN'S EXPLOITATION

On the surface the traditional position appears to be in agreement
with the ideal position. A closer analysis, however, makes it obvious that
many times a biblical principle was exploited to justify societal biases.

Some Scriptures were taken out of context, and the result was practices based on half-truths. The most obvious were those laws, written and unwritten, that made a woman little more than property and gave men rights of exploitation. Double standards emerged allowing men like Karl Marx, who was opposed to biblical truth, to capitalize on the hypocrisy.[1] The traditional system, therefore, had a "form of godliness," but led eventually to a thought process that completely rejected biblical principles.

EMERGING DISTORTION: HUMANISTIC PRINCIPLES

Today we see the family operating under humanistic principles. Humanistic philosophy teaches that man makes himself what he is; he is responsible only to himself in the final analysis. In essence man has made himself a deity, the master of his destiny.

For example, Wayne Dyer, a humanist, seems to incorporate the same view into his psychological therapy. He gives this advice: "Remember that you have no responsibility to make others happy, just as they have no obligation to make you happy. The important thing is to set your own standards."[2]

ISSUE: VALUES

IDEAL POSITION: SUBJECT TO ALL OF GOD'S ABSOLUTES

The ideal position adheres to God's absolutes for family operation. Ethical and value patterns are subject to God's definition, not man's. In this structure man's responsibility is to obey, not to alter the value system.

TRADITIONAL DISTORTION: ARBITRARY SELECTION OF GOD'S ABSOLUTES

We see the traditional outlook arbitrarily selecting the absolutes that society currently finds convenient and supportive of its values. For example, the scriptural admonitions to the husband to love his wife as "Christ loved the church and gave Himself for it" (Eph. 5:25-28) and "to live with your wives in an understanding way, as with a weaker vessel, since she is a woman; and grant her honor" (1 Pet. 3:7, NASB) were far too

1. Sheila Rowbotham, *Women, Resistance and Revolution* (New York: Vintage Books, 1974), 107-8.
2. David Wallechineski and Irving Wallace, "An Analysis of Counseling Processes," *Ladies Home Journal,* vol. 95, no. 10 (October 1978), 229.

often completely ignored. Yet, the scriptural mandates for the submission of the wife were loudly proclaimed.

That thinking of the times was reflected in some early public laws that forbade women to "meet together to babble and talk" (for any reason), and ordered husbands to "keep their wives at home."[3]

Unfortunately, that outlook is far from extinct. For example, a young couple, both Christians, were divorced largely because the husband practiced this terribly distorted view of scriptural mandates. To him, the husband as head of the house meant he was an arbitrary ruler. His wife, a small, quiet, genteel person, apparently submitted to his emotional tirades and abuses until she reached her breaking point; she took their young son and fled, refusing to see or speak to him again. That heartbreaking situation exposed more than just a distorted biblical perspective. It also revealed a complete lack of meaningful communication, without which no marriage can function.[4] By that we mean honesty spoken by both partners—complete and from the heart. We have discovered that in nearly every case of marital difficulties, communication between spouses is superficial at best and in severe cases, nonexistent. This is an area that must continually be exercised, and one that we will deal with more completely in the next section.

EMERGING DISTORTION: NO ABSOLUTES; EXISTENTIALISM

The value system that gives force to the philosophy that man is the master of his fate is modern *existentialism*. It is a self-oriented "do your own thing" philosophy that adheres to no uniform absolutes. The goal of this "me first" value system is individual happiness, regardless of how unhappy our actions will make others in the process.[5] Thus, in adopting this value system, particular interest groups, such as those supporting the feminist movement, have a basis and justification for change at any cost.

ISSUE: INTERPERSONAL RELATIONSHIPS

IDEAL POSITION: UNSELFISH DEPENDENCE

When a husband and wife know Jesus Christ as Savior, they become capable of the ideal marital relationship based on oneness with Christ. A marriage and family based on that unity will produce unselfish depen-

3. Rowbotham, 23.
4. J. Grant Howard, *The Trauma of Transparency: A Biblical Approach to Inter-Personal Communication* (Portland, Ore.: Multnomah, 1979).
5. Wallechineski, 227.

dence. Here we discover what is meant by the passage "the two shall become one flesh" (Gen. 2:24), for in this kind of relationship both partners yield their individualistic identities and develop a new, joint relationship. In this context a wife submits to her husband, not grudgingly, but out of her heart-felt wishes. The husband, in turn, loves his wife as himself and as Christ loves the church (Eph. 5:25).

It is important to reemphasize here that apart from Christ's presence in the marriage, neither party is capable of such attitudes on a steady, stable basis.

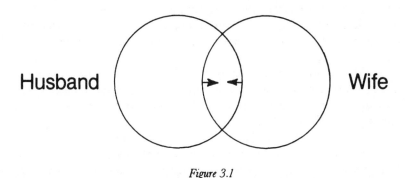

Figure 3.1

TRADITIONAL DISTORTION: ROLE DEPENDENCE

The paramount objective in the traditional relationship is group cohesion. Unity or mutual respect becomes of secondary importance. That is evidenced in history's portrayal of the extremely dominant husband, with the wife sometimes treated as a "second-class citizen."[6]

A young couple, Jack and Jenny, come to mind here. Jack, a big, strong West Point graduate, was the epitome of intelligence and self-confidence. Jenny was a small, bubbly blond with a warm, friendly personality. When we first met them, small problems had already begun to emerge. Again, instead of honest communication, we saw dishonesty and evasion on Jenny's part, while Jack's favorite weapon was the silent treatment. As time passed it became obvious that the main problem was a lack of mutual respect. Jenny's self-image was poor, and Jack, rather than helping her see her importance to the Lord and to him, treated her as a child in mind and emotions.

His attitude was at best patronizing, for when disagreements arose he

6. Simone De Beauvior, *The Second Sex* (New York: Modern Library, 1968), 430.

became degrading and demeaning in his comments. Because that inten-
sified Jenny's poor self-image, she began to let her appearance slip, causing further problems.

But this case has a happy ending. On the verge of bitter divorce, Jack
and Jenny saw the Lord as their only hope and gradually gave themselves and their problems to Him. The road back was not easy, but God
proved Himself faithful.

EMERGING DISTORTION: SELFISH INDEPENDENCE

A marriage and family based on the self-oriented philosophy, promoted by most feminists and traditional power-hungry husbands, will produce selfish independence. The concept of unity is flung aside, and even
though husband and wife cohabit, each strives for an independent set of
goals.

As this self-oriented philosophy continues to make gains, some repu-
table scientists now believe that even actions that seem to be altruistic
have their ultimate roots in selfishness. The theory encourages the
emerging philosophy of marriage.[7]

Significantly, the American Psychiatric Association has recently had
cause to diagnose *narcissism* as a particular personality disorder. It has
caused many to be so consumed with themselves that they cannot communicate effectively with others.[8] This mental disorder may be a contributing factor to a divorce rate escalating at such a feverish pace that census bureau analysts have predicted over 50 percent of all children born
in 1978 will eventually become members of a one-parent family.[9]

ISSUE: BASIC UNIT OF SOCIETY

IDEAL POSITION: THE FAMILY UNIT IS PRIMARY

According to biblical standards, the family is the basic unit of society.
It is a divinely created institution through which God reveals Himself to
mankind. Ethel L. Herr writes:

> In the garden of Eden God laid the foundations for two kinds of families on
> earth. He made marriage the basis on which the whole expanding physical

7. Michael Demarest, "Why You Do What You Do — Sociobiology: A Theory of Behavior," *Time*, vol. 110, no. 28 (1 August 1977), 54-63.
8. The Committee on Nomenclature and Statistics of the American Pyschiatric Association. *DSM III, Diagnostic and Statistical Manual of Mental Disorders*, 3d ed. (Washington,
   D.C.: American Psychiatric Association, 1980).
9. Paul Glick and Arthur Norton, "Over Half of Homes Consist of One-Two People"
   Longview (Tex.) *Daily News*, 12 March 1979.

family would be built. After Adam and Eve sinned, God promised the coming of a Savior who would one day become the cornerstone of God's spiritual family. In the New Testament God used the marriage relationship of the physical family as an analogy to help us understand the nature of the relationship between man and his Savior in the spiritual family.[10]

TRADITIONAL CONCEPT: THE FAMILY UNIT IS PRIMARY

Basically, the traditional concept has adhered to the family as the basic unit of society. In this case, a biblical truth has become a social guide.

The family unit is also the foundational source of individual identity that establishes a healthy society.

Michael Novak, recent resident scholar at the American Enterprise Institute in Washington, D.C. sums up the family:

> The only department of health, education and welfare that works . . . without the family, we would still have to provide for the development of the individual. In no other way could we do the job half so efficiently, half so cheaply, or with half so much affection. . . . There is a kind of moral growth that comes from being married and being part of a family that the individual left to himself or herself, could scarcely attain otherwise, and never so naturally.[11]

EMERGING DISTORTION: THE INDIVIDUAL BECOMES PRIMARY

The family is endangered if its emphasis shifts from the functional unit to an overemphasis on the individual. In an article written for *Psychology Today*, Perry London stated: "The basic unit of society is the individual, who is able financially to live alone and find amiable companionship, sex, and other recreation, without having to provide anything in return."[12]

In this kind of situation the goal of a wife or husband becomes autonomy, in which the greatest portion of attention is placed on the self, rather than on other family members.

10. Ethel L. Herr, *Chosen Families of the Bible* (Chicago: Moody, 1981), 15.
11. Michael Novak, "The American Family, an Embattled Institution," *The Family, America's Hope* (Rockford, Ill.: Rockford College Institute, 1979), 9-18.
12. Perry London, "The Intimacy Gap," *Psychology Today*, vol. 11, no. 12 (May 1978), 40.

IDEAL POSITION: PATRIARCHAL

For harmony to exist in the home, there needs to be an established order of authority and responsibility. Modern psychologists find it hard to accept the plausibility of a line of authority in a marriage. Lucile Duberman, a professor of sociology, states that it is impossible for a couple to build a marriage on both a line of authority and on companionship, as that presents an incongruent concept.[13] Ernest Burgess, also a professor of sociology, holds that a couple can operate under either plan but not both.[14]

IDEAL FAMILY
TRADITIONAL AMERICAN FAMILY

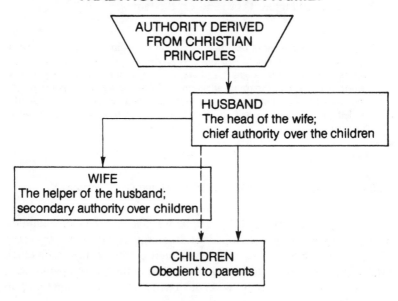

Figure 3.2

The Bible, however, exhorts the Christian family to operate under both a chain of authority and companionship to insure harmony in the home. As stated earlier, the essential key to companionship is heart-to-

---

13. Lucile Duberman, *Marriage and Its Alternatives* (New York: Praeger, 1974), 100.
14. J. Ross Eshleman, *The Family: An Introduction*, 2d ed. (Boston: Allyn and Bacon, Inc., 1978), 120.

heart communication exercised on a regular basis. For some couples that comes naturally. For others, it must be more of a conscious effort. It is a fact that the great majority of married couples spend less than five minutes per day in one-on-one meaningful communication. The *sixteen-minute attention rule* encourages communication. Four times a day the husband and wife spend four totally uninterrupted minutes simply talking to each other. The four times recommended are: first thing in the morning; before the husband or wife leaves for work; when the partners come home from work; and bedtime. A closer and happier companionship is the logical result.

God has ordered the family to live according to the principles of *headship*, where each member of the family lives under the authority of the head God has appointed. The husband lives under the authority of Christ and is responsible to Him for the leadership and care of the family. The wife lives under the authority of her husband and is responsible to him for the way she orders the household and cares for the children. The children live under the authority of both parents. The authority over the children, however, remains essentially one. The dotted line in the above illustration indicates that the authority of the mother is a derived authority. That means her goals and her husband's goals in discipline, love, and guidance are the same. They have been talked through and prayed through together. Each relies on one source—God's Word—for all answers.

TRADITIONAL DISTORTION: PATRIARCHAL

The traditional view has incorporated the same patriarchal line of authority. But apart from the warming, vitalizing power of the Holy Spirit, many times there are cold, unfulfilling relationships for all involved. While it tends to give order, it does not always give stability to a household.

EMERGING DISTORTION: DUAL-ARCHAL

Rejecting the patriarchal concept as totally irrational, those in the feminist movement have accused the apostle Paul (whom they refer to as "savage") of affirming that a woman ought to be "subordinate" to her husband.[15] Here the word *subordinate* has been substituted for the original word *submission*. A misinterpretation of God's Word is made in that *submission* refers to willful subjection, whereas *subordinate* implies second-class position.

15. Beauvior, 97.

In rejecting the patriarchal concept, a double line of authority has emerged in the modern home. The results can be disastrous for children reared in such a household, for many times they learn (consciously or unconsciously) that there are no firm commitments or directions in life, and are left without a concrete foundation on which to build their lives. Without a firm and unified voice, the children can become frustrated, and many times reject their parents altogether. Perhaps that helps to explain why in a survey of 850 junior and senior high students, 75 percent of all boys and 80 percent of all girls responded with a definite *yes* when asked the question, If you were given the opportunity, would you trade in your parents for newer, more glamorous models?[16] Without clear direction and foundation, that double line of authority can break down even further, resulting in chaos in the family.

THE EMERGING AMERICAN FAMILY

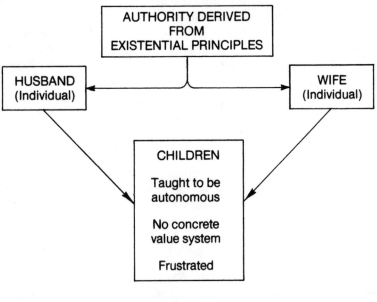

Figure 3.3

16. Abigail Van Buren, "Dear Abby" column, *Longview* (Tex.) *Daily News*, 30 September 1979.

Issue: Roles

IDEAL POSITION: POSITIONALLY EQUAL WITH DIFFERENTIATION OF ROLES

In the very beginning God created woman for man and gave to man the role as head of the woman. That design has not been changed, although some would try to alter it. The biblical design, however, dictates not only how Christians should operate in a marital relationship, but what attitudes should coincide as well.

God says in Galatians 3:28 that in His eyes men and women are equal. God also says, however, that the function of each in the marital relationship differs in accordance with His directions and plan, as seen in Genesis 1-3. There will be no feeling of inferiority or superiority in the ideal marriage because the husband and wife are jointly members of the same Body of Christ. Functioning within the framework of those God-given roles prevents chaos in the marital relationship and will produce unity and harmony in the home.

TRADITIONAL DISTORTION: POSITIONALLY UNEQUAL WITH DIFFERENTIATION OF ROLES

A culture that ordered its male members to "keep their wives in proper place, over-emphasized role differentiation in the home"[17] (the emphasis is on the word *proper*). Those who were obsessed with who did what in the relationship adhere to the idea that the so-called menial tasks were women's work while what they considered stately and more important duties were the responsibility of the man. Again, the improper attitudes of both men and women toward the tasks they performed gave this distortion credence.

Jenny, whom we mentioned earlier, fell prey to this unfortunate way of thinking. Instead of realizing that the role of mother and wife was of far greater value to God than any outside employment she might have, she continually berated herself as "only a housewife" and wished for a job that would give her status and identity. That misshapen value system can creep into our thinking almost without notice if our eyes and ears are tuned to the world system instead of the Word of God. The media, our educational system, and even some of our churches demean the role of the housewife and mother, assuring us that "being fulfilled" is of primary importance, and suggesting that involves "doing your own

17. Rowbotham, 23.

thing" outside the home even if the family must pay a price. In Jenny's case that attitude began to reveal itself in her housekeeping, the care of their children, and even her personal appearance. The flaws in this widely preached social doctrine become evident through a careful study of what the Bible has to say concerning the elevated and precious role of wife and mother.

EMERGING DISTORTION: POSITIONALLY EQUAL WITH NO ROLE DIFFERENTIATION

As can be expected, the inevitable result of a changing society has been the complication of marital roles. One of the major causes of divorce today is a lack of understanding by the spouses as to what specific duties and roles each must perform within the marriage. According to *Changing Times,* "the ramification of the woman's liberation movement in demanding equality in roles has been to alter the traditional family structure." The article goes on to say that "according to some authorities, the only need many families now supply to their members is emotional, leaving one fragile thread to hold together what once was bound by man. The result—more divorce."[18]

The feminist movement has stated that for a woman to be positionally equal with a man there must be an absence of role differentiations. That posture has led many wives to resent the roles God has ordained for them. As a result, those same attitudes can be transferred to daughters, who will then feel resentment toward the men they eventually marry.[19] Even young Christian couples have been drawn slowly into all that this emerging philosophy of the family involves. One young couple in particular vividly portrayed this problem. Those two people, who seemed "the perfect couple," embarked on a course of events leading inexorably and inevitably to divorce. The history of their relationship showed parallels in every area we have discussed. Kitty claimed to know Christ as her Savior, but she did not know Him as Lord. His absolutes meant little to her if they happened to come between herself and what she wanted to do. Generally, what she wanted to do was follow the world's materialistic value system and morals. Kitty's husband was also a Christian, but not strong enough in his faith and emotional makeup to be the spiritual leader and head she needed. He felt guilty about that and made sporadic attempts to be the leader he knew he should be before God, but Kitty seemed to make a game out of getting around him.

18. Sidney Sulkin, ed., "What Future for the American Family?" *Changing Times* (December 1976), 7-8.
19. John D. Frame, *Psychology and Personality Development* (Chicago: Moody, 1969), 98.

They both had expensive tastes and were undisciplined in their spending habits. Because of their indebtedness, she went back to work when their daughter was five months old. She increasingly gleaned her identity from her status in the world, continually striving for higher and better positions, joining various clubs and service organizations. Her time at home dwindled to almost nothing. The few minutes she spent at home were spent with her daughter, leaving little time for effective communication with her husband. Kitty announced that she could not be happy any other way and that she certainly could not make her husband or daughter happy if she herself was not happy. Her husband seemed to realize they were headed for trouble, but he had allowed Kitty free reign for so long that he did not know how to pull the relationship back together.

Kitty's lack of respect for her husband and for God's absolutes led her into extramarital affairs. The latter brought a final bitter separation and divorce. As always, the saddest part of this story cannot be told. No one knows fully what scars a little three-year-old daughter can suffer when parents become more concerned with what they can get than with what they can give.

ISSUE: LOVE

IDEAL POSITION: A GIVING RELATIONSHIP

Based on 1 John and on 1 Corinthians 13, the concept of love asks the question: What can I give to a relationship? Love is a result of a deep commitment and a response to the total person. Thus, love has the quality of self-giving, not exploitation, and is Christlike in its characteristics.

TRADITIONAL DISTORTION: A SUSTAINING RELATIONSHIP

Love in a marriage might be a fringe benefit, but it is conditional on the wife *knowing* her place in the family and the society. The overemphasis on *place* and *duties* will cause the wife to think of herself only as a machine, not as the object of her husband's love or the helper-companion established in Genesis 2.

EMERGING DISTORTION: A SELFISH RELATIONSHIP

Based on modern existential and humanistic principles, What can I get from the relationship? seems to be the question asked when the issue of love is analyzed. Such is the selfish, independent philosophy proposed by such popular songs as "I Want to Be Free."

The ability to say good-bye at will becomes the goal of the emerging family, which can be summed up in the following quote: "In the Civil Rights Movement, you need to have a feeling for the temporary... of making something as good as you can, while it lasts. In a conventional relationship, time is a prison."[20]

CONCLUSION

We have seen how current views on the family have evolved. The philosophical structure of the family has slowly shifted away from God as a result of an inaccurate use of His Word. Today's structure, in rejecting biblical principles, relies on an existential basis for behavior. In family relationships individual goals, rather than family unity, become first priority.

For the Christian, however, the most important idea to be gleaned in attempting to develop an ideal relationship is that God has set the patterns by which He wants the Christian family to operate. They are carefully and fully given in His Word. The biblical perspective is based on mutual giving and serving, respecting and loving, and always within the specific framework of responsibilities.

QUESTIONS TO PONDER

1. Briefly outline the biblical position concerning the family unit.
2. How has society historically distorted God's original intention concerning the family unit?
3. Analyze some emerging trends that will affect the family.
4. Define the following terms:
   a. humanistic principles
   b. selfish independence
   c. roles
   d. dual-archal rule
   e. patriarchal rule
   f. absolutes
   g. values
   h. concept of love
5. From this chapter what conclusions can be made for the evangelical Christian?

20. Kenneth L. Culver, ed. *Social Problems in America* (San Francisco: Holt, Rinehart & Winston, 1974), 223.

4

The Two Shall Become One

We have discussed that the original intention of God in creation was to make a male and a female who would express His glory through their unity of being and diversity of function. They were to complete each other, enabling them to fulfill the purpose of God for procreation and domination of the earth. They were not to seek the other's position, but as half of the whole man they were to complement each other. The Fall of Adam and Eve distorted that relationship and blurred the image. Instead of their working together in unity, competition began. Rather than the pair expressing the glory of God, they expressed the grossness of sin. Their original unity, seen in the proper correspondence of their persons and the sexual union, was superseded by the power struggle initiated in the Fall, which has continued in society ever since. The willing submission of the wife and the loving lordship of the husband, an expression of divine unity, has become distorted and, for some, has ceased to exist.

The distortion we see in husband-wife relationships is not new. Ever since the battle of the sexes began in the Garden of Eden, many men have yielded to the overtly sinful practice of "lording it over" their wives. On the other hand, many wives have failed to submit willingly to the leadership of their husbands. Though they may have yielded outwardly in reaction to pressure from society in general or their husbands specifically, the inward submission has been rare. Husbands and wives are guided by the current secular values that we have called the emerging distortion, and they are being molded by the world rather than by the Word of God (Rom. 12).

In this section we hope to show the proper roles of husbands and wives who are Christians; non-Christians have no power from God to reach the standards laid out in the book of Ephesians. However, before proceeding to Ephesians, we want to explore the status of women in Paul's world as a backdrop to his teaching.

THE ROLE OF WOMEN IN PAUL'S WORLD

The traditional role of women in Western society finds its roots in the western portion of the Mediterranean in the countries of Greece and Italy, but so does the women's liberation movement. In both Greece and Italy women were considered inferior to men, but that was rectified to a considerable degree in later Roman society.

ROMAN SOCIETY

The lot of women changed considerably from the days of the early republic to that of the Roman Empire during the time of Paul. In earlier days, the wife and daughter had little power, economically, domestically, or politically. The changes in the late republic and early empire gave her access to all the areas of life mentioned above, but not without cost. Unfortunately, with her liberation came the destruction of the Roman family, which also was affected by the same social adjustments that gave "freedom" to women.

The right of the father over his wife and children was granted to him in Rome's early history by the Twelve Tables. That power extended to every area of control over his family, even to the power of life and death. The reason for the control over the wife and daughter was because of the assumed weakness and lightmindedness of the female sex.[1] In view of that, a woman was always under the legal protection and authority of a man.

That structure of authority was considered essential to the maintenance of Roman society. The Roman state was perceived as an association of households, and a person's position in a household determined his status in the community. In like manner, a strong parallel existed between the power of the head of the family over his dependents and the power of the community leaders over the citizens.

After the Second Punic War the power of the husband began to weaken because of two basic moves of the state. Dowry rights ceased to pass from the father of the bride to the husband. That tended to give the woman more control of her property and more independence in mar-

---

1. Sarah Pomeroy, *Goddesses, Whores, Wives, and Slaves* (New York: Schocken Books, 1975), 150.

riage. In time, women would be allowed to inherit, make legal contracts and wills, and initiate divorce. The second cause was Augustus's *law of liberation*. To encourage childbirth he decreed that women who bore several children were freed from a male guardian. A modern counterpart to that 'law' would be a recent decision of the French government. Because of the low birth rate in France, the government will give women $300 a month to quit the job force and have a third child. Augustus's decree also had the effect of the reversal of a philosophical evaluation of women mentioned earlier:

> This provision . . . impaired the judicial doctrine of the weakness of the female sex by expressing the notion that at least those women who had demonstrated responsible behavior by bearing the children Rome needed could be deemed capable of acting without a male guardian.[2]

Not only were the laws concerning the guardian instrumental in bringing female emancipation, but various philosophers and moralists began to raise the question of the equality of women and men. Stoicism, first taught by Zeno of Greece, was advocated by Seneca, Epictetus, and the emperor Marcus Aurelius (beyond the time of Paul), who urged the elevation of the position of women. The various religions of the time, including Christianity, also allowed women to participate along with men in most activities, thus heightening the feminine consciousness. Many feared that the growing emancipation of women would bring a deterioration of morals and the destruction of the family. Some women did begin to be more lax in their morals with added freedom as evidenced by a quote from Seneca (A.D. 54): "Is there any woman that blushes at divorce now that certain illustrious and noble ladies reckon their years, not by the number of consuls, but by the number of their husbands, and leave home in order to marry, and marry in order to be divorced?"[3]

Such vices were not restricted to women, however, for even such men as Cicero and Cato were guilty of divorcing their wives for greater wealth. But in women's emancipation, it seems as if a passion developed for a lack of responsibility to a husband and home. The slogan emerged: "To live your own life!"[4]

GREEK SOCIETY

The road to feminine emancipation in Greece was harder and less

2. Ibid., 151.
3. Charles C. Ryrie, *The Place of Women in the Church* (Chicago: Moody, 1958), 6.
4. Jerome Carcopino, *Daily Life in Ancient Rome* (New Haven, Conn.: Yale U., 1940), 93.

successful than that of its Roman counterpart. The woman was sold practically as a slave to her husband. She was basically uneducated except in her home duties. That inferiority of women was fostered by a negative attitude propagated by the scholars of the day. Women were seen to be the embodiment of evil (the myth of Pandora is an example).

Plato is often cited as one who truly considered women to be equal with men. Although he taught that women should have the same education as men, it was for a utilitarian end; that women might be best and most fully used for the state. In *Timaeus* one sees Plato at his most negative point:

> On the subject of animals, then, the following remarks offered. Of the men who come into the world, those who were cowards or led unrighteous lives may with reason be supposed to have changed into the nature of women in the second generation.[5]

Women in most periods of Greek history were very much under the dominion of men and lived very secluded lives. The woman was prohibited from participating in the nondomestic affairs of life to the point that she was really a prisoner in her home. That seclusion apparently was to guarantee that any offspring were her husband's.

Husbands highly honored women, but ordinarily only within the context of being mothers and housekeepers. The woman was a ruler in that realm and possessed a place of honor, but she was not to move from that place given to her by nature. Xenophon, a Greek historian, in the *Oeconomicus*, has Ischomachus say to his wife concerning the vocational differences of man and woman, "And since both the indoor and the outdoor tasks demanded labour and attention, God from the first adapted the woman's nature, I think, to the indoor and man's to the outdoor tasks and cares."[6] Interestingly, no such distinction of sphere exists in the Genesis record when it presents the dominion of the earth by male and female.

The status of women varied in the cultures of Rome and Greece. One thing seems clear: if women were given legal protection, and some given opportunity to pursue many of the privileges enjoyed by men, they never fully achieved recognition as equal persons in the way described in Genesis 1:26-28 and in the way early Christianity viewed them.

---

5. Evelyn and Frank Stagg, *Woman in the World of Jesus* (Philadelphia: Westminster, 1978), 82.
6. Ibid., 73.

PAUL'S TEACHING ON THE ROLE OF HUSBANDS AND WIVES IN EPHESIANS 5

The pinnacle passage on the proper role relationships of husbands and wives is Ephesians 5:22-33. We see there the reciprocal responsibilities of man and woman in the marriage union. The two are to be motivated by the concept of servanthood, but not in identical ways. The husband is called to lead his wife (as Christ leads the church), building her and caring for her needs. The wife is admonished to submit to that leadership as she would submit to the leadership of Christ. Those reciprocal duties express the unity of the two as created by God and illustrate the unity of Christ and the church. That unity may best be served by diversity such as we have with the separate functions of husband and wife or by the separate ministries within the Body of Christ (1 Cor. 12). Diversity in unity may be seen in the example of a football team. If a coach told his team members that they needed greater unity and that he wanted everyone to play quarterback, disaster would occur. Instead, each of the team members plays a different position or role, but with the same goal in view. Thus, unity is served through diversity. Apparently, God views the unity of husband and wife in the same way.

THE UNITY THEME OF EPHESIANS

The teaching of Paul on the unity of husband and wife recorded in Ephesians 5 is only part of the greater unity motif of Ephesians. Only through an examination of that motif will we fully understand Ephesians 5:22-33.

In answer to the yearnings of the first-century world,[7] Paul averred that the world makes sense only through the acceptance of Jesus Christ, who is the goal of all things in the universe (Eph. 1:10). Similar to the Stoic desire for brotherhood, the apostle proclaims that everyone, regardless of race, color, or class has been made acceptable to God through Christ's death on the cross (2:13). Gentiles, who were alienated from the promises and salvation of God could now be "fellow citizens with the saints, and of God's household" (v. 19).

In contrast with the pagan, religious world, Christianity brought a true oneness. The unity of all things in Christ (see the *therefore* of Eph. 4:1), from a cosmic perspective, was the impetus for Christians to maintain spiritual unity (v. 15) and to offer hope to a disintegrating and fragmented society.

The unity of Christians was based on several Christian realities. Paul

7. See G. H. P. Thompson, *The Letters of Paul to the Ephesians, to the Colossians, and to Philemon* (Cambridge: Cambridge U., 1967), 20-22, for a description of the religious and philosophical groupings of the ancient world for which Christianity provided an answer.

said there was one body, one Spirit, one hope, one Lord, one faith, one
baptism, and one God and Father of all (4:4-6). There is not a baptism
for Jews and another for Gentiles; not one for blacks and another for
whites. There are no second-class Christians.

In Ephesians especially, the concept of allegiance to and union with
one Lord is important. Over against the multiplicity of the gods and
lords of paganism, the Christian religion proclaimed only one Lord
(4:5). He alone is the head of the church (1:22; 5:23) and its Savior (5:2,
23). Union with Christ (1:3) has at least three results: (1) resurrection or
enthronement with Jesus (2:6), which is sharing with him in triumph
over the forces of this age; (2) rebirth, which is putting off one's self-
centered nature and putting on true righteousness and holiness (4:22-
24); and (3) the gift of the Holy Spirit of God, the pledge of God's favor
and the promise of future blessings (1:14).[8]

Throughout the book, the major idea is unity. That unity related specifically to the accomplishments of Christ in this world. He conquered
the forces contrary to God, put the universe on a course that will rescue
it from the god of this age, and made Christians participants in His
victories.

THE FORM AND STRUCTURE OF EPHESIANS 5:22-33

This passage constitutes a portion of a larger section of exhortatory
material that biblical scholars call a *haustafel* or table of responsibilities
for a household. The passage develops the responsibilities of husbands
and wives to each other, whereas chapter 6 continues with the duties of
parents and children, and masters and slaves.[9] Notice also that there is
no mention of rights—only responsibilities. (See Appendix 2 for more
detailed background.)

There is a summary statement in verses 22-24 followed by a presentation of the divine activity (of Christ) in verses 25-27, succeeded by the

8. Ibid., 27.
9. Scholars long have argued about the origin of the *haustafeln* as a literary form. Some see
the source as pre-Christian in either Judaism or Hellenism. Cf. Martin Dibelius, *An die
Kolosser Epheser an Philemon* (Tubingen: J.C.B. Mohr [Paul Siebeck], 1933), pp. 48-50
and Karl Weidinge, *Das Problem der urchristlichen Haustafeln* (Leipzig: J. C. Heinrichs,
1928) are major exponents of a Hellenistic origin. David Daube, "Participle and Imperative in 1 Peter," an appended note to E.G. Selwyn, *The First Epistle of St. Peter*
(London: Macmillan, 1964), 467-88, advocates a Hebrew form that was brought into
Greek.
   A more likely origin, based on Old Testament passages, is that of the apostle Paul.
Notice the dependence on the Old Testament in the *haustafeln* of Ephesians 5 and 6:
Ephesians 5:31 has Genesis 2:24 as its background; the husband's exhortation to love
his wife may relate to Leviticus 19:18; the bride imagery may be taken from the rela-
tionship of Yahweh and Israel; Ephesians 6:1-3 has the fifth commandment (Ex. 20:12)
as the authority for its comment. Peter may have copied his *haustafeln* form after Paul.

human (husbands) activity in verses 28-29*b*. The interrelationship of the divine and human follows in verses 29*c*-32. Finally, the passage ends with a summary statement.

At least five emphases may be found in the passage: Christ is the Savior of the body, the church; the Lord is responsible for the purity of the church; the husband's love is for the wife and is an emulation of Christ's love for the church; the wife is to submit to and respect her husband as the church submits to the Lord; and the Genesis text, in Paul's estimation, represents the unity of Christ and the church as one body. The text has Christ-church as the focus and the husband-wife as the expression of that divine relationship.[10] This appears to be the same kind of imagery we discern in Genesis 1 and 2, as expanded in Psalm 8.

THE RELATION OF THE HOUSE RULES TO THE EPHESIAN THEME

The house rules are a superb expression of the motif of unity in Ephesians. The exhortation beginning with 4:1 develops the implications of God's intention to unite all men and all things under the lordship of Christ. This section gives an exalted view of how the new existence in Christ may be lived within the Christian household in contradistinction to the way the Ephesian recipients had lived in their non-Christian relationships (4:17-24). The Christian husband and wife may begin in Christ to undo some of the results of the Fall. Christ has called a truce in the war between the sexes and proclaimed unity and fulfillment to all through His victory over the world.

MUTUAL SUBMISSION AND HEADSHIP IN EPHESIANS 5:22-33

SUBMISSION–PART OF THE CURSE?

Does the Pauline argument recognize a proper hierarchical structure to marriage? Is this structure a result of the Fall that needs to be done away with in Christ, or was this authority structure God's intention in creation? Let us look at the latter question first.

Christian feminists often insist that submission is not proper for Christian wives today because submission, they say, was a part of the curse from which Christ released women. For example, Letha Scanzoni and Nancy Hardesty in *All We're Meant to Be*, understand male authority and female submission as a yoke of sin that needs to be thrown off. In its

---

10. Markus Barth, "Ephesians 4-6," *The Anchor Bible*, vol. 34A, ed. William Foxwell Albright and David Noel Freedman (Garden City, N.Y.: Doubleday, 1974), 700.

place they propose an egalitarian marriage, neither partner being an authority figure, with both partners being equally submissive.[11]

Can such a relationship be maintained? Eventually, one of the partners would have to give direction to the marriage. Does an authority role necessitate inequality of essence? Of course not! Although he has a superior role, the president of the United States is not any more in the image of God than anyone else in America. When God ordained elders in the church to rule and lead the local church, they were not created as superior beings. Parents are not superior to their children in reference to position before God and as heirs to the redemption of God. Authority does not supplant equality.

George W. Knight contends that contrary to Scanzoni and Hardesty all the aspects affected by the curse are already presumed in Genesis 2. The curse on Adam and Eve causes a distortion of already perfectly natural conditions: childbearing (Gen. 1:28), work (Gen. 1:28; 2:15), and authority and submission of husband and wife (Gen. 2:18-25). Is the church to seek to alleviate the effect of sin on childbirth, work under hardship, and the husband-wife friction? Yes, he says, but not by elimination of childbirth, work, or proper husband-wife roles. Rather than remove a husband's headship, he says that through love, one should remove an oppressive rule, which is a result of sin.[12]

Several years ago, one of us knew a man who bossed his wife terribly. He gave her instructions on how she should dress, fix her hair, what to buy, where to go—but he had little genuine concern for her as a person. He did all the things he wanted to do and bought what he wanted to buy, but she was a slave in her house. He was not leading her in love; he was being a dictator. That is not what is meant by *headship* in the Scriptures. That husband should have sought to bring out the very best in his wife and see to it that her needs and some of her desires were being met. Here the church needs to correct the plague of sin on husbands' attitudes toward their wives. Peter sought to do that in his first epistle: "You married men, in the same way, must live with your wives in an intelligent consideration of them" (1 Pet. 3:7, Williams*).

We have already demonstrated that the creation order recognized roles for the husband and wife, but does the teaching of the apostle Paul substantiate such roles? We now turn to our second question posed above: Did Paul recognize a hierarchical relationship between husband

---

* *The New Testament, A Translation in the Language of the People*, by Charles B. Williams.
11. Letha Scanzoni and Nancy Hardesty, *All We're Meant to Be* (Waco, Tex.: Word, 1974), 106-18.
12. George W. Knight III, *The New Testament Teaching on the Role Relationship of Men and Women* (Grand Rapids: Baker, 1977), 43-44.

and wife? To decide that question we must examine his use of the word *submission* (*hypotassomenoi*, Eph. 5:21) and *head* (*kephalē*, v. 23), as well as the house-rules form and the unity motif set forth by him.

IS SUBMISSION TO BE MUTUAL?

The house-rules are considered by most to begin with verse 22. However, because verse 22 does not have a verb, we must decide the relationship of the phrase: "Be subject to one another" in verse 21 to what precedes and follows it. Probably, we should not connect it with verse 22 in a grammatical sense, but we may understand the phrase as setting the tone for the following passage.

The verb *submit* (also translated *subject*) is used in reference to many different relationships in the New Testament, such as wives to husbands (Eph. 5:22; Col. 3:18; Titus 2:5; 1 Pet. 3:1, 5); children to parents (Luke 2:51), slaves to masters (Titus 2:9; 1 Pet. 2:18); Christians to secular authorities (Rom. 13:13; Titus 3:1; 1 Pet. 2:13), church members to church leaders (1 Pet. 5:5), as well as believers to God (1 Cor. 15:28b; Heb. 12:9; James 4:7) and to Christ (Eph. 5:24).

The difficulty in the passage at hand is that if we understand the phrase "Submit yourselves to one another" in verse 21 as referring to verses 22-33, one has mutual submission of husbands and wives, which appears to dilute the idea of hierarchy. That is averred by Scanzoni and Hardesty:

> The usual way of teaching Ephesians 5 suggests that it is the wife who must make the self-sacrifice (just the opposite of what the text says) and unwittingly encourages the husband to be selfish, egocentric, convinced of his right to have his own way, and filled with pride, and a heady sense of power. No person can remain unspoiled by the corrupting effect of power when he is told he holds by divine right a position of superiority in which others are duty-bound to subject themselves to him.
> If the husband's example is Christ, we must remind ourselves of how Christ regards and relates to the believer. He never compels us against our wills; he never forces or coerces. There really is no basis for insisting that wives obey husbands even if it goes against their own better judgment.[13]

The two feminists have interpreted the passage through the mind-set of contemporary society's reaction rather than with the spirit of Ephesians. Certainly a man might become as they describe him, and we might add that a woman rebelling against biblical submission also might

13. Scanzoni and Hardesty, 102.

act in sinful ways. The point of the passage is that in Christ the man can lovingly lead and the woman can willingly submit.

Scanzoni and Hardesty present Christ as one who gives suggestions that the church then may evaluate and choose to obey or disobey, seemingly with either option being acceptable. The problem with that view is that disobedience to Christ's commands is sin. The wife is to fulfill her role to her husband in the same way as the church should to Christ. We must stress that adhering to the biblical roles assigned by God is an act of obedience to Him. Each spouse fulfills his or her role in loving submission to God. Therefore, the faithfulness of a husband's loving leadership is not conditional on the wife's willingness to submit to his authority, nor is the wife exempt from her function if the husband is negligent in his responsibility. Both are responsible before God for their own attitudes and obedience to His design for marriage.

Certainly, if the husband is asking the wife to do something contrary to God's righteousness, she is not under obligation in such instances. In such cases the husband is not giving loving leadership but is, in fact, sinning. If a conflict occurs, then responsibility to obey must be directed to God apart from the authority figure.

For whatever reason, in presenting submission, Paul did not specifically require submission of the husband. Neither in the wider context are parents urged to submit to their children (Eph. 6:1-4), or masters to their slaves (6:5-9). Only the terms *wives, children,* and *slaves* occur with verbs expressing subjection or obedience, and in each case "the obligation is based on the connection of the believer with Christ."[14]

Implicitly, although the *one another* may provide for a mutually submissive attitude by the various classes of the house rules, it is difficult to be conclusive on the question of mutual submission. In reference to the pairs, note the role of authority but also the idea of servanthood:

Submission

Through obedience to authority	*Through special care*
Wives—submit to husbands in everything, respect	*Husbands*—love wives as own body
Children—obey parents, honor	*Fathers*—don't exasperate children, train and instruct in the Lord
Slaves—obey, respect and fear, with sincerity	*Masters*—do not threaten slaves

Whether the mutual submission of Ephesians 5:21 contextually relates to the husband-wife (or parent-child, master-slave) discussion is of small

14. B. F. Westcott, *St. Paul's Epistle to the Ephesians* (Grand Rapids: Eerdmans, 1958), 82.

consequence in light of the servanthood that is a necessary aspect of Christian living. However, we must not assume that servanthood excludes roles of authority. Christ was Lord over His disciples and the church, but He was also the true servant (John 13:13-17; Mark 10:45; Phil. 2:5-8). Certainly, leaders in the local church are to submit them- selves to their people, and yet they are to exercise authority over the church. In like manner, the wife submits herself to her husband by rec- ognizing him as the authority or head in everything, whereas the hus- band places himself under his wife by meeting her needs and fulfilling her (vv. 26-27). That is the expression of *agapē* (love) in the text that the husband is exhorted to do.[15] Joyful submission on the part of the wife toward the husband's authority and the loving headship over the wife on the part of the husband is the correction the apostle gives to the corrup- tion of the husband-wife relationships found in Genesis 3:16.

Part of the difficulty of husband and wife being able to identify prop- erly with each other's roles is that they have not experienced the frustra- tions and specific problems of those roles. To understand better the role of mother and homemaker, a husband should consider periodically tak- ing over the house for his wife. The wife is then able to have greater freedom by being away from some of the responsibilities of the home and children. Husbands can better understand why certain things around the house often are not done (children can wreck our best-laid plans!) and perhaps will seek to pitch in to help more often.

DOES HEADSHIP MEAN AUTHORITY?

How one understands Ephesians 5:22-33 depends considerably on what one understands by the word *head*. There appears to have been no contemporary analogy to Paul's reference to the husband as the head of the wife. The idea probably originated with Paul and must be under- stood in the context of his letter.[16] Why then did he compare the hus- band to a head? Let us look at some reasons given for this metaphor.

Berkeley Mickelsen and his wife Alvera write that the word *head* does not mean "boss" or "final authority." Instead, they say, the common meaning was *source*, like the "head of the Mississippi River."[17] Likewise, Scanzoni and Hardesty argue that source, not authority, is the meaning of *head*.[18]

15. Barth, 621.
16. Ibid., 618.
17. Berkeley and Alvera Mickelsen, "Does Male Dominance Tarnish Our Translations?" *Christianity Today* (5 October 1979), 23.
18. Scanzoni and Hardesty, 30-31.

The idea of source in the word *head* seems to be absent in the classical era of Greece, and probably in the use of the word in the secular world in Paul's time.[19] This *head*, occurring in the plural, could mean the source of something or refer to that which completes something,[20] but the Mickelsens and Scanzoni and Hardesty are incorrect in their other examples and arguments.

The standard lexicon on the vocabulary of the New Testament and early Christianity lists *kephalē* at times as referring to superior rank.[21] *The Theological Dictionary of the New Testament*, a major work, presents *kephalē* as conveying the idea of authority.[22]

A look at Paul's writing will reveal his intended meaning. A study of *head* in the context of three passages in Colossians (1:18; 2:10, 19) reveals that the word refers to rule. But more to the point is Paul's use of head in reference to the creation narratives in 1 Corinthians 11. The authority of the male is seen in his being prior to her and also the source of the female in creation (vv. 8-16). The idea that authority is based on source is argued in Genesis 2 and the view also expressed by Paul in 1 Timothy 2:13, but this does not mean that the word *head* means "source." Finally, there is the use of head in Ephesians. Ephesians 1:22 states that Christ is the head (or source of) and authority over the church.[23]

In conclusion, Paul's use of the term *kephalē* reflects, in metaphorical contexts, the use of the Septuagint where *head* is a synonym for the Hebrew word meaning "the chief ruler." Applied to the New Testament question of the home, the husband is the head or authority over the home and its affairs.

HEADSHIP AND SUBMISSION BRING UNITY

Rather than disharmony coming from role distinctions between husband and wife, Ephesians 5 emphasizes that unity is the result. The

---

19. Wayne Grudem, "Does *Kephalē* ('Head') Mean 'Source' or 'Authority Over' in Greek Literature? A Survey of 2,336 Examples," *Trinity Journal*, vol. 6 (1985): 38-59. See also H. Wayne House, "Should a Woman Prophesy or Preach Before Men?" *Bibliotheca Sacra*, vol. 145 (1988): 141-61.
20. H. G. Liddell and George Scott, *An Intermediate Greek-English Lexicon* (Oxford: Clarendon, 1889), 430.
21. Walter Bauer, *A Greek-English Lexicon of the New Testament and Other Early Christian Literature*, trans. William F. Arndt and F. Wilbur Gingrich (Chicago: U. of Chicago, 1957), 431.
22. Heinrich Schlier, "kephale," *Theological Dictionary of the New Testament*, ed. Gerhard Kittel, trans. and ed. Geoffrey W. Bromiley (Grand Rapids: Eerdmans, 1965), 3:674-75.
23. Cf. Paul Sampley, ed. Matthew Black, *And the Two Shall Become One Flesh* (Cambridge: Cambridge U., 1971), 122.

background of Genesis 1 and 2, as well as the proper understanding of headship, causes the apostle to structure this passage around unity. Rather than the disharmony brought about by the Fall and its results, Paul saw in the new order in Christ a return to the harmony of the creation when God said, "It is very good!" Christians are to have a new order of existence, a way to walk, because they are a new creation of God. They are to be wise and know the will of God (Rom. 12:1-2; Eph. 5:15-17), rather than follow the current spirit of the times. Lenski spoke to that neglected emphasis of unity in the discussion on the male-female roles in the home:

> One point is made to stand out, one that the entire epistle also presents: Unity. One body, which thus has one head (1:22; 4:15). So the married couple is a unity. It can have but one head, even as the Bride, the church, can have but the one head, Christ. Two heads for either would not only cause a duality, it would produce a monstrosity.[24]

So then, we have observed that wives are to submit, not because of the superior nature of the male, but because of the unity of the two, a unity intended by God in creation. The entire epistle of Ephesians speaks of the unity of the body with its head. That theme is reflected again in Ephesians 5 where the husband is urged to love his wife as his own body, for as the Scripture says, "The two shall become one flesh" (v. 31). Unity, not superiority, is what is displayed in submission. The wife's recognition of the husband's lordship and the husband's loving rule of the wife is the mutual submission Paul presented in this passage, a reversal of the curse of Genesis 3:16b. To fail in that regard is to fail to experience the reality of the new creation in regard to marriage. It is to break the unity of the bond that God intends to bring to the male and female, and it destroys the illustration that marriage has of Christ and the church.

We have seen in the biblical portions of this unit that God created man as male and female, equal bearers of the divine image. And we understand that He intended for them to fulfill His purposes of procreation and domination of the earth, culminating in bringing glory to Him. Their equality is expressed by their joint creation in His image; the rule of man over the woman is because woman is derived from man. That original unity was destroyed in the Fall; as a result, woman would desire

24. R. C. H. Lenski, *The Interpretation of Galatians, Ephesians, and Philippians* (Minneapolis: Augsburg, 1937), 626-27.

to usurp man's rule. And man, if he was to rule, would often become domineering. God's original creation seemed marred beyond repair. However, Paul presented in Ephesians the plan of a new creation in Christ. In reference to the husband-wife relationship, provision was made for following the will of God and for believing spouses again to manifest God's creation unity by the woman's voluntary submission to the lordship of the man and the man's meeting the woman's needs by a loving rule over her. In that kind of marriage relationship, a symbol of Christ and the church, God's glory is able to be seen in His world.

Questions to Ponder

1. What are some ways in which the feminist movement of the ancient Roman world parallels that of the feminist movement in America today?
2. In a nutshell, what is the motivation for the demands of the current feminist movement? Is it spiritual, and are the demands biblically acceptable?
3. What are some legitimate concerns of the women's movement to which Christians should speak?
4. Give some examples from your own marriage in which unity is enhanced by diversity. If you are not married, give some complements you might need in a partner.
5. Does the hierarchical form of marriage have to destroy the ingenuity, creativity, and expression of women? Explain your answer.
6. What does Ephesians 5:22 mean by submitting ourselves "as to the Lord"?
7. In living with his wife, how might a husband obey Scripture in a considerate manner?
8. If a husband is not lovingly leading his wife, does that properly allow a wife not to be submissive to him and not to accept his authority over her?
9. How is the husband to love his wife as his own body?
10. Did submission of the wife to the husband come as a result of the Fall? Explain your answer.
11. How can Christ restore the pre-Fall relationship of husband and wife? Will it ever be fully restored in this life?
12. As persons in the image of God, if someone has authority over another person, is there inequality between the two?
13. In what ways may submission be mutual between husband and wife? Give practical examples how each might be a servant to the other and yet both retain a hierarchy in the marriage.

14. What is the meaning of *submission* in Ephesians 5?
15. What is the meaning of *head* in Paul's discussions in 1 Corinthians 11 and Ephesians 5?

5

Confronting the Problem and Its Solution

The four previous chapters of this unit have dealt primarily with the setting of the home concerning the wife and mother.

Marital status is a major factor in determining the responsibilities and priorities of the Christian woman.

It has been substantiated from Scripture that the wife's main work responsibility centers in the home (an internal work priority). That is contrasted to the role of the husband, for in taking on the responsibility of caring and providing for his family, he finds his main work priority to be outside the home. (See figure at the end of this chapter.) That is evident when we analyze the passages concerning *love* in a marriage. While it is true that emotional affections ought to be evident in the husband's life as well as his wife's, Scripture indicates that the *main* emphasis in the love role for the husband is different from that of his spouse. For example, in Titus 2:4, wives are to be taught (note that it does not come naturally) to "love their husbands." The word *love* here is *phileo* and indicates strong affection, one that results from a sense of satisfaction that the needs of the family are met. It also indicates a strong physical and emotional attachment to one's spouse.

In Ephesians 5:25 husbands are commanded to "love their wives, even as Christ loved the church." *Love* in this passage comes from a different Greek word, *agape*, which indicates a benevolent relationship to be demonstrated in the family. Another primary idea involved in the agape love is sacrifice. The husband willingly gives himself for the good of his beloved. That is the main analogy of Ephesians 5:25. One way agape love is to be shown is by the husband's providing for the family in the work world (external work priorities). The apostle Paul, in 1 Timothy

5:8 stated, "But if anyone does not *provide* for his own . . . he has denied the faith, and is worse than an *unbeliever*." *Provide* here refers to the husband's maintenance of the family. This looking out for his own establishes his credibility with his wife and family—the opposite of the infidel (unbeliever) who is untrustworthy in all his actions.

Therefore, the Christian wife then ought to submit herself to the headship of her husband. The unmarried female, on the other hand, ought to submit herself willingly to Christ for direction and meaning in life, and then be free to act independently within the boundaries set by Scripture.

Finally, role differences between the husband and wife were not created to make the male superior to the woman; the opposite is true. Jesus said in Matthew 20:26, "Whoever wishes to become great among you shall be your servant." The world thinks in terms of a ladder development; that is, a leader must always come out on top and that superiority results from status. That philosophy has been filtered down and transmitted to the family unit.

On the other hand, Scripture teaches that all believers are positionally equal in Christ (Rom. 2:11; Gal. 3:26-28). Roles are needed to promote organizational unity and purpose in the marriage relationship. A role does not necessarily signify a hierarchy. A more scripturally compatible view can be seen in a kind of wheel design. We are told many times in the Bible that God is no respecter of persons; He does not see human beings ranked in terms of worth or status.

THE WHEEL, OR HORIZONTAL, VIEW OF MARITAL ROLES

Both husband and wife are a part of the same wheel (positionally equal on the horizontal plane). The King is Christ, not man. The Holy Spirit, at the hub of the wheel, then directs the husband and wife to Christ's leadership (through which they can fulfill their intended roles for the family). Is it not for that reason that Satan is working so hard to destroy the Christian family? It seems frightening, but we must remember God's scriptural principles have not changed, no matter how much society's have. And because of Christ's work at Calvary and the indwelling of the Holy Spirit, the "ideal" in family relationships can be practiced and achieved!

In light of the biblical and sociological background given thus far in this segment, ponder the following commonly asked questions.

1. Should a wife work outside the home? According to her role as set by Scripture, is outside employment a sin, or at best, an acceptable alternative?

That is a complex question, but it can be answered in a simplistic way. No, outside employment for the wife is not a sin. However, her work priorities must be in tune to biblical directives. A close look at the passage in Proverbs 31, which lists the characteristics of a good wife, indicates that work outside the home is affirmed as a positive trait. "She makes linen garments and sells them, and supplies belts to the tradesmen" (Prov. 31:24, NASB).

We see in this verse that the *ideal* wife is involved not only in production, but also in the marketing aspect of her chosen vocation. But we cannot take that verse out of context. For prior to it, an outline of the wife's priorities in life are given.

Her husband comes first (v. 11).
She is the first to rise in the morning; to take care of the
   needs of her family (v. 15).
She takes care of the needy in the community (v. 20).
When all of her above-listed responsibilities are met then she engages
   in employment. So, if the wife is able to fulfill her prior obligations,
   outside employment cannot be considered a sin (v. 24).

2. Are Christians succumbing to the world's views and attitudes?

Even as evangelical Christians, we find ourselves changing our value system ever so slightly on the issue of marital roles and responsibilities. We accept with more and more ease ideas, life-styles, and values that are totally alien to Scripture.

We need to remind ourselves of the illustration of the frog. If the frog is put in a pot of boiling water, it will jump out. If that frog, however, is put in the pot and the water is warmed gradually, the frog will not jump out and thus will be "cooked." As evangelical Christians we need to be aware that changes occur slowly. And, if we are not careful, we can be like a frog being "cooked" in the world's value system. God's directives must never be compromised!

3. What should be said to the wife who says, "I can't be fulfilled staying at home"?

In answering that question, we need to find out what *being fulfilled* means. The world structure defines *fulfillment* for the wife as being independent of any external control (i.e., her husband's authority). She may say, "I can't be fulfilled unless I work outside the home." That indicates a problem of selfishness on her part. This selfishness, which plays on a psychological need of self-identity, is created by our society and tends to persuade the wife that fulfillment in life cannot be achieved in the home setting. A wife with that attitude, however, would have difficulty with Titus 2:1, 4-5, for in that passage "sound doctrine" is manifested in the wife's learning to be a good keeper *at home*, her primary work priority as a wife!

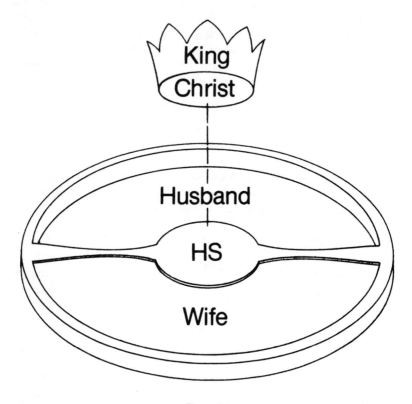

Figure 5.1

Perhaps what the wife needs most is her husband's affirmation and respect for her as the homemaker. She may be taken for granted by her husband and family, or the husband may not hold her position as manager of the household in high esteem. In that case, she truly does not feel fulfilled and seeks an appreciated identity from other skills or persons through an outside job.

In either case, a spiritual-attitude problem probably exists. Whether the problem stems from the wife or the husband, it does not take long for it to permeate the marriage and undermine the family. The fulfillment of God's design for the family structure must always be the priority, must be continually discussed, and must be actively pursued.

For the Christian, then, fulfillment or *self-esteem* can be summed up in the phrase: I'm important . . . but only in relation to the Body of Christ. And when analyzing biblical passages on role demands (Titus, etc.), a wife's fulfillment or self-esteem will *increase* as she yields to the precepts set forth in Scripture. The wife who devotes herself lovingly to serving her family will find fulfillment much easier than the wife who makes fulfillment *itself* her priority.

In the same way, the husband who loves his wife to meet her needs will find fulfillment much easier than the husband who makes lordship his priority.

4. How should the Christian wife respond when her husband grudgingly allows but does not encourage her to seek outside employment?

First, if the husband forbids outside employment, the submissive wife should yield to the demands of her husband. But in the case of the hesitant husband, the wife needs to be very sensitive to him by projecting herself in "his shoes."

His personality may be such that his self-image is threatened. If that is the case, outside employment should not be sought. On the other hand, the husband might be hesitant to accept the wife's idea of outside employment because of a feeling that he is being tested by his wife. By thinking that she indeed does not want to work, the husband might feel an obligation to assert himself by showing some reservation.

The key solution to this question is *communication!* Honest and open dialogue between the couple could eliminate one *assuming* the thoughts and intentions of the other spouse.

5. Does the home situation affect the wife's desire to seek outside employment?

The answer is definitely yes. Some of the factors that may come into play here are:

A. *The present economic need.* Let us suppose that the husband will become incapacitated or need to further his education. Outside employment might be needed. It must be noted, however, that a reversal of roles (between the husband and wife) should, if at all possible, be partial and only temporary. Remember, the children learn their sex identification from their parents!

B. *The situation regarding children.* The illustration at the end of the chapter shows that the needed energies a wife directs toward rearing her children, in effect, determine how much time she can adequately spend in an outside employment situation. Obviously, when all children are in school, she has more free time.

C. *Technology and free time.* Our highly complex and technical society affects the amount of free time a wife does have. As mentioned in a previous chapter, a wife's domestic responsibilities have drastically been altered by technological advances. No longer in our culture are such things as baking bread "from scratch" mandatory. Thus, in caring for her family, a wife can find herself with more free time for other things. Again, the order of work priorities mentioned earlier should be kept in mind.

WORK PRIORITIES FOR THE WIFE (168 HOURS PER WEEK)

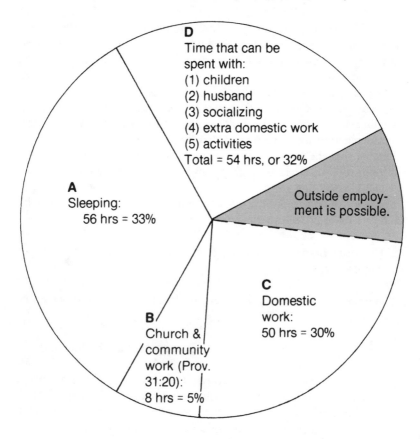

Figure 5.2

For the wife, work is primarily, but not exclusively, inside the home. That is not to say outside work is forbidden, but that outside work for the wife becomes secondary in terms of her priorities. (It is interesting that the order of a wife's work, as found in Proverbs 31, begins with her responsibilities to her family before those outside the home.)

The "gray area" encompassed with C in the chart (Fig. 5.2) thus indicates that outside employment for the wife is contingent on (1) approval of her husband; (2) amount of domestic responsibilities, such as size of the home or the number of children, and (3) church and community work.

Because C and D are not constant, the wife must remain flexible to meet the needs of her family. And, except for the time spent with her children, the wife, to demonstrate *phileo* love (nowhere in Scripture is *agape* used to refer to the wife's love to her husband) to her husband and family, needs to spend section D at home or with her husband and family, and not fill that time with outside employment. For the end result of outside employment many times yields fatigue and stress—two factors that can cause conflict in the family.

It should be noted that in a spiritual sense *agape* love is demonstrated by the wife to her husband (1 John 4:7-11). In her marital role, however, God only demands the *phileo* kind.

WORK PRIORITIES FOR THE HUSBAND (168 HOURS PER WEEK)

Work for the husband is primarily, but not exclusively, outside the home. The *agape* love a husband provides for his family encompasses approximately 35 percent of his time each week (see B and C in the chart, Fig. 5.3).

With about 33 percent of each week spent in sleep, the remaining 32 percent will be spent in the following manner: (1) time with his wife and children; (2) activities such as eating, playing, and watching TV; (3) socializing with friends; (4) extra, outside work; or (5) church and other activities.

For the husband, A, B, and C usually remain constant. D then becomes flexible and subject to many variables. It should also be mentioned that during the time he is at home, the husband should share equally with his wife in caring for their children and helping with the household chores.

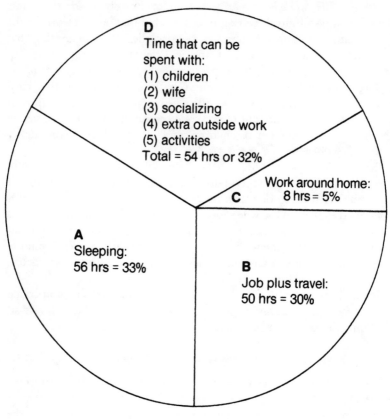

Figure 5.3

Part Two _____
Abortion and Euthanasia

Historically, one of the most important principles of American society has been the sacredness of the life of each individual. We consider primitive, disgusting, and immoral those societies in which the life of the individual is dependent on the whims of the powerful. Yet our society seems, through humanistic thinking, to be on the brink of becoming the kind of people we once detested.

Our societal values and norms have become frighteningly absurd in this age of transition and change. That absurdity takes shape quickly when we compare our country's laws protecting two types of young and unborn. The American bald eagle is protected by law (and rightly so). A person may be fined up to $5,000 for breaking an eagle egg or molesting or killing an eagle. The oddity comes, however, when we realize that the same government passed laws to subsidize the cost of killing an unborn human being.

Dr. Everett Koop believes we are in a "schizophrenic society." He describes a cultural paradox: we will spend large amounts to save the life of a three-pound baby struggling in the intensive care unit, whereas, in the same hospital, we condone the destruction of unborn infants via the abortion route![1]

Koop goes on to say that the Supreme Court, in view of court decisions of the past few years, apparently has shown a higher regard for the humane treatment of murderers than for the rights and life of an unborn infant.[2] At the other end of life's scale, we see a second group of human

1. C. Everett Koop, *The Right to Live: The Right to Die* (Wheaton, Ill: Tyndale, 1976), 17.
2. Ibid., 35.

beings becoming victims of our society's sugarcoated, humanistic philosophy. We are beginning to accept a logical progression of thinking; namely, if abortion is desirable when a child is "unwanted," then terminating the life for the "unwanted" aged also is a real possibility.

That was made vivid when two members of the Euthanasia ("mercy killing") Society, Dr. and Mrs. Henry Pitney Van Dusen, ended their lives together to fulfill a suicide pact.[3] They believed that when life either became totally meaningless for them (as a result of health, etc.), or when they felt society had treated them as unwanted individuals, taking their own lives could be justified.

It is hard for many to relate to those examples because abortion and euthanasia have not directly touched their lives. However, with the increasing disposal of the unwanted, various questions emerge such as, What is the importance of life? How does today's thinking compare to God's thinking as outlined in Scripture? Answers to those questions are needed for a clear perspective of what Christians should be supporting.

First, we will take a brief look at the historical background of the human dignity issue. Next, we will analyze the philosophic structure of a society that allows the unwanted to be terminated. And last, we will question the ethical basis for society's emerging attitude.

3. S. Maculay, "Euthanasia: Can Death Be Friendly?" *Christianity Today* 20 (21 November 1975), 17.

6

The Respect for Life in a Permissive Society

THE HISTORICAL CONTEXT

From extremely primitive societies to those as advanced as the Greeks and Romans were, the termination of unwanted lives has been practiced. Even honored philosophers such as Plato and Aristotle believed that society should rid itself of the frail and the deformed. Both the Greeks and the Romans regularly practiced extensive population control by abortion and infanticide.[1] Reasons for human extermination in ancient Rome included governmental legislation, suppression of the poor by the rich, and superstition. Those may have contributed to the population decline of the third century.[2]

To show the small value placed on human life in ancient Rome, it was customary to put a newborn baby at the father's feet. If he picked up the infant, it meant that he accepted it as his child and as a member of his family. If he did not pick up the infant, the child became a castaway and was left beside the road either to be picked up by a stranger or to die.[3]

It has been estimated that approximately two-thirds of the world's population currently lives in countries that practice active abortion and euthanasia.[4] The lack of respect for human life in those societies is very evident. And to some, the fact would justify the act. According to

---

1. M. Rostovtzeff, *Social & Economic History of the Roman Empire* (London: Oxford Press, 1957), 1:476.
2. Ibid., 2:738.
3. Stewart A. Queen and Robert W. Haberstein, *The Family in Various Cultures*, 4th ed. (Philadelphia: J.B. Lippincott, 1974), 182.
4. "15 Facts You Should Know About Abortion," a brochure distributed by Zero Population Growth, Inc., Washington, D.C., 1979.

anthropologist Marvin Harris, the important population-limiting factors among hunters and gatherers (terms describing primitive cultures) are infanticide and abortion, regardless of the survival risks to the mother.[5] That is because pre-industrial people generally lack effective chemical or mechanical means for preventing conception. However, chemical means and crude mechanical procedures are used once conception takes place. For example, plants and animal poisons are often given to the mother to induce physical trauma. And if chemical means prove ineffective, tying tight bands around the pregnant woman's abdomen, punching, or even jumping on her abdomen is practiced.[6]

If a child is fortunate enough to make it through the first nine months and is born, crisis number two occurs. In many tribes, such as the Toda tribe of South India, female infanticide is extensively practiced.[7] Its rationale is that for the population to remain stable, each woman must rear only one female to reproductive age. According to anthropologists Stewart Queen and Robert Haberstein, unwanted females in the Toda tribe are put in buffalo pens to be trampled to death.[8]

In other primitive cultures superstition continues to allow infanticide. In a few African societies, twins are considered an evil omen for the tribe. Consequently, one or both are killed or exposed to the elements.[9] The Toda tribe will also terminate the life of a child if it is born feet first.[10] That points out how superstition plays a role in the value of human life.

Sociologists consider the turning away from primitive practices to be a characteristic of "civilized" cultures. Turning toward such practices, then, represents a reversion to barbarism. The acceptance of abortion will lead to the acceptance of other uncivilized ways. Dr. Paul Meier of the Minirth-Meier Clinic has explained that in Nazi Germany, "first abortion was legalized, then followed the elimination of the mentally insane, and finally the elimination of the elderly."

According to J. Kerby Anderson of Probe Ministries, once society begins to devalue the life of an *un*born child, it will begin to do the same with a *new*born child. In the past few years doctors have allowed a number of so-called "Baby Does" to die. (Governmental attempts to prevent this have been overruled in the courts.) Surgeon General C. Everett Koop, interviewed by "Focus on the Family," said: "My great

5. Marvin Harris, *Culture, People, Nature*, 2d ed. (New York: Thomas Y. Crowell, 1975), 201.
6. Ibid., 266.
7. Queen and Haberstein, 23.
8. Ibid.
9. Philip K. Bock, *Modern Cultural Anthropology*, 2d ed. (New York: Alfred A. Knopf, 1974), 56.
10. Queen and Haberstein, 23.

concern is [that] there will be 10,000 Grandma Does for every Baby Doe."

Unfortunately the more "advanced" our society becomes, the more we revert to the primitive concepts of abortion and euthanasia. In recent surveys a majority of Americans expressed approval for a more liberal approach to abortion and euthanasia.[11] What has happened to the sacredness of human life on which our country was founded? Could it be that in the wake of immense technological advancements we have become soft and selfish, choosing the easy way rather than what we know to be right? We are operating under a humanistic framework, a framework that permits and encourages one to do what is "right in his own eyes" (Judg. 17:6). That makes it easy to contemplate the thought of terminating life when selfish goals are interfered with.

For example, the women's liberation movement has at its foundation the "hate" of being a woman. The fact that women *have* to be the sex to bear children has been the source of much frustration and hostility for many. Such a rebellion against motherhood and reproduction has been a stimulant to the current abortion philosophy.

We hear politicians and other leaders advocate that each woman must have the right to choose to have an abortion or not. A women's rights leader once stated, "I do not believe in abortion, but I feel the woman should have the right to choose in this matter." That logic is absurd. That is similar to the president of the United States saying that he does not hate Israel, but if another country decided to invade Israel, that would be their choice and we should not get involved or make a value judgment on the situation. Irresponsible? Of course it is. But is that not also our attitude toward the unborn who do not have a voice in their own destiny?

THE PHILOSOPHICAL CONTEXT

Human life. What do we mean by that term? Should the definition be based solely on biological data? Does theology have something to say here? When does life actually begin or end? Questions such as these have been asked and debated for many centuries.

How we answer them depends on our philosophic foundation and framework, that is, our basic understanding of who we are and why we exist. The philosophic foundation of American society is gradually becoming more and more humanistic. A general premise of humanism is that man alone is the measure of all things. In other words, man himself

11. H. L. Wenger, "Should Mercy Killing Be Permitted?" *Good Housekeeping*, April 1967, 84.

becomes a god. What matters is man's ability to control his own destiny and be the master of his own fate. The *Humanist Manifesto* declares: "We can discover no divine purpose or providence for the human species . . . no deity will save us . . . we must save ourselves."[12]

The logical and frightening conclusion is, if each man is in essence a god and responsible only to himself for his actions, each alone shall decree who shall live and who shall not, as it seems good in his own eyes. The humanistic thinking that absolutes do not exist has led to the emergence of *cultural relativism*. By definition, cultural relativism holds that behavior can only be understood "in relation to the accepted practices of the culture in which the behavior occurs."[13] In other words, if a culture accepts the idea that unwanted females should be put in buffalo pens to be trampled to death (as with the Toda tribe), then that action is acceptable behavior. It might not be acceptable in our culture to do that, the relativist continues, but what the Toda tribe does is essentially its business and not our concern. In fact, many humanistically oriented anthropologists would argue against missionary endeavors for that same reason. Those scientists feel that converting these people to Christianity is wrong because it might upset their "cultural philosophic structure." To Christians it should be obvious that cultural relativity is extremely harmful. Let's examine the philosophy of humanism and how it has tainted our responses to these issues.

QUESTION 1: WHAT IS HUMAN LIFE?

Human life is more than mere living. Most evangelical Christians would argue that life begins at conception, and that the *soul* of that being is created at that time also. The humanist, on the other hand, would say *life* involves an act of the will. Joseph Fletcher, a humanist and the popularizer of situation ethics, stated: "To be a human is to be self-aware, consciously related to others, and capable of rationality. When these things are absent, there is neither a potential nor an actual person."[14]

There is a subtle implication to Fletcher's thinking. When others begin to decide, arbitrarily and subjectively, who is self-aware, who is consciously related to others, and who is capable of rationality, then not only the unborn, but also the retarded, insane, and elderly sick, are fair game.

---

12. Nancy Barcus and Dick Bohrer, "The Humanist Builds His House upon the Sand," *Moody Monthly*, September 1980, 24.
13. Clifford T. Morgan and Richard A. King, *Introduction to Psychology*, 5th ed. (New York: McGraw-Hill, 1975), 402.
14. B. Bard & J. Fletcher, "The Right to Die," *Atlantic*, April 1968, 63.

Thus, killing would no longer be murder! And, because man is "god," he would have every right to make that judgment.

QUESTION 2: WHEN DOES HUMAN LIFE BEGIN?

Many primitive societies believe that human life does not begin until the child has received a name or has some other ritual performed for it. The humanist would say that "infanticide may be regrettable but not murder."[15] Here we see a typical humanistic analysis of a primitive situation, for a humanist cannot condemn any action that seems appropriate to a particular culture.

Most humanists believe, as sociologist J. Gipson Wells, that "life is present in the earliest union of reproductive cells, but human life begins with birth."[16] When you are "god" you have the right to decide that issue at will!

The Bible, in opposition to humanistic thought, gives us clear indication that life begins in the womb (Isa. 49:1; Luke 1:15), and that only God has the right to determine when it should be terminated. As Christians our perspective or ideas on any question ought to take second place to what God has to say. That is the real difference between humanistic and biblical positions.

QUESTION 3: WHAT IS MEANT BY THE TERM *UNWANTED*?

Throughout the literature promoted by pro-abortionist groups runs an argument for abortion that says it is better to have an abortion than to bring an unwanted child into the world. From the humanistic perspective that is a logical statement because man is the center of his universe. To the humanist, those who are unwanted represent simply an invasion of his self-centered rights. They pose a threat to his way of life, and when this occurs, abortion or euthanasia becomes a feasible solution.

To the Christian, however, there should be *no* unwanted persons. The apostle John said, "Anyone who does not love his brother, whom he has seen, cannot love God, whom he has not seen" (1 John 4:20). Christians should not only be concerned with the pro-life movement, but also with the care of those children forsaken by their parents or society. Support for orphanages and the handicapped should certainly be a primary consideration.

The book of James tells us that our love for God ought to be demon-

15. Bock, 55.
16. J. Gipson Wells, *Current Issues in Marriage & the Family*, 2d ed. (New York: Macmillan, 1979), 265.

strated in overt actions. The Christian should be *other*-oriented, which is diametrically opposed to the *me* orientation of the humanist camp.

THE ETHICAL CONTEXT

As previously mentioned, humanism holds the view that there are no absolutes regarding good or evil, and that man himself must set the standards for right and wrong. Therefore, what man declares right, becomes right. Christianity takes the opposite stand: there are absolutes and man has an evil nature (Gen. 6:5; 8:21; Pss. 58:3; 51:5; Prov. 6:16; John 8:44). The Bible clearly tells us that apart from salvation man will do the will of his master, Satan (John 8:44). It is ironic that the humanist feels he is acting independently. In reality, he is a slave to sin (Rom. 6:17).

In contemplating the consequences of a system that seeks to give ultimate control to man, various conclusions are obvious. First, euthanasia, like abortion, will no longer be considered immoral. Humanist Joseph Fletcher has asked, "Why is fetal euthanasia all right, but not terminal euthanasia?"[17] The Dutch, whose society has become one of the most liberal, go further than withdrawing life-support systems. For the past few years Dutch physicians have given lethal injections to 5,000-10,000 patients annually. Dr. Ake Grenvik, professor of anesthesiology and surgery at the University of Pittsburgh and director of critical-care training at the university's Health Center, predicts that active euthanasia may also become accepted in the United States within the next decade.

Once the absolutes of right and wrong and good and evil are removed, any charismatic leader can press his ideas on his followers. A close look at Jim Jones and the mass suicide of his cult, or at Hitler's misuse of power that involved nearly the entire globe in war, will bear that out.

Finally, in a society absolutely free of absolutes, one need only rationalize his position to convince himself that his attitudes and behavior are justified. The humanist, for example, finds euphemisms and other "language tricks" helpful in gaining more public support. Words such as *population dynamics* and *pregnancy termination* are substituted to "lessen the blow" of the real action taken—that of killing a human being.[18]

CONCLUSION

Today every group and faction presses on us loudly declaring, "We want our rights." Yet the sanctity of life seems to be ignored. Evangeli-

17. S. Maculay, "Euthanasia: Can Death Be Friendly?" *Christianity Today* 20 (21 November 1975), 36.
18. C. Everett Koop, *The Right to Live, The Right to Die* (Wheaton, Ill.: Tyndale, 1976), 45.

cals agree that God is the ultimate source of human life. God created life and sustains life; we value life — *all* life — because God values it. The humanist, however, never reaches beyond himself in constructing his value system, and ultimately, selfish convenience prevails as the criterion for his behavior. For Christians, Christ and his selfless behavior must be the example.

QUESTIONS TO PONDER

1. Define values.
2. Define norms.
3. What is the difference between exposure and abortion?
4. Describe the similarities and differences in the primitive and civilized forms of abortion.
5. From your research, what does the Bible have to say about the sanctity of human life?

7

The Slaughter of the Innocents

Recently a letter appeared in the "Dear Abby" newspaper column that demonstrates the misunderstanding of many Christians on the subject of abortion. The writer, identifying himself as a Bible student, pontificates on the issue of abortion, seemingly oblivious to the myriad of difficulties in this moral problem:

DEAR ABBY: Since so many women and ministers read your column, I would like to present the biblical view on abortion.

A woman has the right to abort an accidental pregnancy if she so chooses. The fetus is not a living soul, but a living organism. It is a part of the mother's body—connected by the umbilical cord. The fetus is not a human soul until the umbilical cord is severed and the fetus takes its first breath of air and is able to survive on its own outside its mother's body.

The Bible clearly states: "God breathed into Adam's nostrils the breath of life, and man *became* a living soul" (Genesis 2:17).

BASIS FOR BEHAVIOR

Unfortunately that simplistic and inaccurate statement on a Christian view of abortion too often is held by Christians, even though it is completely out of accord with biblical and theological evidence and is contrary to known scientific evidence about the unborn.

We propose to present the arguments against the practice of abortion from the fields of law, ethics, medicine, and theology to obtain a full-orbed understanding of this major moral question.

THE SUPREME COURT RULING OF 1973

HISTORY OF THE DECISION

On January 22, 1973, the Supreme Court of the United States took an action contrary to two thousand years of universal concern for unborn life in the Western world. With almost dictatorial power, or "raw judicial" power in the words of a dissenting justice, the Court made an unprecedented legal decision against the unborn. The decision of the court was logically faulty, morally devoid, historically inaccurate, legally unsound, constitutionally irresponsible, and without true justice, because the ones condemned by this act (unborn children) were not allowed a hearing in court. We turn now to demonstrate the accuracy of that assessment.

THE SLIDE TO LEGAL ABORTION

The repeal of anti-abortion laws by the Court in 1973 came after the sexual revolution of the sixties and the rise of the feminist movement. Sex outside of marriage necessitated a foolproof method of birth control so that one would not have to be encumbered with the consequences of supposedly immoral actions. Others factors also came into play. Much was said in the sixties and early seventies of overpopulation. It almost became a patriotic duty to restrict families, even though it is not our purpose here to argue that question. Planned Parenthood became an organization dedicated to the good of mankind, it appeared, although it evolved into an organization almost exclusively given over to abortion. Furthermore, the inhumanity of abortion quacks was emphasized with supposedly numerous women dying at their hands (figures that Dr. Bernard Nathanson, famous former abortionist, says were blown out of proportion and lacking in empirical evidence).[1] Those women must be "saved" from almost certain butchery or death, it was argued, by allowing them safe abortions. Additionally, the women's movement, as already argued, recognized *required* pregnancy as a burden that would greatly dissipate the intended results of making women and men interchangeable partners in society. All of those factors (and probably more) led to that fateful day of January 22, 1973.

The slide to convenient abortion was not favored by the majority of Americans. After the liberalization of abortion laws in New York, public sentiment became strongly anti-abortion. The New York legislature

1. Bernard Nathanson, *Aborting America* (Garden City, N.Y.: Doubleday, 1980), 193.

repealed the pro-abortion law in 1971, one year after its enactment, but Governor Nelson Rockefeller, an abortion supporter, vetoed it. Michigan and North Dakota placed easy abortion laws on their ballots in 1972, which were rejected by the voters two-to-one and three-to-one respectively.

Even in view of the evidently wide sentiment against non-life-saving abortions, the anti-abortion laws enacted by the majority of state legislatures were overturned by the Supreme Court in 1973. The path leading to that infamous ruling is filled with deceit from abortionists and seeming collusion between the courts and those seeking repeal of the anti-abortion laws.

DISTORTION OF THE FACTS

Before the liberalization of abortion, pro-abortionists spoke loudly about the supposed 5,000 to 10,000 deaths per year by illegal abortions. Dr. Nathanson, a leader in the currently named National Abortion Rights Action League (NARAL), says that he knew those figures were false, but the statistics were useful for the cause. He comments that the federal government listed only 160 deaths from illegal abortion, and in 1972 only thirty-nine were recorded. Since bodies are difficult to hide, and deaths difficult to explain, Nathanson says a maximum number of 500 deaths per year is probably accurate.[2]

In reality, due to improved abortion methods, deaths of mothers receiving illegal abortions have greatly declined. In 1937, 2,113 deaths were reported; in 1940, 1,682; in 1955, 266; and in 1960, 289. Now observe the statistics from 1961 through 1971:

1961	324	1967	160
1962	205	1968	168
1963	272	1969	132
1964	247	1970	128
1965	235	1971	99[3]
1966	189		

One may observe that the reported deaths of mothers having abortions has greatly decreased over the years, probably because of improved techniques and better conditions; but let us not forget that successful abortion has a 100 percent mortality rate because a baby is always killed!

2. Ibid.
3. Burke Balch, "How Many Illegal Abortions Were There *Really* Before 1973?" *National Right to Life News*, vol. 8, no. 9 (19 May 1981), 5.

STACKING THE DECKS

In the courts, the unborn have had little chance for justice. Basile Uddo, a professor of law, has written of the ways the federal courts have transgressed the fairness expected of jurisprudence and seemingly with blind lack of reasoning have favored abortionists. He begins his article with a quote from Sarah Weddington, the lawyer for the defendant in the infamous *Roe v. Wade* case:

> The hearing on the case before the panel of three federal district judges was my first contested case. I was petrified. I remember that Sarah Hughes . . . was one of the judges. At one point during the hearing, when my nervousness was obviously showing, Sarah winked at me as if to say, "It's going to be all right." Sure enough, it was.[4]

Uddo gives numerous examples of the kind of favoritism shown by the courts for the abortion position, prefacing the examples with these remarks:

> When Sarah Weddington delivered those remarks at a national conference on abortion she gave us an insight into how the whole judicial involvement in abortion got its start: with a wink from the bench! Of course it's not surprising that *Roe v. Wade* has its roots in such a non-decorous exchange between judge and counsel since without a strong shove by the judiciary *Roe v. Wade*—on its merits—would never have gotten off the ground. But, as clear as it is that personal judicial preferences created a constitutional impetus for the abortion decisions few would have predicted that the progeny of those ill-conceived decisions would have been more illegitimate, and evidence of even greater judicial bias. Today, however, it is clear that the federal judiciary's treatment of abortion litigation is uniquely accommodating to the pro-abortion position. In virtually every instance—from the most minor state abortion regulation, to the more significant congressional attempts to limit federal expenditures for abortions—federal judges have shown an uncanny ability to torture the constitution into a pro-abortion document. The ensuing examples are only the tip of a very large iceberg, so large that the time clearly has come for Congress to limit the jurisdiction of the lower courts in abortion cases.[5]

Pressure from extremists within the women's movement and elitists from the legal and medical professions had considerable impact upon the Supreme Court justices. Bob Woodward and Scott Armstrong, authors of *The Brethren: Inside the Supreme Court*, reveal inside pressure from law clerks and even the wives and daughters of the judges. So, with

4. Basile J. Uddo, "When Judges Wink, Congress Must Not Blink," *Human Life Review*, vol. 5, no. 3 (Summer 1979), 42-60.
5. Ibid., 42.

myopic vision they passed a decision contrary to medical and scientific reality, legal fairness, the law of God, and the wishes of the majority of Americans.

ANALYSIS OF THE RULING

Now, let us briefly review the actual case of *Roe v. Wade*. The court decided (by a vote of 7 to 2) that abortion may be performed at any time of pregnancy up until birth. Although the decision divides pregnancy into three trimesters (unknown to physicians)[6] and *seems* to allow protection of the unborn child in the third period, in reality the child may be aborted for the emotional, physical, or familial health of the mother at any time. Obviously, since those terms are so vague, unborn children are totally without protection under the present law.[7]

The Court's decision was based on several inaccuracies. First, it held that it is not possible to know when human life begins. However, without question, human life begins at fertilization; that is a biological fact.[8]

Second, the Court said that abortion laws are of recent origin and therefore unnecessary. Remember that laws against slavery, and even our own Constitution, are of recent origin. However, the Court overlooked eleven centuries of Roman law against abortion.

Third, the Hippocratic Oath, which forbade abortion, was considered to be too influenced by Christianity to be of value. Pagan pre-Christian thought apparently is viewed as more objective!

Fourth, supposedly anti-abortion ideas cannot be found in the Constitution, whereas somewhere within the Constitution is a "right to privacy" for the woman, giving her the right to an abortion. Neither abortion nor right to privacy is found in the Constitution.

Fifth, only when the state has compelling interests should it interfere with the right to privacy. The state may have interest in the unborn when the unborn has "capability of meaningful life." Coupled with that is the dangerous view that right to life is not a natural right, as the Declaration of Independence states, but something invested by the state.[9]

That brief look at the Court's holdings and rationale (or lack of it) shows that something is terribly wrong with our present judicial system.

The only way effectively to overcome such an unjust and immoral

6. Nathanson, 213.
7. Note the findings of world-famous geneticists at the Senate hearing conducted by Sen. John East, "When Does Human Life Begin?" *National Right to Life News*, vol. 8, no. 9 (4 May 1981), 1-3, 8. Recent dissents by Justices White and O'Connor reveal that *Roe* is unraveling and would perhaps be overturned by a prolife majority on the Court.
8. *Roe v. Wade, U.S. Supreme Court Reports* (22 January 1973), vol. 35 Lawyer's Edition, Second Series (San Francisco: Bancroft-Whitney, 1974), 193.
9. Ibid.

ruling is by a constitutional amendment. Unfortunately, many believe that once the Court has spoken, we should not try to change its decision. But the Court has made errors before, so we must be guided by other considerations, such as the Judeo-Christian worldview. That the Court may be challenged, and sometimes should be, is best seen from a similar ruling of the last century.

The Dred Scott case of 1857 is an example of an infamous decision. The Supreme Court ruled that a black man or woman did not have equal protection under the Constitution, that he or she was not a *person* under the law. We reject that Supreme Court decision, as did the Fourteenth Amendment. And yet, the parallel between the slavery arguments and those culminating in the decision in *Roe v. Wade* are practically identical. Professor Patrick Derr of Clark University examines that correspondence:

1. Although he has a heart and a brain, and is human from a biological perspective, a *slave/fetus* just is not a legal person under the Constitution. The Supreme Court made this perfectly clear in the *Dred Scott/Roe v. Wade* decision.

2. A *slave/fetus* becomes a legal person only when he is *set free/born*; before that time, as the courts have ruled, he has no legal rights and we need not be concerned about him.

3. A *man/woman* has the right to do whatever *he/she* pleases with *his/her* personal property, the *slave/fetus*.

4. The economic costs, direct and indirect, of prohibiting *slavery/abortion* will be absolutely catastrophic.

5. The social consequences of prohibiting *slavery/abortion* will be disastrous.

6. What is more, both the social and economic burdens which will result from prohibiting *slavery/abortion* will be unfairly concentrated upon a single group: *slaveholders/pregnant women*.

7. Is not *slavery/abortion* really something merciful? Is it not really better never to be *set free/born* than to be sent ill-equipped and unprepared into an environment where one is unwanted, unloved and bound to be miserable?

8. Those who believe that *slavery/abortion* is immoral are free to refrain from *owning slaves/having abortions*; they should give the same freedom to those who have different moral beliefs.

9. Accordingly, those who believe that *slavery/abortion* is immoral have no right to try to impose their personal morality upon others by way of legislation or a constitutional amendment.

10. The claim that *slaves/fetuses* are like us is simply ridiculous; all

one has to do is look at them to see that they are completely different.

11. *Anti-slavery/anti-abortion* is nothing but a *Quaker/Catholic* conspiracy, which violates and undermines the separation of Church and State.

12. The members of the *anti-slavery/anti-abortion* movement are nothing but a bunch of hypocrites. If they really cared about human beings, they would work for *all* humanitarian causes, and they would never resort to violence.

13. The *anti-slavery/anti-abortion* movement is in fact a small band of well-organized religious fanatics who have no respect for democracy or the principles of a pluralistic society.

One could continue the list ad nauseum, for the parallel is thorough. But three more examples—those formulated from the other side of the argument for contrast—will suffice:

14. The question of whether *slavery/abortion* should be tolerated is not a matter of personal or religious belief; it is a question of protecting the civil rights of millions of innocent human beings who are not in a position to protect themselves.

15. The attempt to characterize the *anti-slavery/anti-abortion* movement as nothing but a *Quaker/Catholic* conspiracy is a scurrilous appeal to the very basest sort of religious bigotry.

16. The humanity of *slaves/fetuses* cannot be denied simply because they look different from us; there is no morally defensible way to draw a line somewhere along a continuum of *skin color/development* and claim, "This is where humanity starts, this is where it stops."[10]

LAWS OF GOD V. LAWS OF CULTURE

Abortion is one of the major moral issues with which we have to deal today. The question of the unborn not only concerns the institution of family and the meaning of it within society, but raises the very meaning of the sanctity of and the right to life. When the Supreme Court fails to reflect the laws of God upon which this country was founded, Christians have a higher allegiance.

The gravity of the problem may be seen in the following observations.

---

10. Patrick G. Derr, " 'The Argument' and 'The Question,' " *Human Life Review*, vol. 5, no. 3 (Summer 1979), 77-83.

Obedience to the Laws of God and Man
Satan's Distortion

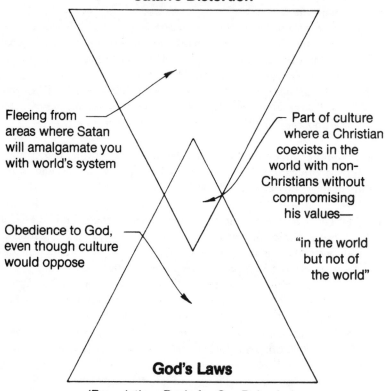

Fleeing from areas where Satan will amalgamate you with world's system

Part of culture where a Christian coexists in the world with non-Christians without compromising his values—

"in the world but not of the world"

Obedience to God, even though culture would oppose

God's Laws

(Foundation: Basis for Our Behavior)

Figure 7.1

RIGHT TO LIFE AS A DIVINELY ENDOWED RIGHT

The acceptance of abortion as it is generally advocated in America today is a rejection of the basic right to life provided within the Scriptures, Western tradition, and our own country's documents of freedom. Human life is not simply a mechanistic product; it is the creative act of God. Majority vote or sociological opinion do not alter that truth. Just laws cannot be made without appeal to morality, a morality built on the laws of God. To the framers of our nation, founded on a Judeo-Christian worldview, certain truths were self-evident: life, liberty, and the pursuit of happiness. Justice Blackmun felt that the so-called right to privacy, located somewhere in the Fourteenth Amendment, was not an indelible right.[11] The most basic of all rights is the right to life, for it contains the right to have rights. Such an almost absolute right (to use Professor Noonan's term) must be surrendered only by free choice (excluding the necessity of society to protect itself justly against a murderer, etc.) and when a higher ethic necessitates. The subordination of fetal right to that of the mother's choice, on the premise of right of privacy, argues property rights over the right to life. The Grants rightly say:

> Christianity has become so secularized that it is sometimes difficult to distinguish it from atheistic humanism. In such a situation the very foundations of the doctrine of rights have been eroded. All men are not created equal; they are not created at all. Justice can become a privilege society grants to some of its people, if they are the right age, and sufficiently like most other people. One can foresee a time when before one can qualify for rights, a kind of means test may be used: "Are you human in the fullest sense of the word?" "Are you still enjoying quality of life?" And here is the crunch; as the fetus loses out on this ethic, so will the weak, the aged, the infirm, the unproductive. If we come to believe that we are not creatures, but accidents, rights will no longer be given in the very nature of our legal system. The most powerful among us will then decide who are to have rights and who are not.[12]

WILL THE DOMINOES FALL?

The domino theory purported by the Grants, Koop, Schaeffer, and others becomes all the more likely when one recognizes the growing number of the economically unproductive aged who will prove to be a gradually greater economic burden to the growing minority of the young. If America succumbs at the point of abortion we are initiators of a process. Malcolm Muggeridge understood that well, for he wrote:

> Our Western way of life has come to a parting of the ways; time's takeover bid for eternity has reached the point at which irrevocable decisions have to be taken. Either we will go on with the process of shaping our own destiny without reference to any higher being than Man. . . . Or we draw back, seeking to understand and fall in with our Creator's purpose of us rather than to pursue our own; in true humility praying, as the founder of our religion and civilization taught us: Thy will be done. This is what the abortion controversy will be about when, as must inevitably happen, it arises.[13]

11. Sheila and George Grant, "Abortion and Rights," *The Right to Birth*, 7-8.
12. Ibid., 7-8.
13. Malcolm Muggeridge, *Human Life Review*, vol. 1, no. 3 (Summer 1975), 5.

SECULARISM CONFRONTS THE CHRISTIAN

The humanistic force behind the abortion decision and practice is a clear foe for the church. We need not have any misunderstanding about the reality of this confrontation and the importance of its outcome. A rejection of the sexual distinctions and functions purposed by God in the beginning is but a rejection of the Creator and an exaltation of the wisdom of man. A more blatant humanistic and anti-Christian view of the unborn is the opinion of Justice Blackmun in *Roe v. Wade.* Wittingly or not, he clearly preferred the ethical teaching of pre-Christianity to that of Christianity. "Ancient religion," Blackmun says, "did not bar abortion." What further challenge must be given before we act? Pagan religion is the guide for public policy in the United States.

The solemnity of the abortion question also may be seen in the possible repercussions of such barbarity as awareness of the problem pricks our consciences. The Civil War is a possible paradigm of the potentiality of the crisis in view of the magnitude of the issue. At the beginning of the slavery controversy in the United States few were truly acquainted with the atrocity of slavery. But when public awareness grew, the intenseness and incendiary nature of the situation precipitated a civil war that shook and almost destroyed our nation. From that struggle came the overturning of the Dred Scott decision and the establishment of the Fourteenth Amendment. Such a confrontation is not beyond possibility. The civil rights movement of black people or the rejection of the Vietnam conflict by the young brought tremendous struggles and effects into our society. Who knows how damaging the results would have been had not various civil rights acts been passed, or had the war continued? Similarly, if something peaceful cannot be done to stop the slaughter of the innocent, society cannot possibly hold together as though nothing were happening. Can Christians support a government at the point of abortion on demand? Passivity in this issue may be seen as an ethical crime in itself!

In line with the statement of support for government is the fact of our sharing the guilt for the evil being done. When we support men and women who allow such evil to continue with impunity, justice cries out from the ground. Immoral leadership causes us to do evil, according to Psalm 125:3.

PAST CHRISTIAN CONSENSUS

In view of our present predicament we desperately need to develop the kind of consensus that Christians of past centuries have possessed. Let us examine some of the testimony of early Christians on the subject of abortion.

The early church was unambiguous on abortion. One of the earliest noncanonical Christian writings is the *Didache* or *Teaching of the Twelve Apostles*, dating at the end of the first or at the beginning of the second century. An exposition of the Second Great Commandment ("You shall love your neighbor as yourself," Matt. 22:39) says: "You shall not commit murder; you shall not commit adultery; you shall not commit sodomy; you shall not commit fornication; you shall not steal; you shall not use magic; you shall not use philtres [dangerous drugs]; you shall not procure abortion, not commit infanticide. . . ."[14] Infanticide and abortion are more closely joined by Minucius Felix, an apologist of the third century:

> Among you I do see newly-born sons at times exposed to wild beasts and birds, or violently strangled to a painful death; and there are women, who, by medicinal draughts, extinguish in the womb and commit infanticide upon the offspring yet unborn.[15]

In line with the foregoing is the cogent statement of Tertullian, the great church Father:

> For us murder is once for all forbidden; so even the child in the womb, while yet the mother's blood is being drawn on to form the human being, it is not lawful for us to destroy. To forbid birth is only quicker murder. It makes no difference whether one take away the life once born or destroy it as it comes to birth. He is a man, who is to be a man; the fruit is always present in the seed.[16]

Without modern understanding of genetics, Tertullian understood that humanness is resident from the beginning in the unborn: all the human will ever be is in the child at conception. Further testimony is found in the ancient church. Athenagoras, a Christian apologist of the second century, said:

> When we say that those women who use drugs to bring on abortion commit murder, and will have to give an account to God for the abortion, on what principle should we commit murder? For it does not belong to the same person to regard the very foetus in the womb as a created being, and therefore an object of God's care, and when it has passed into life, to kill it.[17]

In a similar vein, Clement of Alexandria commented:

14. *Didache*, ii.2.
15. Cited by Harold O. J. Brown, "What the Supreme Court Didn't Know," *Human Life Review*, vol. 1, no. 2 (Spring 1975), 15.
16. Ibid., 15.
17. Athenagoras, *A Plea for the Christians*, 35.

If we should but control our lusts at the start and if we would not kill off the human race born and developing according to the divine plan, then our whole lives would be lived according to nature. But women who resort to some sort of deadly abortion drug kill not only the embryo but, along with it, all human kindness.[18]

That emphasis, reiterated through numerous ancient Christian writers, finds its true exemplar in the biblical teaching on the fatherhood of God. In reference to that, one may see the emphasis of Christ on the fatherliness of God. God is concerned about His children, and that serves as our example, as Fairweather says:

The Christian world, taught by its Lord, reverences their very helplessness as the emblem of its own condition in the presence of God, and recognizes in their dependence an appeal to its unselfish devotion, that it may be an imitator of God.[19]

In contrast to the low regard toward nascent and newborn life in the ancient Graeco-Roman world, one should not be surprised that a church moved by the concern of its Lord for children should rigorously seek to protect and promote protection for children, born and unborn. That act of love for neighbors is seen in an early Christian writing, *The Epistle of Barnabas*, which says: "Love your neighbor more than yourself. Do not kill a fetus by abortion, or commit infanticide."[20]

Children, unborn and born, continued to enjoy that favor until recent years. The Greek physician Hippocrates maintained a view later bolstered by Christian support. The noted authorities on English common law—Bracton (13th century), Coke (17th century), and Blackstone (18th century)—considered abortion a crime.[21]

It is ironic that past centuries have had less scientific evidence for the nature of the human life and development of the fetus than we have today, but harmoniously maintained a consensus of opinion against abortion.

PRESENT LACK OF CONSENSUS

Considering the importance of the subject of abortion, the lack of consensus among Christians is a point of perplexity for those who strongly support an anti-abortion position. Evangelical Christians are substantially unanimous in their rejection of sexual sins, graft in church and

18. Clement of Alexandria, *Christ the Educator*, II, 10:96. Cited by Fairweather, 43.
19. Eugene Fairweather, "The Child as Neighbour," *The Right to Birth*, 41.
20. *Epistle of Barnabas*, 19:5.
21. Ian Gentles, "The Unborn Citizen," *The Right to Birth*, 14.

government, infanticide, and other crimes against the person. Why should the abortion issue be different?

When all the reasons for advocating abortion have been given, and all the shibboleths have been set aside for lack of sincerity, it appears that the dominant reason for abortion in American society today is the surge of feminist ideology. Feminism has not developed beyond the trite cliche "I gotta be me," a reflection of current narcissism, and a rejection of the biblical teaching on sexual roles within marital unity. Abortion is seen as a cure-all that allows for the fulfillment of personal aspirations. In some Christian circles abortion may even be done in the name of God. Note this statement by Scanzoni: "The Christian physician will advise induced abortion only to safeguard greater values sanctioned by Scripture. These values should include individual health, family welfare, and social responsibility."[22]

Also note the following reason: "An additional child might hinder its (the Christian family's) corporate and individual task to serve God in the world."[23]

We are led to believe that preserving the creation of God in the womb of the mother may be in antithesis to the good of a family and society. With such pronouncements we are being led, along with Alice, into Wonderland, where words are what we make them. We are told that we serve God by destroying the persons He creates in the wombs of mothers. To accept such reasoning is to be sucked into a moral black hole from which no light of God's truth issues. We must not buy the spirit of the times advocated by those professing to speak for evangelical Christians, but instead we must make a stand with our moral consciences chained to the Word of God.

So then, there is a clear need to develop a consensus among Christians. The Scripture unobtrusively teaches that society is to protect the innocent and punish the guilty. Seeking simply to avoid the problem will not make it go away, but rather will put us under the discipline of God. Observe the admonition of the sage in Proverbs 24:11-12:

> Rescue those being led away to death;
> hold back those staggering toward slaughter.
> If you say, "But we knew nothing about this,"
> does not he who weighs the heart perceive it?
> Does not he who guards your life know it?

22. Cited by Jeremy C. Jackson, "The Shadow of Death: Abortion in Historical and Contemporary Perspective," in *Thou Shalt Not Kill: The Christian Case Against Abortion*, ed. Richard L. Ganz (New Rochelle, N.Y.: Arlington House, 1978), 94.
23. Jackson, 94.

Will he not repay each person according to what he has done? (NIV*)

However legitimate many of the complaints of today's feminists may be, abortion as a feminist cause is dwarfed by the need to see the taking the lives of the unborn as a human cause. The civil right of the woman to a private choice must not be allowed to override the civil and moral right of the unborn child to be protected against aggression. With one child in four a likely victim in the abortion mania, now is the time to speak and act; if we do not, we in America can properly expect the judgment of God.

CHRISTIAN WITNESS OF LAW AND GOSPEL

In the midst of the controversy the distinctive contribution should be made by Christians and more specifically by those who have learned to bow only at the altar of God, by those who have been willing to stop up their ears to the Sirens' call of this world and to hear only the Word of God.

But to those who truly hear the voice of God, it becomes incumbent on them to proclaim the Word—a Word that burns in their bones even as it did in Jeremiah's. However, the Word of God may come forth in either judgment or grace, and whether a person or society is given judgment or grace largely depends on the condition or contriteness of the heart. Grace is to be preached to the brokenhearted, but judgment to the proud and unrepentant. There is every indication that our narcissistic society sees itself above being judged. America needs a statement of God's law. In the words of Brown:

> I think that at this point in America's social, legal, and spiritual history it is important to perceive the matter clearly and say that it is our duty as Christians in late 20th century America to preach to society the law of God. We must challenge our fellow Americans not to pollute the land wherein we live: "For blood defiles the land and the land cannot be cleansed of the blood that is shed therein but by the blood of him that shed it."[24]

A world apart from God has not been willing to listen to the truths about abortion, but what of the Christian? In giving this message outwardly we must also look among our own ranks to see if we have really come to grips with the reality of abortion. Gentles says:

---

* *New International Version.*
24. Harold O. J. Brown, "Legal Aspects of the Right to Life," in *Thou Shalt Not Kill*, 124-25.

If abortion is an issue for conscience, ought we not, in the first place to take steps to ensure that our own consciences are fully informed? Central in the debate on abortion, as we have seen, is a question of over-riding importance: what is the true nature of human life before birth? There are evidences in the current debate that a diminished view of human life in general results from habits of thought that take no real account of the nature of life within the womb. This tendency overlooks an important sector of the ethical horizon and seriously limits the field of moral vision. Can convinced Christians accept this "blind spot" in moral reasoning? Moreover, our approach should be theological, and our theology biblical.[25]

We must accept the challenge of Gentles if we are to call ourselves Christians. We must not allow the real questions to be clouded by issues that properly are secondary. The nature of life in the womb must be understood before value judgments are made about when that life may be extinguished and for what reasons. As well, our decision must be based on the teaching of Scripture as it is discerned through sound principles of exegesis and logic, not on pronouncements of "Dear Abby theology."

We should first look at Scripture, at what God's Word has to say about abortion. Then, as we are accountable to God for His truth revealed to us, we must address those directly and indirectly involved in the abortion issue.

THE BIBLE ON ABORTION

The Scriptures do not discuss abortion in any detail. However, they do provide clear evidence as to the nature of the unborn so that one may recognize the wrongfulness of taking the life of the child in the womb. To our knowledge, the biblical writers make no distinction between a born or unborn child. Every passage we examined either attributes human characteristics to the unborn child or speaks of the child in a personal way. In the spectrum of life—conceptus, embryo, fetus, baby, child, adolescent, adult, senior adult—there is a continuity. Any discontinuity is in the language or world view, not in the biological or personal reality. The continuity in Scripture indicates that God is not only forming and caring for the unborn child, but forming him as a specific individual for a specific postnatal calling. It is dangerous to separate or draw distinctions between fetal and postfetal life.

The demands of space will not allow for an in-depth look at every passage of the Bible that supports our argument that unborn life is to be

25. Gentles, 14.

honored and protected. We will turn to two major passages, Psalm 139 and Exodus 21:22ff., and refer briefly to some other passages.

PSALM 139—LOOKING INSIDE THE WOMB

No portion of Holy Writ provides the vivid and beautiful portrayal of the work of God in the creation of the unborn as does Psalm 139:13-16:

> For you created my inmost being; You knitted me together in my mother's womb.
> I praise you because I am fearfully and wonderfully made; Your works are wonderful, and I know it very well.
> My bones were not hidden from You when I was made in the secret place, when I was woven together [as] in the depths of the earth.
> Your eyes saw my embryo!
> And in your book all (my unformed parts) were written;
>   daily they were being fashioned
>   before the whole was complete.

God is not only the Creator of the heavens; He is also involved in the unseen world of the womb. Ronald Allen, a professor of Hebrew exegesis, says:

> The Bible never speaks of fetal life as mere chemical activity, cellular growth or vague force. Rather, the fetus in the mother's womb is described by the psalmist in vivid pictorial language as being shaped, fashioned, molded and woven together by the personal activity of God. That is, as God formed Adam from the dust of the ground, so He is actively involved in fashioning the fetus in the womb.[26]

Bernard Nathanson, in his book *Aborting America*, comments that the reason the unborn have so little protection is partly because they are unseen. If wombs had windows, much argument would fall by the wayside. And yet the psalmist artistically gives us a view inside the mother and praises God the Creator, who skillfully and wonderfully is developing a child (vv. 13-14). To reject a child by abortion is not only rejecting the product of a man and a woman; it is rejecting the work of God.

At times, those who advocate abortion do so with seeming sympathy for the unborn who is handicapped or mentally deficient, as though right to life depends on measuring up to some standard of physical or mental perfection. We need to remember that if God is bringing a child into the world, the child may be measured only by God's standards. Consider the

---

26. Ronald Barclay Allen, *In Celebrating Love and Life!* (Portland, Ore.: Western Baptist, 1977), 6.

man in John 9:1-3 who had been blind from birth and healed by Jesus
Christ. Verse 3 indicates that the purpose of the blindness—quite different from the evaluation of the ones questioning the Lord—was "in order
that the works of God might be displayed in him."

The formation of the bones of the child, according to Psalm 139:15,
although not visible to the mother or the outside world, were never hidden from God. Tiny embryonic persons are the subjects of God's superin-
tending love and concern.[27]

The translation of verse 16 has been a problem to interpreters for centuries. David used a word that is translated in the King James Version as
"My substance, yet being imperfect," whereas the *Revised Standard Version*
and the *New American Standard Bible* read, "My unformed substance."
Mitchell Dahood translates the word *galmi* as "my life states."[28] The best
understanding in our opinion is to follow the standard Hebrew diction-
aries and so understand the word as "my embryo."[29] We should understand the word *embryo* by dictionary definition in terms of the child from
conception to the third month of pregnancy.

Not only does God behold and form the unborn from conception on,
but all the parts of the child are written daily in God's book as they are
formed until the embryo is complete. Dahood is right in relating "all of
them" to *galmi* (embryo or life stages) rather than to days.[30] The psalm
portrays Him as the transcendent One, but at the same time depicts His
nearness to His Creation.

EXODUS 21:22-25—PROTECTION FOR THE UNBORN

Christians who have viewed abortion as an acceptable moral action
often have used Exodus 21:22-25 as biblical justification:

> If men strive, and hurt a woman with child, so that her fruit depart from
> her, and yet no mischief follow: he shall be surely punished, according as
> the woman's husband will lay upon him; and he shall pay as the judges
> determine. And if any mischief follow, then thou shalt give life for life, eye
> for eye, tooth for tooth, hand for hand, foot for foot, burning for burning,
> wound for wound, stripe for stripe. [KJV*]

* King James Version.
27. Curtis J. Young, *Abortion and Psalm 139, Man's Destruction of God's Handiwork* (Washing-
    ton, D.C.: Christian Action Council, n.d.), 3.
28. Mitchell Dahood, *Psalms*, The Anchor Bible (Garden City, N.Y.: Doubleday, 1966),
    3:295.
29. Francis Brown, S. R. Driver, and Charles A. Briggs, *A Hebrew and English Lexicon of the
    Old Testament* (Oxford: Clarendon, 1907), 166; and Ludwig Koehler and Walter
    Baumgartner, *Lexicon in Veteris Testamenti Libros* (Leiden: E.J. Brill, 1958), 426.
30. Dahood, 3:295.

Three basic interpretations have arisen from the study of that passage.

Ronald Allen argues that the text at hand concerns a miscarriage, because a live premature birth was unlikely in the ancient world. The condition of the woman would be the determining factor in whether there was a retaliation against the man who struck her. He continues that although the unborn died in that particular encounter without the guilty man being killed, that should not be a sign that the Hebrews considered the fetus a nonperson. In Exodus 21:20-21 a slave's death did not bring a penalty beyond a fine, and no one considered a slave a nonperson in the Old Testament. He concludes, "Hence, the argument is in error that the payment of a fine rather than the death of the guilty denotes less than the loss of a human life in the case of the fetus."[31]

Allen continues that because the law in question is case law (casuistic law), or *what if* law, it is not a universal law. In this case, he says, if the crime produces death, it is considered manslaughter rather than murder.[32]

The text does not indicate whether or not the blows against the woman were intentional, but the penalty exacted is broad enough to cover everything from a fine, if no injury occurs, to life-for-life if death ensues. And we would contend that the injuries refer to the unborn as well as the mother, a point to be made later.

Allen makes one major error in his reasoning. He says concerning the casuistic law in Exodus 21:22-25, "This is not descriptive of the kind of thing that would happen with regularity. This is rather a 'what if . . . ?' kind of situation."[33] On the other hand, one reason he discounts a premature live birth is its rarity: "The concept of a premature live birth is a relatively modern one anyway; few premature live births could have survived in an ancient world."[34]

As we shall see in the following presentation, the premature-birth view is a superior explanation for the events recorded in the passage at hand.

The next explanation for Exodus 21:22-25 is a very ancient one, but one propounded by many today who approve of abortion. The major presentation of this argument in *Christianity Today* and *Birth Control and the Christian* was by Bruce K. Waltke. To Waltke's credit, he has changed his views on abortion since his earlier works, but unfortunately has stated that he believes his earlier analysis of this particular passage is still the better one.[35] Waltke states in *Birth Control and the Christian:*

31. Allen, 3.
32. Ibid.
33. Ibid.
34. Ibid., 2.
35. Bruce K. Waltke, "Reflections from the Old Testament on Abortion," *Journal of the Evangelical Theological Society*, vol. 19, no. 1 (Winter 1976), 3.

[An] argument in favor of permitting induced abortion is that God does not regard the fetus as a soul ... no matter how far gestation has progressed. Therefore, the fetus does not come under the protection of the fifth commandment. That he does not so regard the fetus can be demonstrated by noting that God does not impose a death penalty for the destruction of a fetus.[36]

Several lines of argument militate against Waltke's understanding of Exodus 21:22-25: (1) The meaning of *come* or *go out;* (2) the meaning of *child;* and (3) the idea of *harm.*

What the King James Version translates "her fruit depart" the *New American Standard Bible* translates "she has a miscarriage." That latter translation of the Hebrew is not in harmony with the intention of Moses. The Hebrew word for *come out* or *depart* is used in Genesis 25:25-26 and 38:28-29 for childbirth (see also Job 1:21; 3:11; Eccles. 5:15; Jer.11:5; 20:18). The authoritative *A Hebrew and English Lexicon of the Old Testament* by Francis Brown, S. R. Driver, and Charles Briggs lists the meaning in Exodus 21:22 as "untimely birth," not miscarriage.[37] Similarly, the *New International Version* reads "premature birth." That a premature birth is to be preferred over miscarriage will be apparent in subsequent argument. One point needs to be mentioned before we pass from this particular line of argument. If Moses had desired to mean *miscarriage* by the Hebrew word translated "come out" in the English text, the Hebrew language has a perfectly good term he could have used to express that idea. He used this word several times in the Pentateuch (e.g., see Gen. 31:38; Ex. 23:26; see also Hos. 9:14). Because he used another word often occurring in contexts of birth rather than a word meaning miscarriage, the idea of birth (premature) in Exodus 21:22 is preferable.

Is the child of Exodus 21:22 a person on a par with the mother in the incident? Some have sought to draw a distinction between an unborn child and a human being: "God does not regard the fetus as a soul ... no matter how far gestation has progressed."[38] However, there is no evidence that the Hebrew society ever distinguished between an unborn and born child. The word for *child* in Exodus 21:22 is defined in the Hebrew dictionary as "child, son, boy, youth."[39] There is no more reason to assign arbitrarily a different status to the child of Exodus 21:22 than to the child of Isaiah 9:6. As we will see momentarily, the same penalty

36. Bruce Waltke, "Birth Control and the Christian," *Old Testament Texts Bearing on the Controversy of Human Reproduction,* ed. Walter Spitzer and Carlyle Saylor (Wheaton, Ill.: Tyndale, 1969), 10-11.
37. Francis Brown, 422-25. This view has been held by several authorities such as Geiger, Keil, Delitzsch, Jacob, and Cassuto.
38. Waltke, 10.
39. Francis Brown, 409.

applies for hurting the child as for hurting the mother. Moses understood no difference! Waltke comments:

> No evangelical would deny that a baby is a human being and that it is made in the image of God, that is, that it has the capacity for spiritual, rational and moral response. The question, then, is "Does the fetus have that capacity?" The answer is that it does and that this capacity was already present at the time of conception.[40]

To whom does the harm refer in verse 22? In our opinion the harm may refer either to the mother or the child and may be anything from a minor injury to death.

The *New American Standard Bible* implies that the harm to the unborn is of little consequence. Supposedly, whatever happened to the unborn would bring only a fine, whereas if the mother was hurt the *lex talionis*, or law of retaliation, would be enforced. That is simply reading into the text. The Hebrew text does not have the word *further*, and if the author had intended only the woman to be in view, he could easily have said "to her." Since this is a general statement, we should understand harm either to the woman or her child.

The best understanding of the meaning of *harm* and the subsequent retaliation is that a fine was exacted on the liable person because of either the mental or physical discomfort the striker had caused. If bodily harm of any significant amount (eye, burn, bruise) occurred against the mother or child, the principle of retaliation took over. As Cottrell concludes, "The text will permit no other understanding."[41]

We have demonstrated in brief that Exodus 21:22-25 does not concern induced abortion or miscarriage. Instead, the purpose of its inclusion is to protect the rights of a mother and her unborn child. Both are seen needing protection in the Mosaic legislation and are not differentiated in their humanness. Although many scholars interpret the text differently, as Cottrell put it, "The weight of scholarly opinion . . . is outweighed by the text itself."[42]

We would like to offer an interpretative translation of Exodus 21:22-25 that would sum up the discussion presented in this section:

> And *if* men struggle with each other and strike a woman with child so that she has a premature birth, yet there is no significant bodily injury to the mother or child, he shall surely be fined (in view of initiating the traumatic

40. Waltke, "Reflections," 13.
41. Jack W. Cottrell, "Abortion and the Mosaic Law," *Christianity Today*, vol. 17, no. 12 (16 March 1973), 9.
42. Ibid.

experience) as the woman's husband may demand of him; and he shall pay as the judges decide. But if there is a significant bodily injury to the mother or child, then you shall appoint *as a penalty*, and according to that which applies, life for life, eye for eye, tooth for tooth, hand for hand, foot for foot, burn for burn, wound for wound, bruise for bruise.[43]

Exodus 21:22-25, then, gives no support whatsoever to the legitimacy of abortion.

ARE THE UNBORN IN THE IMAGE OF GOD?

Several other passages could be offered to show the humanness of the unborn but only brief mentionings of a few will be made. The concern of God for the unborn in identifying them before birth reveals the humanity of the little ones; for example, Jeremiah (Jer. 1:5), the apostle Paul (Gal. 1:15). Another powerful passage is Psalm 51, where David says the moral law of God was present in him in his unborn state. In the inward parts, his mother's womb,[44] he had a spiritual nature. Note the words of the Hebrew scholar E. R. Dalglish:

> In the depths of the womb the psalmist was wrought in the context of sin (v. 7) [English v. 5]; but there is another factor: the psalmist knows full well the divine desire for truth to be a moral imperative even in the formulative stages of his being within his mother's womb and is conscious that even there wisdom was taught him, i.e., his embryological state in the closed up chamber of the womb, the moral law was inscribed within his being.[45]

The image of God appears to be already resident in the child even before birth.

WHEN IS THE "SOUL" CREATED?

Some have sought to identify the *soul* as coming into existence usually sometime after fertilization. Some common views as to at what stage that happens are: (1) at the time the fetus attaches itself to the uterine wall; (2) when the baby's heart begins to beat; (3) when quickening (the mother feels movement) happens; and (4) at birth, when the baby inhales air for the first time. Thus, each new person at some arbitrary stage is created directly by God in reference to his or her spiritual essence.

A major Scripture used by those who believe God puts an individually

---

43. H. Wayne House, "Miscarriage or Premature Birth: Additional Thoughts on Exodus 21:22-25," *Westminster Theological Journal*, vol. 41, no. 1 (Fall 1978), 123.
44. Waltke, "Reflections," 13.
45. Ibid.

created soul into each body is Genesis 2:7. The text reads: "Then the LORD God formed man of dust from the ground and breathed into his nostrils the breath of life; and man became a living being." The passage nowhere implies that that became the pattern for the creation of men. Literally, the text reads: "God breathed into him the breath of *lives*, and man became a living being." He was not an animated and functioning being (as an unborn baby is) until that animating breath from God. At that initial stage of creation God invested Adam with all the necessary elements for the spiritual-physical beings that would follow him. Romans 5:12-21 teaches that the whole human race was in Adam and that our beings have come totally from him.

Scripture portrays human beings as part of a long spiritual-physical chain that can be traced all the way back to Adam. That view is known as traducianism. The spiritual, as well as the physical, aspects of our nature are transmitted seminally, through procreation.

First, although the Bible clearly teaches that God shapes the unborn, he does not create biological and spiritual life individually. That we know from Genesis 2:2. There we have evidence that God has ceased His creative work. That passage would lose all meaning if He were separately creating all people today. Today God is providential and preserving, not creating out of nothing.

Second, the apostle Paul taught that the human race is a unity. Christianity has always taught the essential unity of body and spirit for humanness; thus, the need for a resurrection. If each life was to be created separately and injected into a body, the unity of humankind would be impossible. Note Paul's words, "He made from one [Adam], every nation of mankind to live on all the face of the earth."[46]

WHAT IS MAN?

In non-Christian circles, evolutionary humanism has added its deadly potion to the debate on *what is man?* With human beings considered as only quantitatively different from animals, rather than qualitatively, humanness is only a matter of definition, not intrinsic quality. Garrett Hardin, a professor of human ecology, makes this point: "People who worry about the moral danger of abortion do so because they think of the fetus as a human being and hence equate feticide with murder. Whether the fetus is or is not a human being is a matter of definition, not fact, and we can define any way we wish."[47]

46. Acts 17:26, NASB.
47. Garrett Hardin, "Abortion—Or Compulsory Pregnancy," *Journal of Marriage and Family* (May 1968), 250-51.

That position is diametrically opposed to the thinking of Christianity. Christians know from God's Word that man is a creation of God and is made after God's image. Francis Schaeffer, eminent theologian and philosopher, said that man is separate from the animal, plant, and machine in that he is a person, able to commune with God. Only his finiteness places him alongside the rest of creation.[48]

All life that comes from the union of a father and mother is human life. All living organisms belong to some species; there is no third category. If the fetus is alive, then what species is it, if it is not *genus homo?* Women do not bear anything but humans!

A human being does *not* come from a one-cell organism. All of us *were* that one-cell organism, for that is how humans *are* at that stage in the development of human life. There is a continuum from fertilization to death in the human species, although we vary from some members of the species according to what stage of development we have attained.

The question of *what man is*, rather than when life begins, is the crux of the abortion controversy. As hearings in the Senate Subcommittee on the Separation of Powers demonstrated in 1981, there is practically total unanimity on the beginning of human life: fertilization. What abortionists are now arguing is that being a person and being human are not to be interpreted as interchangeable.

Scripture and science both indicate the humanness of the unborn. Acknowledging that, the Christian must also respond. He must address abortionists with the evidence or direct them to where they can find the evidence. We propose that we must address the unborn, the mother, the father, the church, society, God, and lastly, ourselves concerning this issue to expose the meaning and ramifications of the question of abortion. All of those elements are asking the Christian for his response—what shall the nature of that response be?

How Shall We Respond?

TO THE UNBORN

Are you one of us? When we address the unborn entity in the womb of the woman, our question must be, *Are you one of us?* That is the very question not addressed in preference for the desires of the mother, but we must give it priority. For if there were no doubt as to its humanness, its personhood, its being an individual creature of God, what would be our

48. See Francis A. Schaeffer, *Pollution and the Death of Man: The Christian View of Ecology* (Wheaton, Ill.: Tyndale, 1970), 49.

concern? None at all! Such was the grave lack of reasoning exhibited by
the Supreme Court in 1973 in its avoidance of the question of the
humanness and personhood of the fetus. Why should the state want to
protect a nonhuman entity in the mother any more than protect her
appendix? If she needed it out for her benefit, who would prohibit it?
And if that entity was a separate organism from the mother, its humanness was the important—really the only—issue to be discussed initially,
for in law and morality, human life is an absolute value, taking prece-
dence over property or convenience. The Court simply was not willing to
face squarely the crucial question. So in asking the fetus, Are you one of
us? we are seeking to know if it is human life, and if it is, does one who
has human life naturally have personhood?

We do not intend to rehearse thoroughly all of the arguments from
medicine on the humanness of the fetus. Others have done so, with
greater expertise than we possess.[49] There is no real medical debate as to
the human life intrinsic in the unborn. The scientific evidence for the
humanness of the unborn is overwhelming. The prescientific understanding of human life's beginning at "quickening" or some other period several months after conception (the evidence adduced by the Supreme
Court) is no longer defensible. Also, those who understand the fetus as
only "a blob" either are living in a prescientific world or are being inten-
tionally deceitful. To consider the unborn as only another part of the
woman's body, in the words of Nathanson, is "biological nonsense."[50]
The following data that scientists know about fetal life demonstrate the
accuracy of viewing the unborn as possessing a separate human life:

1. The heart begins to beat between the eighteenth and twenty-fifth day
   after conception.
2. Brain waves have been recorded as early as forty-five days.
3. The baby's movements can be felt by the mother as early as six
   weeks.
4. At eight weeks the baby possesses the fingerprints it will have for life.
5. All bodily systems are present by eight weeks and are functioning by
   eleven weeks.
6. At eleven to twelve weeks a baby can suck its thumb.
7. At twelve weeks the baby weighs one ounce, at sixteen weeks six
   ounces, and at twenty weeks approximately one pound.[51]

The criteria established by the Harvard Medical School for a defini-

49. Nathanson, 195-205.
50. Ibid., 188.
51. Bill Crouse, "Abortion Notes," handout by author, 2 (Probe Ministries Seminar, Dal-
    las, Tex., 1981), photocopy.

tion of death may be used in reverse to demonstrate human life at the early stages of pregnancy (although we would push the beginning of human life to fertilization for additional reasons). Those criteria are: no response to external stimuli (e.g., pain); no spontaneous movements or respiratory efforts; no deep reflexes; and no brain activity as indicated by a flat electroencephalogram (EEG). Reversed, that criteria would indicate that the unborn is alive by the sixth week of pregnancy.

The father of fetology, Sir William Liley, reveals the humanness of the unborn child when he writes:

> We know that he moves with a delightful easy grace in his buoyant world, that foetal comfort determines foetal position. He is responsive to pain and touch and cold and sound and light. He drinks his amniotic fluid, more if it is artificially sweetened, less if it is given an unpleasant taste. He gets hiccups and sucks his thumb. He wakes and sleeps. He gets bored with repetitive signals but can be taught to be alerted by a first signal for a second different one. And finally he determines his birthday, for unquestionably the onset of labour is a unilateral decision of the foetus. . . . This then is the foetus we know and indeed we each once were. This is the foetus we look after in modern obstetrics, the same baby we are caring for before and after birth, who before birth can be ill and need diagnosis and treatment just like any other patient.[52]

Are you my neighbor? A second major question we must raise for the unborn is, *Are you my neighbor?* Do you deserve the same kind of right to life that all other human creatures of God deserve? Indeed, a further consideration is proffered by Louis Dupre: "At any early stage of development a person is all the more entitled to full protection, since he is totally dependent on others for his survival."[53] More than that, if the unborn is a person and is weak and subject to exploitation, as Christians, do we not have an obligation to consider the fetus as a neighbor and be a neighbor to it? The slurs of pro-abortionists that pro-lifers are fetus lovers is in reality a statement of blessing. Not that we do not have concern for the mother—we must help her to act responsibly and lovingly—but we must recognize the dignity of humanness that the unborn share with us since they too are *imago Dei.*

The special situation of a helpless child being allowed to live takes on special meaning in view of the favored position children had in the earthly life of Jesus, which reflected the love of the Father for His children. That concern should spur us on to emulate our Lord in our

---

52. Ibid.
53. Louis Depre, "A New Approach to the Abortion Problem," *Theological Studies*, vol. 34, no. 3 (September 1973), 487.

attempt to turn back the Herodian tide in our day of rejection of the unborn.

When, if ever, may the child be aborted? That is the proper question to address after, and only after, we have established our view that the unborn are persons created by God. When we have decided that question, the problems that arise are not nearly so difficult to solve.

Some have sought to gain concessions on abortion by positing hypothetically "hard" cases in which (they think) abortion is certainly allowable. A popular argument is offered by philosophy professor Judith Thomson. She recognizes that parents who do not practice birth control have responsibility to the child, but "if they have taken all reasonable precautions against having a child, they do not simply by virtue of their biological relationship to the child who comes into existence have a special responsibility for it."[54]

She compares a woman who accidentally has become pregnant to the following parable. Let us suppose that a famous violinist has a fatal kidney ailment. One morning you wake up to discover against your will that you are confined to bed and that the violinist has been plugged into your body for the next nine months sharing your kidneys. If you unplug him he will die. You, in this parable, are the mother and the violinist stands for the unborn child. Should you be expected to maintain the life of the violinist against your will? Thomson thinks not; having a right to life does not guarantee having either a right to be given the use of or a right to be allowed continued use of, another person's body.[55] She feels that nobody is required by society to make such an inordinate sacrifice for nine months. Even though pregnant women might be Good Samaritans to do such a thing, society and law require only that they be "minimally decent Samaritans."[56]

An obvious problem with Thomson's example is that the analogy really is not parallel enough with pregnancy. As Nathanson says:

> This casts an unfair and wrong-headed prejudice against the consideration of the state of pregnancy and skews the argument. Pregnancy is not "sickness." Few pregnant women are bedridden and many, emotionally and physically, have never felt better. For these it is a stimulating experience, even for mothers who originally did not "want" to be pregnant. It seems that pregnancy must be cast as a very heavy disability (albeit one of limited nine-month duration) in order to make abortion seem justifiable.[57]

54. Judith Thomson, "A Defense of Abortion," in *The Rights and Wrongs of Abortion*, ed. Marshall Cohen, Thomas Nagel, and Thomas Scanlon (Princeton, N.J.: Princeton U., 1974), 21.
55. Ibid., 12.
56. Ibid., 19.
57. Nathanson, 220.

Two further observations on the inadequacy of the parable must be noted. First, we need to recognize the distinction that the illustration does maintain. Even if it were ethical for a woman to separate herself from the unborn child, that does not give her the right to have the child killed.

Second, in reality the parallel of the sick violinist to a mother with child is totally unacceptable. John T. Noonan, Jr., a law professor, calls the similitude to pregnancy "grotesque." Noonan continues, "It is difficult to think of another age or society in which a caricature of this sort could be seriously put forward as a paradigm illustrating the moral choice to be made by a mother."[58]

Noonan offers a parallel of a woman with child, which is much more accurate than that presented by Thomson, taken directly from tort law:

> On a January night in Minnesota, a cattle buyer, Orlando Depue, asked a family of farmers, the Flateaus, with whom he had dined, if he could remain overnight at their house. The Flateaus refused and, although Depue was sick and had fainted, put him out of the house into the cold night. Imposing liability on the Flateaus for Depue's loss of his frostbitten fingers the court said, "In the case at bar defendants were under no contract obligation to minister to plaintiff in his distress; but humanity demanded they do so, if they understood and appreciated his condition.... The law as well as humanity required that he not be exposed in his helpless condition to the merciless elements." Depue was a guest for supper although not a guest after supper. The American Law Institute, generalizing, has said that it makes no difference whether the helpless person is a guest or a trespasser. He has the privilege of staying. His host has the duty not to injure him or put him into an environment where he becomes nonviable. The obligation arises when one person "understands and appreciates" the condition of the other. Although the analogy is not exact, the case seems closer to the mother's situation than the case imagined by Thomson; and the emotional response of the Minnesota judges seems to be a truer reflection of what humanity requires.[59]

The only question that warrants consideration on whether to abort is a value that is equal to the value of the child as a person specially created by God for a purpose in life. Certainly there are times when the equal rights of two persons are in competition and one of the person's rights must give way. At such times values must be equally considered and not denied before making a decision. But the overwhelming majority of abortions performed today are not done with those factors in mind. The

---

58. John T. Noonan, Jr., "How to Argue About Abortion," *A Private Choice—Abortion in America in the Seventies* (New York: Free Press [Macmillan], 1979), 2.
59. Ibid., 2-3.

statistics indicate that fewer than twenty out of 100,000 women die as a result of pregnancy.[60] According to Nathanson, out of 250,000 abortions performed in 1978 only 1,857 were approved for life endangerment, only 385 for health danger, and only 61 for rape or incest—*not* a life or death cause.

> This shows the degree to which abortions are being performed on other than medical grounds. In practice, it is not possible to spell out every probable element in medical practice and each case of a particular disease will vary. What we need—and can develop—is a workable ethical standard.[61]

The preponderance of non-life-saving abortions indicates four things: (1) the denigration of God's order of motherhood for women; (2) the rejection of God's creation within the mother; (3) the unwillingness to accept responsibility for one's sexual actions and its results; and (4) the denial of one's responsibilities as a neighbor to the weak.

TO THE MOTHER

In view of the above mentioned responses we must have a word from God to the mother. Obviously the time to speak to the woman is before she becomes pregnant. In our contemporary cultural setting, with the strong feminist emphasis, the woman is in control over her own body. Certainly God's standard for the single person is sexual purity. But we recognize the realities that sexual purity will not be maintained by many; as well, many abortions (though not the majority) are sought by married women. That being the case, one may offer alternatives to pregnancy. She can choose sexual continence, contraception, sterilization (or make sure her sexual partner makes that third choice).[62] Even though those choices may involve difficulties, any of them is preferable to abortion.

However, if the woman is already pregnant and seeks an abortion, there is another proclamation. If the fetus is truly another person residing inside the mother, and if the mother's life is not at stake, we must speak the law of God to her—"You shall not murder." She must be made to understand that the sin is great, even rising in the heart before the act is performed. In the words of Thielicke, it "begins with the renunciation, the wishing away of the embryo . . . for here is a person who refuses to

60. Nathanson, 243.
61. Ibid., 244.
62. Ibid.

say Yes to a gift bestowed by God and a responsibility imposed by Him."[63]

God's active Word to the pregnant woman is that the decision is not whether she will become a parent or have a child, but whether she will accept the child she already has as a gift of God. Or as Thielicke says, "Whether one dares to brush aside the arm of God after this arm has already been outstretched."[64]

When dealing with the mother who has aborted a child and is contrite about her sin, one may give a message of good news. Often one does not think through actions before doing them, either from lack of information or because of the trauma of the experience. So is the case with much abortion today. Many are not aware of the sinfulness of the act and do not understand what is really inside them. Also, often parents, friends, or the sexual partner urge abortion of the fetus. The number of women having guilt after an abortion is great. In view of all that one must speak to the woman that God forgives. The church has often been unwilling to minister to these women; God is more merciful in His judgment than men.

TO THE FATHER

Often women are unfairly blamed for the evil of abortion. Actually, polls have revealed that men are much more pro-abortion than are women. The fathers of newly conceived children frequently desire to put the burden solely on the woman they impregnate, and so be released from responsibility. Although the Supreme Court has presently taken away the rights of a father over the decision on abortion, it is to be hoped that that decision will be overturned. Laws should be enforced that require the men in such cases to be responsible for their actions.

Christian husbands (as well as wives) must seriously consider the responsibility given by God in the Genesis mandate to procreate and dominate the earth (Gen. 1:22). Knowing that the godly family is also a model for the world of Christ and His church (Eph. 5:22-33), we must ask ourselves if God's design for marriage and the family can be disregarded or permanently postponed because of economic or personal inconvenience.

TO THE CHURCH

Today the church must respond in several ways to the abortion issue.

63. Helmut Thielicke, *Theological Ethics, Sex* (Grand Rapids: Eerdmans, 1964), 2:229.
64. Ibid., 227.

First of all, it must speak out loud and clear against that terrible sin against God and humanity. Fairweather comments:

> The abortion controversy, then, presents an inescapable challenge to the Christian church, as a responsible teacher of faith and morals. If the question were a narrowly legal one, the case would be different; the church has no particular talent for drafting statutes. But when philosophical, religious and ethical truths and values are at stake, she has no right to keep quiet. Whatever the law may say or fail to say, she must try to discern and speak the mind of Christ.[65]

The church is called to be the light of the world, to speak truth in the midst of error. Yet, Christians often have been reluctant to speak on abortion boldly. It is to be hoped that the situation is now changing.

The church also should be involved in greater care for unwed mothers who desire to give birth to their children, both in spiritual and financial support. More counseling centers should be set up for those contemplating abortions. Counseling young people on this issue would be helpful. Last, the church must make a more conscious effort to emulate the compassion of her Lord in ministering to the wounds of those who have aborted their children.

TO SOCIETY

Society must be addressed also. The cries of separation of church and state should not hinder the denunciation of abortion in our country. The Christian conscience is not the slave of the state. Furthermore, because ours is a government of the people, Christians should fulfill their obligation to government by being involved in the lawmaking to protect the innocent. Gentles says:

> Christians, then, need not be ashamed to support a law that gives solid legal protection to the unborn child. Legal protection of the unborn implies that abortion would be permissible only when continuation of the pregnancy would result in the death of the mother. To adhere to this position is not to indulge in a censorious moralism. It is simply to take seriously the principle that an innocent person's most fundamental right is the right not to be killed. As Christians we are perhaps more deeply touched by the abortion issue because of our convictions about the preciousness of human life. We are told that the face of God is reflected in each human being. We are told that every hair on our head is counted, and that the value of each one of us is so great in God's eyes that it cannot be reckoned. Nevertheless, when we

65. Fairweather, ii.

advocate a law against abortion we do not merely speak out of our private religious vision. We also speak from a conviction that innocent life must be protected if a healthy society is to endure.[66]

Human beings do not exist for the state, but the state for human beings. Rather than promoting love for a neighbor as moral law, the state, instead, often may promote an elitist ethic. Note the following:

> The ill-conceived love of neighbor has to disappear, especially in relation to inferior or asocial creatures. It is the supreme duty of a national state to grant life and livelihood only to the healthy . . . in order to secure the maintenance of a hereditarily sound and racially pure fold for all eternity. The life of an individual has meaning only in the light of that ultimate aim, that is, in the light of his meaning to his family and to his national state.[67]

Does that not sound like a statement from a modern proponent of abortion, infanticide, or euthanasia? Very much so! However, that was a statement by the Nazi director of public health, Dr. Arthur Guett, in 1935. We must always be on guard for that kind of attitude among people in power in our government.

TO GOD

Our response to God must be to pray to receive His forgiveness, both in a personal and intercessory manner. We cannot help but share in the guilt of a people that kills the marvelous creation of God. Our guilt is no different from that of ancient people whose cultures practiced child sacrifice. We have shared in that guilt by silence and inactivity. As well, we must seek the face of God to spare our nation from His judgment, realizing that if we turn from this wickedness, His mercy is everlasting and He may turn away His wrath.

After forgiveness must come the attempt to see this world from the standpoint of God. We must express appreciation for His creative work, honoring His masterful work of life through us.

TO US

Last of all, we must address believers. What practical response should we make as Christians? The Bible speaks much to those who are only

---

66. Gentles, 22-23.
67. Bill Crouse, "Abortion and Human Value," *Insight* (Dallas: Probe Ministries International, 1979), 4-5.

hearers of the Word and not doers. Here are some actions that we can take:

1. Individually join movements and political action committees concerned with the subject of abortion
2. Participate as Christians in passive acts, such as sit-ins at abortion clinics
3. Write to newspapers and state a rejection of abortion in the editorial page
4. Write to our congressmen before proposed pro-abortion legislation makes it to the floors of the Senate and House
5. Pray that soon this crime will be no longer a curse on our land.

CONCLUSION

America has received a Trojan horse. With the promise of sexual freedom and fulfillment has come the undoing of our society. The slaughter of the innocents on the altar of convenience will not go unnoticed by a God of justice. This slide toward moral evil began once society took down the banner of absolute ethics and replaced it with situation ethics. Then moral sexual choices became personal, hindered only by the dangers involved. With the coming of the pill, sexual irresponsibility no longer seemed threatening. As well, procreation became a secondary purpose of sexual relations, if indeed it was a purpose at all. With the threat of population explosion, that view received an air of altruism. The role of mother seemed less important, and feminism filled the vacuum. Children in this "new world" pose a problem, a popping of the balloon of womankind come of age. When the hope of the pill—maybe the ultimate friend of women in that mindset—proved to be an unfriendly ally, abortion came forth as a panacea.

With the advent of better birth control methods and abortion on demand came the means for women to disassociate sexual activity from childbearing. Feminists desired to free themselves from the oppression of sexism, the view that role and functions are distributed according to sexual differences. The identity of woman with motherhood was seen as the last obstacle to overcome—and abortion on demand has done that.[68]

Lest we be viewed as sensationalistic in so closely identifying feminism and abortion, note the statement of feminist Lucina Cisler:

---

68. Marnie de Varent, "Feminism and Abortion," in *The Right to Birth: Some Christian Views on Abortion*, ed. Eugene Fairweather and Ian Gentles (Toronto: Anglican Book Centre, 1976), 61.

Those who caution us to play down the woman's rights argument are only trying to put off the inevitable day when the society must face and eradicate the misogynistic roots of the present situation. And anyone who has spoken publicly about abortion from the feminist point of view knows all too well that it is *feminism*—not abortion—that is the really disturbing idea.[69]

From Ms. Cisler's vantage point, then, abortion and feminism are tightly knitted. Abortion is the great equalizer in the eyes of secular feminists, for bearing of children is the "ultimate punishment of sex"[70] that men do not have, and that inequity must be eliminated if women are to compete on a par with men. One feminist carries that social equalization to an extreme: "I happen to think that science must be used to either release women from biological reproduction—or to allow men to experience the process also."[71]

Most women who have abortions do not use the philosophical reasonings of the previously mentioned feminists. Instead, most represent the "convenient society," to use Surgeon General Koop's designation.[72] If the conceived child would hinder one's own aspirations, then it is a disposable commodity. Or, in the case of a handicapped unborn child the aspirations the parents have for the child may be unfulfilled and cause inconvenience to them throughout the child's life. Reasons for abortions are many, but usually they are never considerate of the unborn child.

Our Western civilization is at a crossroad. How we react to the current crisis on abortion may well determine the outcome of our society in the next few years. A disregard for human life cannot help but be a teaching tool that will further erode the American perspective of morality and rights. The dignity of life is the cornerstone of freedom and democracy, and the building is already crumbling.

The question remains, How will we, as Christians, respond? We have offered some guidelines for our approach. Although the issues of abortion are not easy, one must ask the right questions. Before we can talk about women's rights or exceptions that will permit abortion, we must ask whether the unborn is one of us and is our neighbor. If we believe that both of those questions should be answered in the affirmative, to remain silent in view of this sin is to fight against God. We challenge Christians to speak out against this evil of our times, to bear a Christian witness of

---

69. Lucina Cisler, "Unfinished Business: Birth Control and Woman's Liberation," in *Sisterhood Is Powerful* (New York: Vintage, 1970), 309.
70. Lawrence Lader, *Abortion II: Making the Revolution* (Boston: Beacon, 1973), viii.
71. Phyllis Chesler, *Women and Madness* (Garden City, N.Y.: Doubleday, 1972), 299.
72. We sent for a packet from Planned Parenthood on birth control and found abortion strongly suggested.

law and gospel to a world that desperately needs the Word of God on the subject of abortion.

1. What trends in society gave rise to the lax view of abortion?
2. Why do radical feminists consider abortion rights so important?
3. Have abortionists distorted data to make abortion rights more compelling? How?
4. How have the courts favored abortion advocates?
5. When may a baby's life be taken in the womb?
6. What reasons did the Supreme Court give for striking down anti-abortion laws?
7. What parallels are there between the slavery and abortion questions?
8. How does one weigh the rights of some people over against the rights of others?
9. What was the position of the early Christian church on the subject of abortion?
10. How should the law and gospel (judgment and grace) be used by the church in reference to the abortion issue?
11. What two questions must be addressed to the unborn before any other questions are considered regarding abortion?
12. What medical evidence is available that the unborn are human and alive?
13. How does Psalm 139 portray the unborn?
14. Does Exodus 21:22-25 reveal God's concern for the unborn? How?
15. What is the problem with the view that humanness is determined by stage of development?
16. Which is the real crux of the abortion controversy: *what man is,* or *when life begins?*
17. When does human life begin?
18. Do unborn children have an inherent right to live?
19. How must the mother be addressed in the abortion dilemma?
20. Whom have polls showed to be the most pro-abortion—men or women?
21. What is the responsibility of the church toward the evil of abortion?
22. How should society be addressed?
23. What is our responsibility to God?
24. What things might each of us do in fighting abortion?

8

When Do We Pull the Plug?

Today the subject of euthanasia is receiving widespread attention in the media. Unlike abortion, which usually centers on the rights of women to reproductive freedom, the euthanasia presentation appeals to the rights of suffering persons (usually elderly) to die "with dignity." Death is viewed as good according to that position. The term *euthanasia* means "good death" (*eu*=good, *thanasia*=death). Most arguments focus on the phrase "quality of life." When one's quality of life falls below a certain level, proponents of euthanasia consider death to be better than life. Especially relevant to their argument is this question: When may life-sustaining systems be removed from a person who will die without them?

Each new television season for the past several years has brought a powerful drama on "the right to die," stacking the cards heavily in favor of euthanasia and depicting opponents as smug and shallow. Characters and situations are controlled so as to put in a negative light all who believe in the sanctity of life, and to make those who lean toward euthanasia into shining heroes, struggling bravely against an unfeeling society. In reality, those who determine to live with adversity and pain are far more brave and heroic.

THE BIBLICAL PERSPECTIVE

In Scripture death is viewed as an enemy. In the Garden, Adam and Eve were told that if they ate of the tree of the knowledge of good and evil, they would die. The process of death began on that eventful day recorded in Genesis 3, and has equalized every human being since: "It is appointed for men to die once" (Heb. 9:27, NASB).

The sorrow that comes with death is a part of our experience. No matter how much we wish otherwise, our friends, family, and we ourselves face that inevitable foe. Jesus faced it. At the death of His friend Lazarus, Scripture says, "Jesus wept" (John 11:35). Even though He knew that Lazarus would be raised alive momentarily, the tragedy of death overcame Him. And in the Garden of Gethsemane we find Him recoiling from the fate of His own death. On the cross, death, with its separation, caused not only physical, but emotional pain as well.

No, death is not a friend. There is no "good death." It is an enemy that has caused people of all ages, through every means, to fight against its coming. In this life it must come, but Christ has secured ultimate victory over it through His resurrection. With that view before him, the apostle Paul could exclaim, "O death, where is your victory? O death, where is your sting?" (1 Cor. 15:55, NASB).

At the opposite pole from euthanasia is the Judeo-Christian view that life is precious. God is the giver of life. Innocent human life must be protected and preserved. The right to life finds its way into our Declaration of Independence. Even life that is "less meaningful" (to use arbitrary standards) than our own deserves protecting. That includes life that is in some way limited physically or mentally, and life the days of which are numbered. *All* life deserves continuance.

THE PHILOSOPHICAL PERSPECTIVE

An individual's response to euthanasia reflects the deep-seated roots of value and ethical presuppositions. Behavior and attitudes always reflect a philosophy of life. And, in this instance, the commitment to life represents an adherence to a basis of biblical absolutes, whereas a commitment to life termination reflects an adherence to a relative or situational standard.

A PRESUPPOSITIONAL BASIS FOR BEHAVIOR

The two views can be analyzed in the following manner:
Standard of Conduct.

Relativism: The situation determines the proper action; there are no absolutes; and the end justifies the means. Proverbs 14:12 states: "There is a way which seems right to a man, but its end is the way of death" (NASB).

Absolutism: Scripture sets the standards; man cannot deviate; absolutes provide stability and direction. First John 2:3 states: "And by this we know that we have come to know Him, if we keep *His* commandments."

Value Judgments

Relativism: In evaluating the euthanasia question, it is essential to extract all ethical judgments from the equation (value-free, decision-making philosophy).

Absolutism: Ethical and value judgments are necessary in solidifying a position on the euthanasia question.

Attitude Toward Right to Life

Relativism: Pro-euthanasia ultimately is a narcissistic attitude (selfish), for the relief either of the sufferer or of the sufferer's family (and, in some cases, the government).

Absolutism: Pro-life from a biblical viewpoint is an unselfish attitude that relies on God's sovereignty and power. God acts on the behalf of the sufferer in accordance to His own pleasure.

View on Ultimate Authority

Relativism: Man ultimately plays the role of "god" as he makes the final decision on life and death.

Absolutism: God ultimately is supreme as He does what is best for His children. Jeremiah 17:7 states: "Blessed is the man that trusteth in the Lord, and whose hope the Lord is."

Based on those distinctions, the Christian's motivation to terminate life for convenience' sake cannot originate from God.[1] Dr. Everett Koop, in his treatise on the subject, stated, "It does not change the fact that the motivation was to kill, no matter how one explains the deed in terms of compassion and empathy."[2] In reality then, killing equals murder. The statement in Exodus 20:13, "Thou shalt not kill" (KJV) is an emphatic negative imperative (i.e., a prohibition). The Hebrew word *kill* implies the idea of premeditated intent or murder.[3] *Baker's Dictionary of Christian Ethics* endorses the above premise by stating, "Euthanasia is the act of putting to death a person suffering from incurable, distressing disease. It is a violation of the Sixth Commandment, 'Thou shalt not kill (murder).' Such consent does not relieve the killer of guilt for the sin of the murder."[4]

Millard J. Erickson sums up what Scripture teaches on euthanasia by listing the elements in the biblical concept of murder: it is (1) intentional, (2) premeditated, (3) malicious, (4) contrary to the desire or intention

---

1. The law in the Old Testament did distinguish different varieties of homicide-murder, excusable killing, and even mandatory killing. An exegesis of this is found in Millard J. Erickson and Ines E. Bowers, "Euthanasia and Christian Ethics," *Journal of the Evangelical Theological Society*, vol. 19, no. 1 (Winter 1976), 16-19.
2. C. Everett Koop, *The Right to Live, The Right to Die* (Wheaton, Ill.: Tyndale, 1976), 91.
3. Erickson and Bowers, 16.
4. S.M. Reynolds, "Euthanasia," in *Baker's Dictionary of Christian Ethics*, ed. C. F. H. Henry (Grand Rapids: Baker, 1973), 222.

of the victim, and (5) against someone who has done nothing deserving of capital punishment.[5]

Euthanasia seems to fulfill criteria 1, 2, and 5 in most cases. Number 3 and 4 may or may not apply depending on the circumstances. Obviously, the millions of Jews killed during the Holocaust surely did not opt for life to be terminated! However, when any group or society goes from the absolute to the relative, there can be no security in any given area. Thus with Pandora's box wide-open, the situation or climate of the day can dictate when life ought to be terminated.

And along those same lines Koop warns:

> Perhaps in the not too distant future, there could be termination of life that is considered "unworthy" not because of physical or mental incapacity, but because of what might be considered to be unworthy life in the field of ethnic origin, economic capacity, political activity, productivity potential, or any other form or function currently considered to be undesirable.[6]

EXTENSION OR EXTINCTION OF HUMAN LIFE

With the advance of technology in today's world, a real dilemma arises as to what constitutes ethical treatment for one with an incurable disease or illness, or in an irreversible comatose state. To help create an understanding of this issue, four terms have been employed:

1. *Voluntary, passive euthanasia*. In this form of euthanasia, medical personnel, at the patient's request, merely allow nature to take its course.
2. *Voluntary, active euthanasia*. This means that the physician, by request, hastens death actively (e.g., by lethal injection). This raises the controversial issue of whether nonmedical personnel would be permitted to end the suffering of a spouse, another close relative, or friend.
3. *Involuntary, passive euthanasia*. Here the patient either has expressed no willingness to die or cannot do so. The medical personnel do not go to any extraordinary measures to save the patient, and they may withhold food (by removing nasogastric tubes), antibiotics, or life-support systems (respirator).
4. *Involuntary, active euthanasia*. This begins to blur into genocide. The physician actively hastens death, regardless of the patient's wishes, citing humanitarian, economic, or genetic considerations.[7]

5. Erickson and Bowers, 17.
6. Koop, 91.
7. J. Kerby Anderson, "Euthanasia: A Biblical Appraisal," *Bibliotheca Sacra*, vol. 144 (1987): 209-10.

Several inferences can be made from the above definitions:

1. Voluntary euthanasia can be viewed as suicide. "Under the present law, voluntary euthanasia would, except in certain narrow circumstances, be regarded as suicide in the patient who consents and murder in the doctor who administers."[8]
2. If euthanasia is legalized, people who are already fearful of the physician's capabilities "may shrink from him in fear and anxiety at a time when they need his services most."[9]
3. Passive euthanasia is not free from ethical questions. The issues are not as clear-cut as many Christians would like. For example, Koop argues that if a twenty-year-old needs a kidney dialysis machine for survival, that treatment would be considered "normal" and "ordinary." On the other hand if in a ninety-year-old individual the same kidney shutdown took place and was the result of a disease process that inevitably would take his patient's life, the institution of dialysis would be an "extraordinary procedure."[10]
4. There is a correlation between the technology God has given for man to use, and the application of that technology to prolong life. And because God is sovereign, He can will a recovery, or allow death to occur. Thus, our responsibility is to see that what physically can be done be performed, leaving the decision of who lives and who dies to God.
5. Although one of the goals of euthanasia is to provide an "easy" death for the sufferer, it contradicts the Christian's calling to an expected life of suffering (2 Tim. 2:12; 3:12). We are to expect suffering until we enter eternity (Rev. 21:4). However, Jesus does promise peace and strength to meet the trials that come on us in this life.
6. Finally, euthanasia opens up the opportunity for fraud, deception, and deceit where financial position, social status, age, and so on become determining factors in who lives and who dies.[11] On the other hand, care must be taken to minimize the temptation to provide superfluous medical treatment that stems from greed rather than from a genuine concern for the well-being of the patient.

CONCLUSION

The crux of the euthanasia issue centers on the question "Has the con-

---

8. D. Yates Bingham, *Crises in Morality*, C. W. Scudder, ed. (Nashville: Broadman, 1964), 60.
9. Bingham, 69-70.
10. Koop, 93.
11. Ibid., 97.

trol for life been placed in the hands of man, or has God reserved it for Himself alone?"[12] We can only agree with Thomas Wood who said:

> The right to life is God-given, and it is not within the moral competence of man deliberately and directly to take the life of any innocent human being either with or without his consent . . . . A man is not the absolute owner of his life. It belongs to God who gave it. A man has the right to preserve and prolong it, but not the right willfully to destroy it.[13]

For centuries Western civilization in general and Christians in particular have believed in the sanctity of human life. The disabled, retarded, and infirm were seen as having a special place in God's world. Unfortunately this view is beginning to erode. Today some medical personnel judge a person's fitness for life on the basis of what they perceive to be the quality of that person's life.

This so-called "right to die" denies God the opportunity to work sovereignly within a shattered life and bring glory to Himself. When Joni Eareckson realized that she would spend the rest of her life as a quadriplegic, she asked in despair, "Why can't they just let me die?"

Her friend Diana, trying to comfort her said: "The past is dead, Joni. You're alive!"

"Am I?" replied Joni. "This isn't living."

But through God's grace Joni's despair gave way to her firm conviction that even her accident was within God's plan for her life. Now she shares with the world her firm belief that "suffering gets us ready for heaven."

In his research on euthanasia, J. Kerby Anderson concludes:

> Modern medicine defines death primarily as a biological event; yet Scripture defines death as a spiritual event that has biological consequences. Death, according to the Bible, occurs when the spirit leaves the body (Eccles. 12:7; James 2:26).
>
> Unfortunately this does not offer much by way of clinical diagnosis for medical personnel. But it does suggest that a rigorous medical definition for death be used. A comatose patient may not be conscious, but from both a medical and biblical perspective he is very much alive and treatment should be continued unless crucial vital signs and brain activity have ceased.
>
> On the other hand Christians must also reject the notion that everything must be done to save life at all costs. Believers, knowing that to be at home in the body is to be away from the Lord (2 Cor. 5:6), long for the time when they will be absent from the body and at home with the Lord (2 Cor. 5:8). Death is gain for Christians (Phil. 1:21). Therefore they need not be so tied

---

12. Bingham, 73.
13. Erickson and Bowers, 20.

to this earth that they perform futile operations just to extend life a few more hours or days.

In a patient's last days, everything possible should be done to alleviate physical and emotional pain. Giving drugs to a patient to relieve pain is morally justifiable. Proverbs 31:6 says, "Give strong drink to him who is perishing, and wine to him whose life is bitter." As previously mentioned, some analgesics have the secondary effect of shortening life. But these should be permitted since the primary purpose is to relieve pain, even though they may secondarily shorten life. . . .

Difficult philosophical and biblical questions are certain to continue swirling around the issue of euthanasia. But in the midst of these confusing issues should be the objective, absolute standards of Scripture, which provide guidance for the hard choices of providing care to terminally ill patients.[14]

QUESTIONS TO PONDER

1. How does euthanasia differ philosophically, socially, and spiritually from the abortion issue?
2. In your opinion, is there such a thing as a "good death"? Explain.
3. Research the Judeo-Christian view of human life and its importance. How do your findings differ from some modern dogmas?
4. Name some underlying values that direct your actual behavior.
5. Research additional differences between the postures of relativism and absolutism.
6. Is there ever a point (even with the advancements in technology) that medical intervention ought not be implemented? If so, what factors must be considered?
7. What are some legal problems that have arisen as a result of pro-euthanasia propaganda?
8. What effects on society will euthanasia have if it becomes legal in our country?
9. Should the evangelical Christian try to stop the euthanasia movement?

14. Anderson, 216-17.

Part Three —————————
Homosexuality

If we as Christians think we are untouched by the growing problem of homosexuality, we need to take a second look. That will not be difficult, because homosexuality is out of the closet. It is blatantly blasted over our TV sets and upheld as a human right to be protected by antidiscrimination laws. More disturbing is the watering down of certain church denominations' standards, making homosexuality acceptable for laymen and ministers to practice, along with divorce, remarriage, and abortion.

We are not naive, we say. It is common knowledge that in every major city in our country is a gay community complete with a strip of homosexual bars. We have heard stories of people who have driven down one of those strips in broad daylight and watched male street hustlers, often runaways in their early teens and in women's clothing, climb into cars and limousines, prostituting themselves to other homosexuals for money or desire. Periodically we hear of a gay wedding that takes place. We may even be aware that one out of every ten Americans may have homosexual tendencies. We shudder and are appropriately disgusted and righteously indignant, but are we really so worldly wise as we think?

Are we aware that homosexuality has spread beyond the cities into the smalltown roots of our society, into many of our schools and churches?

It is not a new phenomenon; homosexuality was in existence before Sodom and Gomorrah. However, it has never been as open in America as it is today.

The imagination and speculation of situation comedies has given way to hard reality. Gay communities, albeit small and quiet in places, are growing in most small cities and towns.

The results of the open acceptance of homosexuality and gay rights has added another burden for American teens to cope with. According to a public school counselor in one small city of 60,000 people, homosexuality has become a popular and fairly common option to be added to the list of temptations such as drinking, smoking, using drugs, practicing premarital sex, or vandalizing public property. Many American youth are neither embarrassed nor repulsed by the option. They discuss sexual preference, experiment, visit homosexual bars, and seek to be educated in homosexual practices without any more amazement than they have for electronic games or home computers. For them, it is an accepted fact of life.

It is sad that homosexuality has also entered the lives of Christians through the front door of the church. The Christian attitude toward homosexuality, as with feminism and the abortion issue, has evolved from the secular view of tolerance to the humanistic voice of acceptance. Liberal theologians proclaim that practicing homosexuals can love and serve God well in their own sexual life-style. The root of this sad phenomenon is sin, and it grows in the fertile environment of today's homes—homes where God's intended family structure has been altered to suit the personal convenience of the husband and wife.

It is clear that homosexuality is an epidemic that must be confronted in the light of God's Word. The intention of this section is to examine the homosexual issue—its roots, causes, and effects. We will also consider biblical principles and explore a compassionate view of men and women caught in the homosexual movement.

9

Homosexuality: A Contagious Epidemic

Homosexual behavior, once considered to be an unfit subject for discussion in many Christian circles, has emerged in recent years as an issue that cannot be ignored by the evangelical. As a result, the need has arisen for creating a foundation or basis of approach for analyzing the question of homosexuality.

When one sees that America is a humanistically oriented society, it becomes obvious how the view that downplays the evils of homosexual activity has evolved. Its roots are deeply embedded in the nonabsolute structures of this philosophy, and without a concrete basis of right and wrong, individual accountability becomes drastically minimized (that is the underlying theme contained in most current psychology texts).

To put the pieces of this puzzle together, this part will briefly cover three areas: the portrait of a homosexual; popular theories regarding the causes of homosexuality; and the effects of homosexuality in our culture.

THE PORTRAIT OF THE HOMOSEXUAL

Contrary to the belief of many, male homosexuals are not necessarily effeminate, and lesbians are not always more aggressively masculine than other women. Picking homosexuals out of a crowd is really quite difficult in some cases, especially with the complexity of individual personality patterns that exists. Psychiatrist Alfred A. Messer found that homosexuals need to use gestures and body language to identify themselves because of the difficulty in classifying those of "their kind."[1]

1. Alfred A. Messer, *When You Are Concerned with Homosexuality* (St. Meinrad, Ind.: Abbey, 1980), 12.

The homosexual is motivated by a definite erotic attraction to members of the same sex (either by fantasy or by physical sexual relations). According to Irving Bieber, "Male homosexuals differ from each other as do heterosexuals, but they have in common the homosexual inclination, and an inability to form or sustain an orgastically effective, romantic heterosexual relationship."[2]

Bieber also states that homosexuals tend to gravitate toward large urban centers and have formed a subcultural social system, identified by both the visible and hidden elements of the homosexual world.[3]

The homosexual also tends to be a lonely individual who has a compulsive preoccupation with sex. Studies reveal that this strong drive leads to early sexual encounters. For example, 35 percent of all homosexuals began their sexual practices with members of the same sex by the time they were ten years old, and 80 percent became active by the age of sixteen.[4]

Finally, Bieber's research found the most popular choice of homosexual partner is the masculine type or the male who has traits that symbolize masculinity. Only a minority of homosexuals look for feminine characteristics in a partner.[5]

It can be concluded then that very few homosexuals ever "marry" or have a prolonged relationship with a homosexual mate. Most never even know the name of the persons they encounter sexually. The homosexual is preoccupied with an animalistic drive for sex in many cases, and is forced to communicate via disguised secret gestures and body language. It can be said that even though there are certain geographical pockets of the country where homosexuality is accepted and a large homosexual community has developed, in most areas societal norms do not accommodate that life-style. Hence, many homosexuals live with extreme stress and guilt.

CAUSES OF HOMOSEXUALITY

Through the years the question of homosexual causation has been tossed to and fro in the scientific, psychological, and theological communities. However, because it is now a popular and accepted presupposition that man is not ultimately responsible for his actions, the conclusions reached by many researchers reflect such deeply cherished ideas without ample search for other possible answers and solutions. When a

2. Alfred M. Freedman, *Comprehensive Textbook of Psychiatry* (Baltimore: Williams & Wilkins, 1967), 964.
3. Ibid., 964.
4. Ibid., 965.
5. Ibid.

theory is proposed, acceptance is expected to occur. Such blind approval of theories quickly leaps to a so-called acceptance of facts (evolution, for example, is considered a fact in most textbooks today). Why? Under the umbrella of science, if an expert announces to the world an idea, the layman is expected to accept that idea as the "gospel truth." For example, in 1937, a British psychologist named Cyril Burt referred to all left-handers as being clumsy, retarded, stammerers, stubborn, criminal, neurotic, or homosexual.[6] Absurd? Yes, but much of the material in our textbooks today reflects that kind of research: starting with the desired conclusion; then finding data to support that conclusion.

We will now direct our attention to some popular theories on the cause of homosexuality and conclude by presenting the evangelical explanation.

THEORY: HOMOSEXUALITY IS AN INBORN GENETIC DISORDER

Explanation of theory. Most of the evidence for this view was derived from a study on twins by Alfred Kallman. He reported that when the twins were of the same sex, if one was homosexual, so was the other. If the twins were of the opposite sex, the degree of homosexuality was cut in half.[7] That supposedly proved to him and others that homosexuality was genetically based.

Objections to theory. In further research on identical twins conducted at the New York Psychiatric Institute, results did not support Kallman's findings of 100 percent concordance.[8] Masters and Johnson have also reported no difference in the sexual physiology of homosexual males or females and that of their heterosexual brothers or sisters.[9]

THEORY: FREUD'S HYPOTHESIS

Explanation of theory. Sigmund Freud accepted the bisexual theory of his day, which held that when one is born, the tendency toward either homosexuality or heterosexuality was equal. "Freud also believed that the sexual practices in homosexual relationships symbolized regressions to the earliest libidinal level (selfishness)."[10]

Objections to theory. Since Freud's time, "it has been determined that in

6. Atuhiro Sibatani, "The Japanese Brain: The Difference Between East and West May Be the Difference Between Left and Right," *Science 80*, December 1979, 24-27.
7. Alfred M. Freedman and Harold Kaplan, *Modern Synopsis: Comprehensive Textbook of Psychiatry* (Baltimore: Williams & Wilkins, 1972), 415.
8. Evelyn M. Duvall and Sylvanus M. Duvall, eds., *Sex Ways — In Fact and Faith* (New York: Association, 1961), 169.
9. Charles W. Keysor, editor, *What You Should Know About Homosexuality* (Grand Rapids: Zondervan, 1979), 147.
10. Freedman, *Modern Synopsis . . . Psychiatry*, 415.

the normal organism, bisexuality is a fiction. Sex is clearly differentiated at the moment of conception, and there is no evidence to support Freud's theory of homosexuality."[11] Even though Freud's referral to the libidinal level cannot be substantiated at every point, there is a significant correlation of homosexuality to selfishness (i.e., narcissism: an unhealthy love for self[12]).

THEORY: HOMOSEXUALITY IS A GLANDULAR DISORDER

Explanation of theory. A number of researchers have attempted to prove that homosexual behavior results from a glandular imbalance. The development of an effeminate body build and psychological temperament is thus produced.[13]

Objections to theory. Even though a percentage of homosexuals do demonstrate a body build that fits the popular stereotype, investigators have concluded beyond any doubt that "there is no difference between the physique and glandular functionings of the homosexual and heterosexual by any tests."[14]

THEORY: THE INVERSION HYPOTHESIS

Explanation of theory. The Inversion Hypothesis, more commonly referred to as "the accidental theory," argues that homosexual behavior results from an absence of heterosexual possibilities (i.e., boys at an all-boys school; sailors at sea; prisoners in jail; etc.), and should not be considered a disorder. Thus, homosexuality becomes a substitute for normal intercourse.[15]

Objections to theory. Here we see a classic example of humanistic reasoning in the attempt to blame the environment for what in reality is a deliberate personal choice. Even though society would like to conclude that man is not ultimately responsible for his behavior, we must not forget that one deliberately chooses to succumb to the unnatural drives fostered in homosexual practices.

THEORY: HOMOSEXUALITY IS A LEARNED PATTERN OF BEHAVIOR

Explanation of theory. From our viewpoint, it has become increasingly

11. Ibid., 415.
12. For an excellent review of the narcissistic problem in America, we would suggest your reading of Christopher Lasch's bestseller entitled *The Culture of Narcissism* (New York: Warner Books, 1979).
13. Duvall, 169.
14. Duvall, 169.
15. Fred Brown and Rudolf T. Kempton, *Sex Questions & Answers*, 2d ed. (New York: McGraw-Hill, 1970), 233.

clear that homosexuality is not only learned but is also accepted (by the act of the will) and thereby desired by those involved.

An interesting study conducted in Japan by Tadanobu Tsunoda provides some new insights into this line of thinking. In his book *The Japanese Brain: Brain Function and East-West Culture,* Tsunoda's thesis concluded that culture modifies brain function, not vice-versa (biological determinism). He asserts that "language shapes the neuro-physiological pathways of the brain." Also, "the language one learns as a child influences the way in which the brain's right and left hemispheres develop their special talents."[16]

The next step in this reasoning process would be that as language and culture are learned, giving the brain a running pattern so to speak, so homosexuality is learned behavior that is actually programmed into the brain pattern. And once the brain is programmed in that direction, it is very difficult (apart from Jesus Christ) to change its behavioral pattern. Homosexuals themselves will agree to that when asked, What things do you think made you become homosexual? They respond in the following way:

	Homo-sexuals	Lesbians
Early homosexual experience	24%	17%
Homosexual associates	9%	23%
Poor relationship w/mother	16%	14%
Poor relationship w/father	11%	17%
Anti-heterosexual	7%	9%
Unhappy heterosexuality	2%	13%
No heterosexual partners	16%	8%
Social ineptitude	10%	6%
Born homosexual	11%	6%
Lazy/character or moral defect	10%	6%

(Note: Each respondent could check more than one category.)

Lorne E. Brown, M.D., in a recent interview, summed up how one actually becomes a homosexual.

I would like to encourage you in your writing of the book on social issues. I am deeply disturbed at the apparent acceptance of the false notion that homosexually active people are made that way and cannot help it.

I have never seen such evidence in any of the medical literature supporting the theory of biological determinants for homosexual activity. Were

16. Sibatani, 24.

there any valid evidence of biological determinants for this behavior, you may be sure the psychiatric literature would be full of it because psychiatrists are so regularly baffled and defeated by this problem.

Homosexuality is not determined. The homosexual becomes one by a series of choices. These choices may seem imperceptible to him because they are not at first conscious choices to homosexual activity. Most frequently they are those of social attraction, for reasons other than sexual, to a person of the same sex. As the friendship becomes more intimate, some sexual stimulation occurs and if there is not a prior commitment to the wrongness—or at least the undesirability of homosexual conduct, this develops into overt acts.

The pattern, if not abruptly broken off, develops more rapidly if the person or persons with whom the novice associates is already practicing homosexual activity. As the friendship deepens, the values and lifestyle of his friends are accepted. Then one day he "discovers" that he really has a preference for the same sex which has no basis whatever in his genetic, anatomic or physiologic make-up.

Homosexuality can be compared to the act of stealing. Stealing is an activity that occurs quite spontaneously in childhood and is influenced by numerous parental and environmental factors. If the parent, or parents, have few scruples against dishonesty, or if they practice deceitful or devious ways, or if unfortunate circumstances cause a child to gravitate toward dishonest friends, then it is easy for him to become an habitual thief and much harder to become honest. In the same way, parental and family factors, notably a domineering and possessive mother, tend to cause the child to drift toward the kinds of relationships that lead to homosexual activity. Add to this an environment tolerant and accepting of homosexuality and the chances of the person falling into the same trap are reinforced. However, these unfortunate factors of environment and parental, sibling or peer relationships cannot cause one to be either a thief or a homosexual without his co-operation and personal response.

Homosexuality is a harmful condition causing great mental and emotional suffering—a disease if you will. (It also opens doors to a host of other diseases, sexually transmitted, but that is another story.) It is an acquired disease; not genetic or congenital. In addition it is contagious—and to a degree is approaching epidemic proportions.

Homosexuals desperately want to believe, and have us believe, that their state is "gay," normal and acceptable. They would believe that it is genetic and/or congenital, or at least predetermined as in some way imposed upon them by either God or fate. They would deny that it is in any way contagious. Endorsement of these propositions, all of which are false, can only add to the current epidemic.

Certainly believers must as never before be filled with compassion for those already entrapped and have deep concern for ourselves and young people not yet "infected." We must learn and understand the biblical principles, which are not as obscure as many seem to think. Finally, we can have hope, for in the light of these principles and in the power of the indwelling Holy Spirit, it is not as hopeless a condition as many think.[17]

EFFECTS OF HOMOSEXUALITY

As was pointed out earlier, homosexuality is not determined, but rather learned and accepted by the act of the will. It becomes necessary then to look at how it becomes learned behavior in our culture. To do that, a brief analysis of various social institutions needs to be made.

THE FAMILY

Because individuals are born biologically male or female, homosexuality may result when heterosexuality is disturbed in certain observable ways. And in our culture the number one disturbance occurs in the family setting. What kind of home climate is necessary for one to choose homosexuality as a way of life? Ray B. Evans, a professor of psychiatry, states:

> I have never interviewed a male homosexual whose relationship with his father was discernibly loving, non-competitive, and free of mutual hostility. Conversely, I have never observed a single case where an affectionate, constructive father had a homosexual son. I have consistently observed an unremittingly disturbed relationship with males in the early life of homosexual men, beginning with the father, extending to brothers, and almost always involving peer-mates up to and including the preadolescent era.[18]

Howard Hendricks, a seminary professor, has found in his counseling that homosexuals come from homes where the father is detached, passive, hostile, an absolute "zero" in terms of leadership in the home. (At the office he may be totally different.) The mother on the other hand can be described as being aggressive, smothering, dominating, and overprotective as well as demasculinizing. That combination forms a lethal atmosphere for homosexuality to develop.[19]

It must be reinforced here that the odds against one becoming a homosexual are great if that individual is raised in a loving family where God's rules are employed.[20] The tragedy is that many parents who fail in

17. This material was sent to us by Lorne E. Brown, member of the medical faculty, the University of Nebraska Medical Center, Lincoln, Nebraska.
18. Ray B. Evans, "Homosexuality & the Role of the Family Physician," *Medical Aspects of Human Sexuality*, vol. 13 (September 1979), 31.
19. Howard Hendricks, cassette tape "What Is Love?" (San Bernardino, Calif.: Campus Crusade, 1978).
20. For further information on how the family plays a part in the development of a homosexual, we recommend Clyde Narramore's book *Encyclopedia of Psychological Problems* (Grand Rapids: Zondervan, 1970), 114-15.

providing the proper home environment for their children will have to give an account before God someday.

SOCIETY

In sociology, *norms* are defined as accepted ways of doing things. In reality, what becomes accepted in the world system is masterminded by Satan himself (John 8:44), and thus conflicts with God's directives.

On the homosexual issue we have seen society's attitude change from one of intolerance to tolerance. That is evident in the media, courts, the educational structure, and in the medical profession. The American Psychiatric Association no longer classifies homosexuality as a sexual disorder. Many militant feminists have adopted female homosexuality "as a way of proving to themselves and to the world that they need not feel subjugated by men under any circumstances."[21]

Tolerance on the topic of homosexuality has also come to our colleges. According to a 1978 *New York Times* article, homosexual organizations now exist at more than 200 colleges.[22]

We live in a society that is rapidly changing its normative and value structure. Society is telling us to "do our own thing." To advocate morality at any level is taboo. In a recent television appearance evangelist James Robison denounced homosexuality as a sin. His program was canceled, and the courts backed up the station's decision.[23]

Fighting the strong current of today's society that preaches homosexuality as an acceptable alternative life-style is very difficult for the evangelical to do, but very necessary.

MEDICAL

The effects of homosexuality today, from a medical standpoint, are unparalleled in American history. Never before have Americans faced a more serious threat to their health. With homosexual activity raging, AIDS (Acquired Immune Deficiency Syndrome) has become the new killer disease to spring from the immoral activity common to homosexuality. First reported in 1981, AIDS has become the most dangerous of the sexually transmitted diseases, because it is both fatal and, at present, incurable.

Otis Bowen, Secretary of the Health and Human Services Department, has identified AIDS as "the most serious health threat facing our

21. Messer, 75.
22. G. Hechinger and F. Hechinger, "Homosexuality on Campus," *New York Times*, 12 March 1978, 15-17.
23. "How to Call Sin Sin Noncontroversially," *Christianity Today* 23 (4 May 1979), 45.

nation."[24] According to conservative estimates, at the end of 1986 29,000 Americans were infected with AIDS.[25] By the next summer, the number of people infected with AIDS was about to be 1.5 million in the United States and 10 million worldwide.[26] By the 1990's millions are expected to be infected, with hundreds of thousands dying from the disease.

AIDS is not the first plague in history. Five major outbreaks of fatal disease have been recorded. The Black Death killed 25-50 million people in three years. Smallpox was a major killer for centuries. The flu killed half a million Americans in 1917-18. Typhus took approximately 3 million people from 1918 to 1922. Polio killed 22,000 Americans from 1943 to 1956.[27] Obviously AIDS is not the first plague even in twentieth-century America.

Despite the seriousness of this epidemic, Americans are not being taught to give AIDS the "respect" it deserves. Some medical research indicates that the AIDS virus is far more serious than has been publicly admitted by a majority of the medical community. This research indicates that casual transmission cannot be entirely ruled out[28] until we more fully understand the workings of the disease. Meanwhile, common sense would dictate that caution (for example, allowing medical personnel to wear gloves and masks, even if it does make some AIDS patients feel discriminated against)[29] is not inappropriate.

Thomas Sowell believes that school officials should be much more cautious. "Why are children with much milder contagious diseases kept out of schools, but not children with AIDS?," he writes. "This disease has already killed half the people ever known to have it, and with no cure in sight for the other half. . . . The schools' decision cannot be explained on medical grounds but is readily understandable on political grounds. Mothers of children with measles or scarlet fever are not organized politically, but homosexuals are."[30] Sowell is neither an alarmist nor homophobic, as critics of his view like to label it. His approach to AIDS is based on reason and common sense. If this disease is as serious as the

24. *Dallas Morning News*, 20 June 1987, 9A. For a British viewpoint see John Seale, "Memorandum," in the "Third Report from the House of Commons Social Services Committee" (London: Her Majesty's Stationery Office, 1987), 142-48. Seale, a member of the Royal Society of Medicine, pleads with British politicians "to force scientists to speak clearly, precisely and honestly about the Aids epidemic." The AIDS virus, argues Seale, "has the properties of a skilled, devious, hidden and implacable invader with the capacity and willingness to kill every man, woman and child in our country."
25. *U.S. News and World Report*, 12 January 1987, 60.
26. *Dallas Morning News*, 29 June 1987, 4F.
27. *U.S. News and World Report*, 12 January 1987, 69.
28. Gene Antonio, *The AIDS Cover-up? The Real and Alarming Facts About AIDS* (San Francisco: Ignatius, 1986), 95-124.
29. David A. Noebel, Wayne C. Lutton, and Paul Cameron, *AIDS: A Special Report* (Manitou Springs, Col.: Summit Research Institute, 1987), 108-11.
30. Syndicated column, 27 September 1985.

evidence allows, then serious measures must be taken to guard people from it.

So far, those who oppose extreme measures insist that no evidence now exists to indicate that casual contact can transmit AIDS. They consider the chances of infection from casual contact, insect bites, and miscellaneous body fluids (tears, sweat, saliva) to be highly improbable. The problem with this approach is that it rests on uncertainties and indefinite conclusions. How ironic that people go to great extremes to eliminate nuclear arms because of the threat of human annihilation, but adopt a laissez-faire approach to a disease that is already causing thousands to die horrible deaths. This problem, like many others, is better handled through prevention than cure.

Some medical facts about AIDS are:

1. It strips the body of its immunity defense system.
2. It is transferred from victim to victim via bodily fluids — blood, semen, saliva, and possibly bowel matter.
3. It is a fatal disease.

In addition to AIDS, gay sex may also have other consequences:

1. Homosexuals have a rate of infectious hepatitis 8 to 25 times higher than heterosexual males.
2. Two-thirds of all homosexuals have had at least one venereal disease.
3. Twenty percent of all homosexuals hospitalized in San Francisco carried rectal gonorrhea.[31]

POLITICS

Homosexual lobbyists in Washington, D.C., and in our local governments are making steady headway in getting our laws changed to suit their life-style. They are becoming a strong power base as was evident in a mayoral election in San Francisco. Some states now have laws to protect homosexuals so they can have the right to teach our children in schools.[32] And even though unrelated subject matter may be taught, over the course of the school year the homosexual values of the teacher are bound to be transmitted to the students. Considering that the homosexu-

---

31. "The Gay Plague: Homosexuality and Disease." A pamphlet published by the Alert Citizens of Texas, 2-3.
32. Roger M. Williams, "Turning the Tide on Gay Rights," *Saturday Review*, 17 February 1979, 21-24.

als in America control 19 percent of the spendable income in the United States, the political implications become much more frightening.[33]

With the advent of AIDS, however, many Americans are becoming increasingly fearful of homosexuals, and several groups have begun to bring suit against the homosexual community.[34]

The homosexual sub-culture, however, continues to use its political clout to restrict legal actions that would inhibit the practice of homosexuality, even though such activity spreads disease, most notably AIDS. Laws allowing homosexual activity have been upheld. Homosexual bathhouses, a prime source of sexual diseases, are legally protected.

What about the obligation of public officials to protect the public? Legislators have passed laws that prohibit smoking in many public facilities, ban smoking commercials from television, and require drivers to wear seatbelts. Legislators have *not*, however, done all they could to protect people from AIDS.

Many argue that lawmakers have no right to legislate morality. We must remember, though, that to enact any law is to legislate morality. The law against murder legislates morality. The law prohibiting marriage between close relatives legislates morality. Absolute freedom is anarchy and disorder, resulting eventually in slavery. Well-reasoned laws that protect society morally and physically are absolutely necessary, even when they must restrict the freedoms of some.

"When there is no restraint, when mere experience is the touchstone of what should be permitted," wrote Daniel Bell, "the impulse to explore everything, to seek all sensations, even when sanctioned on aesthetic grounds, leads to debauchery, lust, degradation of others, and murder."[35] When the political and judicial communities protect the right of homosexuals to practice under conditions that promote disease, these communities are contributing to the breakdown of public health.

CHURCH

In accepting the values and norms of the world system, many theologians and denominations are now reflecting the tolerant view of homosexuality. It was reported that a majority of the United Methodist fifty-five member general board proposed that the denomination loosen its official position on homosexuality.[36] Other denominations are following close behind in that shift.

33. "Gays: A Major Force in the Marketplace," *Business Week*, 3 September 1979, 118-20.
34. "Litigation Imminent on AIDS Issues," *The National Law Journal* 25 July 1983, 3.
35. Daniel Bell, *Cultural Contradictions of Capitalism* (New York: Basic, 1978), 277.
36. "Methodists: Choosing Love or License," *Christianity Today*, 7 December 1979, 15.

When official positions on homosexuality change, theology must adapt to that change. At a "biblical feminist" workshop held at Fuller Theological Seminary, one of the speakers, Letha Scanzoni, was quoted as saying:

> Homosexuality is a state of being. It appears to be irreversible. . . . In all fairness both to homosexual people and the apostle Paul, I think we need to distinguish between what I've been describing and what Paul is talking about in the first chapter of Romans. There the focus is on deliberate actions and rebellion against God, in a context of idolatry, where heterosexual persons capable of fulfilling God's plan for their sexual expression in a covenantal union of marriage reject that plan.
>
> Surely such a situation differs from cases where a person's own nature is homosexual. The Scriptures are silent on that topic. Is it possible for two homosexual Christians to live together in a relationship which displays these very qualities, of integrity, justice, tenderness, love and faithfulness? Some are already doing so.[37]

In the same report, another conference speaker, Dr. Virginia Mollenkott added: "If homosexual behavior is neither sickness nor sin, which science is showing, we cannot expect healings. We have refused to build a theology of sexuality on Genesis 1 and 2."[38]

If we begin with humanistic presuppositions we can always rationalize our conclusions. That is the trap into which liberal theology has fallen.

QUESTIONS TO PONDER

1. Until recently, why was the topic of homosexuality a taboo subject in evangelical circles?
2. Why do you suppose this taboo has changed? Is it good to study this topic? Why?
3. What was the traditional stereotype of a homosexual? How might that have been harmful?
4. What viewpoint did science and psychology take as recently as thirty years ago in regard to the cause of homosexuality?
5. What other causes of homosexuality have you read about?
6. How has the inversion hypothesis in effect reflected accurately our cultural values? In what other ways is the inversion hypothesis used to justify behavior?
7. Summarize and make conclusions to Lorne E. Brown's treatise on the subject of homosexuality.

37. "Women Convene at Fuller Seminary," Moody Monthly, September 1978, 17.
38. Ibid.

8. In what further ways have the institutions of our culture (media, politics, church, etc.) begun to accommodate homosexual philosophy?

9. Contrast the typical homelife structure of a homosexual to biblical commands for family and interpersonal relationships. What conclusions can be made?

10. Create a journal in which you analyze various television situation comedies for prohomosexual thought.

11. Create a journal in which you record newspaper articles that pertain to the issue of homosexuality. Conclude by categorizing them in the pro- and antihomosexual camps.

10

Two Halves Do Not Necessarily Make a Whole

What does God's Word say about homosexuality? Is homosexuality contrary to the purposes God intended for His creation?

Is there a difference between temptation toward homosexual acts and actual participation in those acts? Are homosexuals our "neighbors"? Does homosexuality exclude one from the kingdom of God? Such are the kinds of questions being posed to the evangelical community today.

Our purpose in this chapter is to examine God's position on homosexuality as it is revealed in the Bible. We want first to look at the cases of Sodom and Gibeah where destruction came upon individuals desiring homosexual relations. Next we will examine the law of Moses on the subject. Then we will turn to the New Testament, where several passages condemn homosexual acts as sin. Finally, we want to look at two major issues that must be considered in studying this question—the nature of sexuality and the relation of the creation order to homosexuality.

THE OLD TESTAMENT ON HOMOSEXUALITY

Nowhere does the Bible condemn persons who are tempted to commit homosexual acts. It is not sinful to be tempted (James 1). However, we are responsible for how we respond to temptation. Although we are sinful creatures without the ability to perform acts worthy of salvation, we have the freedom to resist acts of sin. Examples of resisting and not sinning may be seen in the accounts of Cain and Esau. Cain did not control his anger, but was mastered by it so that he killed his brother. In contrast, Esau controlled his feelings of anger. In the same way one who has

homosexual leanings should resist those feelings so as not to sin. The
Bible clearly condemns the one participating in homosexual activities.

THE CASES OF SODOM AND GIBEAH

Two accounts are recorded in the Old Testament about judgment on
homosexuals (i.e., those practicing homosexuality rather than those who
have homosexual tendencies).

The accounts bear several points of resemblance: (1) male visitors
were welcomed into a host's home; (2) townspeople asked to have homosexual relations with the visitors; (3) the hosts offered a female substitute;
and (4) the homosexuals were punished for their sin.

Those Old Testament examples reveal the ultimate obsession and perversion that results when God's law is rejected, as described in Romans
1.

Let us first look at the Genesis 19 account of Sodom. Lot invited the
two angelic guests into his home. Afterward, the men of Sodom asked to
"know" them. Lot wrongly sought to turn their request aside by offering
his two virgin daughters to them. As a result, God destroyed the city.

The Judges 19 account of Gibeah in ancient Palestine is similar. A
visitor was taken in by an Israelite. Afterward, the townsmen desired to
know the visitor sexually. The host offered (again wrongfully) a concu-
bine for sexual abuse. The townsmen, apparently bisexual, raped her
throughout the night; she was found dead the next morning. Because of
that, Israelites were gathered to kill those men involved.

Some have offered an alternative explanation for Sodom's and Gibeah's
destruction. D. S. Bailey, in his book *Homosexuality and the Western Christian
Tradition*, argues that Sodom and Gibeah were punished for breaching
the rules of hospitality, not for homosexual assault. Their intentions
were hostile but were not homosexual. He says the word for *know* refers
to acquaintance, not to sexual relations.[1] Their sin was not homosexuality, but the failure to accept and treat the guests with dignity.

Ralph Blair, possibly the most articulate theologian of the homosexual
movement, expands on Bailey's position.

> The Biblical story demonstrates the seriousness with which these Eastern
> people took the important customs of Oriental hospitality. It appears that, if
> necessary, they would even allow their own daughters to undergo abuse in
> order to protect guests. The sexual aspect of this story is simply the vehicle
> in which the subject of demanded hospitality is conveyed. It is clearly inter-

---

1. D. Sherwin Bailey, *Homosexuality and the Western Christian Tradition* (New York:
Longmans, 1955), 5.

preted in Ezekiel 16:49, "Behold, this was the guilt of your sister Sodom: she and her daughters had pride, fulness of food, and prosperous ease, but did not aid the poor and needy."[2]

Bailey bases his interpretation of the account of Sodom in Genesis 19 on three factors: (1) the number of times the Hebrew word *yadha* is used in a normal sense of know over against only fifteen times in a sexual sense; (2) arguing from pyschology, he argues that intercourse requires more than physical sexual experience as a way to personal knowledge; and (3) he understands Lot to be a *ge{cron}r*, a resident foreigner, who exceeds his rights by entertaining two foreigners whose credentials had not been examined.[3]

Bailey's first argument is not substantial because a word count does not determine the meaning of a particular word in a given context. If a term is used by an author in an abnormal way, he must be allowed that privilege. The word *yadha* ("to know") is clearly a word for *coitus*, even homosexual coitus.

There is no question that *yadha* is intercourse in Genesis 19:8 and Judges 19:25. Note that on both occasions the host offered a female substitute for obvious sexual abuse. The suggestion of John Boswell that the offering of Lot's daughters was "simply the most tempting bribe Lot could offer on the spur of the moment to appease the hostile crowd"[4] stretches credulity.

Philip Ukleja, in a doctoral thesis, has a more likely view. "It is much more probable that Lot's offer was motivated by the thought that however wrong rape is, homosexual rape was even worse. Lot's offer was simply what he thought to be the lesser of two evils."[5]

A major substantiation of Sodom's sin being sexual is that the New Testament, in reference to Sodom, identifies the sin as sexual sin (Jude 7). In fact, the word for sexual immorality is a strengthened form in the Greek, emphasizing the sinfulness.

Old Testament scholar Derek Kidner contends, "The doubt created by Dr. Bailey has traveled more widely than the reasons he produces . . . . Not one of these reasons, it may be suggested, stands any serious scrutiny."[6]

Blair's previous statement is as unacceptable as Bailey's. His argu-

2. Ralph Blair, *An Evangelical Look at Homosexuality* (Chicago: Moody, 1963), 4.
3. Ibid., 3-5.
4. John Boswell, *Christianity, Social Tolerance, and Homosexuality* (Chicago: U. of Chicago, 1980), 95.
5. Philip Michael Ukleja, *A Theological Critique of the Contemporary Homosexual Movement*, Ph.D diss., Dallas Theological Seminary, 1982, 148.
6. Derek Kidner, *Genesis* (Chicago: Inter-Varsity, 1967), 137.

ments that Sodom fell because of its unconcern for the poor and needy is
a half-truth. He quotes Ezekiel 16:49, but does not proceed to verse 50
where the prophet states the Sodomites did "detestable things" before
God. The word for *detestable* is the same word used in Leviticus 18:22
(cf. 20:13), where a man is forbidden to have intercourse with a man; it
is an abomination or "detestable." More on this word will be discussed
on Levitical laws.

Greg Bahnsen, in his book *Homosexuality, a Biblical View*, sums up the
inadequacy of viewing the offense as one of inhospitality:

> It calls for a strange mentality to see (1) how a simple desire of the
> townsmen to get acquainted would be a breach of hospitality, (2) how it
> could be deemed seriously wicked (especially in light of the city customs,
> which Lot certainly understood), and (3) why it would be so vile as to war-
> rant dramatic divine punishment.[7]

Virginia Mollenkott and Letha Scanzoni, previously noted feminist
authors, have argued that the Sodomites were judged because they
expressed lust rather than love: "To use street language, the apparent
intention is gang rape."[8] However, there is nothing in the text that indicates the intention of the townsmen was homosexual rape. There is no
evidence they anticipated the guests of Lot to resist.

Mollenkott and Scanzoni would have us believe that "love" between
consenting participants (whether homosexual or heterosexual) is not
adultery or sin. Obviously, that definition of love is little more than lust,
which, according to God's law, is sin.

THE TEN COMMANDMENTS AND THE LEVITICAL LAWS

The Ten Commandments are a general statement of the moral law of
God. The commandment against adultery probably should be understood as including an injunction against homosexual sin, a point we will
further explain from the New Testament use of the Decalogue. The
Levitical laws express specific understanding of the general code.

In Leviticus 18:22 and 20:13, homosexuality is called an abomination, punishable by death. Mollenkott and Scanzoni seek to dilute that
denunciation of homosexuality by trying to tie it to the culture of Israel.
They say that Leviticus 20:13 means that if a man lies with a woman
during her menstrual period, he is to be cut off. The rebuke against

7. Greg Bahnsen, *Homosexuality: A Biblical View* (Grand Rapids: Baker, 1978), 33.
8. Virginia Mollenkott and Letha Scanzoni, "Homosexuality: Two Perspectives," *Daughters of Sarah*, vol. 3 (November-December 1977), 6.

homosexuality and intercourse during menstruation are to be identified, in their view, as equal transgressions. They explain:

> Yet our contemporary culture sees nothing wrong with intercourse during menstruation; and several evangelical Christian authors in the field of sexual counseling have recently been assuring Christians that such acts are in no way contrary to the will of God. But the same authors use Leviticus 20:13 to place all homosexual love under an eternal interdict. It is hard to avoid the suspicion that the attitudes of our culture have caused many Christians to become very selective in their application of the Leviticus Holiness Code.[9]

The simplistic understanding of the Levitical code betrays the kind of biblical interpretative method characterized by Mollenkott and Scanzoni. First, they seek to interpret the biblical text from a modern, relativistic, cultural understanding of the nature of right and wrong. Our purpose should be to interpret the Word of God in its setting, not by the current spirit of the times. Second, they fail to notice the difference between the kinds of Levitical laws—civil, ceremonial, and moral.

Civil law concerns responsibility toward one's fellow citizen. For example, if one knew his bull to be dangerous and yet did not take necessary precautions to keep it from harming anyone, the owner was liable (Ex. 21:28-32). Such teaching may find parallels today.

Ceremonial law sought to teach spiritual truths about God's Person, His redemption, and so forth by concrete examples from daily activities such as dress and food. Ultimately, those were shadows of the coming Messiah who brought reality to the symbols of His Person and work.

Moral law has no qualifiers and conditions and is intended for all times. It deals with moral offenses against God, others, or even oneself.

Although those three kinds of laws are interspersed in the Old Testament, they cannot be related to one another as the same. Contemporary readers must distinguish between them even as the Israelites did. John Oswalt, a professor of Old Testament, lucidly states how.

> The most obvious way is in the penalties. A breach of the ceremonial law results in separation from cultic activity [religious participation] for a stated period. Breaking the moral law results in death or expulsion from the camp. Thus there is a qualitative difference between eating pork (Lev. 11:7) or shaving (Lev. 9:27) and cursing one's parents (Lev. 20:9), adultery (Lev. 20:10), incest (Lev. 20:11-13) and homosexual practice.[10]

Abstinence from intercourse during menstruation was a ceremonial

9. Ibid., 6.
10. John N. Oswalt, "The Old Testament and Homosexuality," *What You Should Know About Homosexuality,* ed. Charles W. Keysor (Grand Rapids: Zondervan, 1979), 54-60.

law, possibly representing the need for purity (menstruation was seen as physical uncleanliness) in the marriage union. As explained earlier in this book, the physical union is a symbol that represents the union of Christ and His church. In contrast, homosexuality was an abomination because it broke a moral law that was punished by death or banishment (an attitude also expressed in the New Testament).

Before passing from the Levitical laws, let us observe the meaning of abomination and its significance to the study at hand. The Hebrew word *to'evah* is used considerably in the Old Testament, and refers to something repulsive to God. It is the word used of homosexual and other sexually abhorrent conduct in Leviticus 18 and 20. The reason for the abomination of a given practice is that it is contrary to or false to the world as God created it. Oswalt elucidates:

> "Abomination," then, does not merely define something thought to be done by pagans. Rather, paganism is abhorrent because it involves abominations—attitudes and practices that are false to the creation order. Idolatry is false to creation because it makes God in man's image and suggests we can manipulate God without reference to our own ethics. Adultery is false to creation because it is falseness embodied, that is, it is to be false to the one who has given himself or herself to that person. Homosexuality is false because it denies the distinction between male and female. Beastiality is false because it denies the distinction between human and animal.[11]

Specifically, homosexuality is wrong because it is contrary to God's work in creation. Humanity is presented in the creation narratives as male and female, and they are essential to one another for real humanity to exist. They are essential for the creation mandate of filling and dominating the earth. We will discuss that in more detail later.

THE NEW TESTAMENT ON HOMOSEXUALITY

Several New Testament passages reveal homosexuality to be contrary to the moral law of God. First Corinthians 6:9-10, 1 Timothy 1:8-11, and Romans 1:24-27 all have strong words against homosexual acts.

THE KINGDOM OF GOD AND HOMOSEXUALS

Homosexuals are among the unrighteous in 1 Corinthians 6:9 who shall not inherit the kingdom of God. The apostle was tying all homosexual behavior together in this passage. There is no distinction between homosexuality out of love or lust or between inverts or perverts. He used

11. Ibid., 68.

the Greek word *arsenokoites,* meaning sexual intercourse with a male. Some translators and scholars have sought to soften the word, but to no avail.

FIRST TIMOTHY 1 AND THE TEN COMMANDMENTS

First Timothy 1:8-11 is a Pauline rendition of the Ten Commandments. Note the comparison.

Exodus	*1 Timothy 1*
Commandment 1. You shall have no others gods	Ungodly and sinful
Commandment 2. You shall not worship idols	Ungodly and sinful
Commandment 3. You shall not profane the name of Yahweh	Unholy and irreligious (v. 9)
Commandment 4. You shall keep the Sabbath holy	Those who regard nothing as sacred
Commandment 5. You shall honor your parents	Those who kill fathers and mothers (opponents of honoring)
Commandment 6. You shall not murder	Murderers
Commandment 7. You shall not commit adultery	Adulterers and perverts (homosexuals)
Commandment 8. You shall not steal	Slave traders (thriving slave trade at Ephesus, the distinction of 1 Timothy, v. 10)
Commandment 9. You shall not give false teaching	Liars and perjurers (v. 10)
Commandment 10. You shall not covet	Whatever else Paul does not discuss here: the sins of the mind and heart (v. 10)

One may see from the above chart that Paul had the Ten Commandments in mind. Homosexual sin is viewed by Paul as a violation of the moral law of God given at Mt. Sinai. But additionally, scholars have recognized for a long time that the Decalogue has its roots in the creation teaching of Genesis, to which issue we will soon turn our attention.

THE PERVERSITY OF HOMOSEXUAL SIN

The most graphic text against homosexual acts is found in Paul's letter to the Romans. In Romans 1:24-27 Paul revealed that the rejection of the Creator, and necessarily His intentions in creation, has caused humans to become involved in practices that Moses called abominable. The natural use of sex was that of a husband and wife in loving relationship. The rejection of the Creator brought sexual sin. The greatest expression of that depravity was and is the sexual acts between women and women and between men and men. Certainly adultery is wrong, but homosexual acts are a step further; they are perversion. Harold Greenlee, noted New Testament and Greek scholar, makes this point well:

> Advocates of homosexual behavior as a legitimate life style overlook one logical prerequisite: the legitimacy of extra-marital and promiscuous heterosexual behavior. The logic of this is that fornication and adultery are, after all, only one step removed from what is proper by New Testament standards. That is, they consist of a type of sexual act that is legitimate but under circumstances that are not legitimate. Homosexual behavior, on the other hand, is two steps away from what is proper: not only does it involve illegitimate circumstances, but it also involves sexual acts that in themselves are perverted and grotesque.[12]

So then, both adulterous heterosexual acts and homosexual behavior are improper uses of sex. Heterosexual activity outside of marriage is wrong because a husband-wife kind of relationship is established (1 Cor. 6:16) between those who are not husband and wife. The reason homosexual acts are wrong is because a husband-wife kind of relationship is set up between two who cannot be, by creation intent, husband and wife.

Romans 1:18-32 moves toward a crescendo. Those who refuse to obey the Creator seek to suppress the truth of God. This move from a God-centered world view to a man-centered one can only end in a total misunderstanding of our place in God's world. Sex is a powerful force in our lives. The corruption of our natures finds a perverted ending in unnatural sexual involvements. They are indicative of God's approaching judgment. Bahnsen lays before us some frightening consequences of our growing tolerence for homosexual sin:

> In a sense, homosexuality is the cultural culmination of rebellion against God. It represents the "burning out" of man and his culture. Paul described accompanying aspects of a culture that reaches this stage in verses 29-31. The vices enumerated by Paul accompany the open practice of homosexuality and characterize a society in which homosexuality is practiced and tolerated. Therefore, homosexuality that is publicly accepted is symptomatic of a society under judgment, inwardly corrupted to the point of impend-

12. J. Harold Greenlee, "The New Testament and Homosexuality," in *What You Should Know About Homosexuality*, 88.

ing collapse. Paul the apostle regarded it as the most overt evidence of that degeneracy to which God in His wrath gave over the nations.[13]

THE UNDERLYING THEOLOGY OF THE BIBLICAL TEACHING ON HOMOSEXUALITY

What is the nature of sex that makes heterosexual relations natural and approved (in marriage) and homosexual ones unnatural? Certainly the particular sexual acts that two people perform—whether they be the opposite or same sex—are not the distinguishing marks. Most Christian counselors have recognized that no marital sexual act is taboo—the marriage bed is undefiled!

Sexual intercourse between a husband and wife is relational and procreational. Intercourse and other forms of love play also are recreational. Those aspects are inherent in the creation of male and female.

SEXUAL INTERCOURSE AS RELATIONAL

Eve was not created for Adam simply because he was lonely. As we have seen, only through the union of male and female did a true unity begin. Sameness does not bring completeness and unity; two halves do not make a whole! Two males contribute to the relational and procreational purposes of God no more than two left shoes contribute to comfortable walking. Unity is seen in differentness according to Genesis 2. As God said, it is not good that man should be alone. Was that loneliness to be solved by companionship? Yes, in part. But something in addition to companionship was required. The man needed someone to whom he could fully express himself emotionally, intellectually, and sexually. Only woman can fulfill that for man even as only man can fulfill that for woman.

SEXUAL INTERCOURSE AS PROCREATIONAL

The male and female also were created to procreate. The command is to fill the earth. Obviously that command is restricted to the opposite sexes. This is an obvious argument against homosexuality; homosexuals cannot procreate. That is also what is unsettling about homosexual growth in our country. We would not argue, as some do, that homosexuals commit more sexual crimes than do heterosexuals. But whereas heterosexuals corrupt other heterosexuals primarily, homosexuals usually corrupt heterosexuals. To put it more bluntly, homosexuals must recruit or die out!

13. Bahnsen, 34.

The idea that homosexuals are by nature that way from birth has little acceptance among those who truly study the subject. People become homosexuals by an act of the will, a yielding to the sinful nature in the appropriate circumstances. Homosexuality, therefore, cannot be viewed merely as a variant sexual preference or accidental variation within creation (as is left-handedness). There is no third natural sex in God's creation. Homosexuality represents a choice contrary to nature. Bahnsen comments:

> God the Creator gives created things their essential identity and function and defines man's proper relationships. Man's sexual function has been defined by God as male-female behavior. This fact refutes the claims of homosexual apologists who say that all human beings have the right to self-definition. Such an existentialist rationale (existence preceding freely chosen essence) reflects an autonomous desire to replace God's intended distinctions and created designs for man with the relativistic will of the creature, who would be worshipped as his own creator.[14]

CONCLUSION

The Bible gives absolutely no justification for the view that homosexuality is compatible with a Christian view of the created world. In reality, homosexual behavior is contrary to God's intentions for His world, and a repudiation of His leadership. God intends for a male and female to join in unity of persons and to fill the earth and dominate it. Homosexual relationships are a circumvention of that divine intention. Toleration of the sin, although we need compassion for the sinner, is an indication of a low view of God's standards of righteousness.

In seeing the trend toward societal toleration, the believer should remember that God's Word is absolute and unalterable even in the wake of a social revolution. Taking a biblical stand on this issue may indeed be one area of persecution for the believer in the future. At the same time, the evangelical ought not have a vendetta against the homosexual but rather show genuine love and concern for the homosexual as an individual, all the while attacking the problem of homosexuality as a sin against God.

QUESTIONS TO PONDER

1. Are there any differences between temptation toward homosexual acts and actual participation in those acts? If so, how?

14. Ibid.

2. Are there degrees of sin in God's eyes? If so, where does homosexuality fit in?
3. In the Old Testament, homosexuality was punishable by death. Why the severity?
4. Should Christians strive (by getting involved in politics) to have homosexuality classified in the courts as a crime?
5. Research and expand on the comparison of the Ten Commandments to 1 Timothy 1:8-11.

11

A Look from the Other Side of the Fence

We have had the opportunity to interview at length a Christian man whom we will refer to as Dave. Dave, with God's help, overcame a homosexual life-style. Dave would quickly affirm that the reversal of relationships, attitudes, and values did not come easily, and that the temptations to "slip back" continually haunt his mind. But God has given victory in Dave's life. He now is married to a fine Christian woman and has two children.

Dave was asked some in-depth questions. What is revealed in this interview should aid in a greater understanding of homosexuality and how to deal with it.

QUESTION: HOW DOES ONE BECOME A HOMOSEXUAL?

DAVE: Many homosexuals I have known felt that they were designed that way. That is the way I felt because I cannot remember when my sexual orientation was any different. I can recall at five years of age being sexually stimulated over my father's friends. Thus it was easy for me in later years to actually conclude I was born that way. Now, however, I am convinced that homosexuality is a learned behavior, where at some point I had to choose that path.

I can remember when I was ten years old watching a TV program on homosexual behavior. After viewing the show I can recall saying to myself that I had the problem of homosexuality. I told my parents and they responded by saying, "Dave, you don't have that problem; you just saw something that upset you." They made it sound as if it were bad if someone had that problem, so I was glad when they told me I didn't have it. I never again mentioned the problem to my parents until I was twenty-three. How I wish they would have believed me at that time and sought help for me!

A side note about my family background. My parents had a rotten marriage. Mom and Dad used to fight all the time, mostly about sex. Mom did not want to engage in sex, but Dad did. As a result I did not have a positive role picture of how a husband and wife should act in a family.

QUESTION: WHAT PROCESS LEADS TO HOMOSEXUAL ACTIONS?

DAVE: The environment had to be conducive for my first homosexual encounter. I never acted out my fantasy until I was twenty-one years old. My parents taught me honesty; to do what was right. Because I had been saved in my early teens I knew that it was wrong to have homosexual relationships, so I did not act them out until later.

I remember the events that led up to the first night I had sex with another man. My life was empty; nothing was going right. I had just graduated from an evangelical Bible college and returned home. (I found the Bible college to have an artificial and unrealistic atmosphere.) I was confused and began to give in to the drives I had had all along. One thing led to another and, before I knew it, I was caught in the trap. And once I got hooked, the process of reversal was a hard one for me.

I recall telling myself at Bible college that I needed to talk to someone about my problem, because I was so preoccupied with those homosexual fantasies. I went and talked to one of my professors in my first year at college, and he, like my parents, said I didn't really have the problem. For the second time in my life I was reassured that I was indeed "normal." Unfortunately, in my senior year, my fantasies still persisted. I then went to the head of the psychology department, and that, too, was a dead-end street. I had tried to find help, but somehow the Christian community would rather pretend I did not have the problem than help me face it.

Upon graduation from Bible college I figured I would become active in a local church. At that point in time, I was succumbing to my urges about once a month. That would satisfy the drive for another several weeks at least. As is the case when a Christian sins, guilt began to plague me. I went to the pastor about it, and the first (and only) thing he did was take away all my responsibilities. He alienated me totally without offering any help. I became bitter. That went on for several years. Some members of the church tried to help, but their assistance consisted of a pat on the back, a reading of a favorite Scripture verse, and an assurance they were praying for me. But I wasn't *helped!*

QUESTION: WHAT KIND OF SELF-IMAGE CAN CHARACTERIZE A HOMOSEXUAL? CAN IT BE STEREOTYPED?

DAVE: The majority of the homosexuals I have known have very poor self-images. At times a bad self-image resulted from some physical or social inadequacies that bothered them, but that was not always the case. For example, I knew one fellow who was an extreme extrovert, but if you knew him, you would soon find out that it resulted from a cover-up of his true inner feelings of worthlessness.

I have also known some to engage in homosexual activity to boost their ego; to get the feeling "that somebody wants me" (even if a member of the opposite sex doesn't).

QUESTION: WHAT PERSONALITY CHARACTERISTICS DOES A HOMOSEXUAL HAVE? CAN THEY BE STEREOTYPED?

DAVE: In a way I think a homosexual can be stereotyped as having a melancholy temperament (as Tim LaHaye would classify it). I fit that classic definition to a *tee,* as did most of my homosexual acquaintances. I did a lot of thinking (too much!), I was very sensitive, overly concerned about relationships, moody, pessimistic, and depressed much of the time. It is interesting now that I can look back and realize that my two brothers and one sister are all heterosexual and never had homosexual tendencies. But their temperament was definitely not melancholy either! That is one reason I am positive certain temperament types are more prone to homosexual behavior.

QUESTION: FOR THE HOMOSEXUAL, HOW BAD IS THE PROBLEM OF GUILT?

DAVE: Most of the non-Christians I had sexual contact with had little if any guilt. As a Christian, the guilt I had made me so depressed that I was almost brought to suicide twice. And even now that I have victory over this problem, when I am tempted, I quickly condemn myself for those thoughts. It is hard sometimes to separate the temptation itself from my submission to those thoughts!

QUESTION: WHAT IS INVOLVED IN THE REHABILITATION PROCESS?

DAVE: I believe, in accordance with the AA philosophy on alcoholism, that once a homosexual, always a homosexual. The key in rehabilitation is running from the sin, and not pretending mastery over it. I must admit that I still have homosexual desires at times, but as long as I ask the Holy Spirit to protect, He alone keeps me from being enticed.

I am thankful, however, that it has been five years since I have sinned in this area. Before, when the drive became so intense, I had to find a partner. But now I have control over that drive!

When I counsel others on this problem, the first step I take is to tell them the most important aspect in rehabilitation is to *obey the Lord!* Realize that God is sovereign and that His Word is absolute. If they will not acknowledge that fact, there is little hope for change. Second, it needs to be clearly set in the mind that homosexuality is a sin. I have observed that heterosexual immorality is just as bad of a sin, but for some reason it is tolerated more by the church.

Third, prayer to take away the desire is necessary. I have found, however, that it is not right to ask God to take away the temptation, but rather to give me the ability to resist that temptation. If I am tempted physically, at times my only recourse is to run! About a year ago a man came to my office on business. He was a homosexual. In feeling that I might fall, I had to literally dismiss him quickly from my presence and run from the temptation.

Last, I find great help from God when reading the verse "When I am weak, He is strong." God has become a real source of strength for me.

QUESTION: HOW DOES SATAN STILL HAUNT YOU WITH THE PROBLEM?

DAVE: I still have the problem with my self-image. I notice when I am doing the Lord's will, witnessing, and so on, that I will be tempted much more at that time. The temptations are much stronger when I am involved with the church and being effective for the Lord. At times that bothers me.

You cannot imagine how important certain close friends are when Satan begins to haunt me with my past problem. They are able to edify and give me encouragement.

QUESTION: HOW DO YOU COUNSEL ANOTHER HOMOSEXUAL WHO PROFESSES TO BE A CHRISTIAN?

DAVE: As mentioned earlier, I start by telling them to obey God. You cannot get to first base until you have hit the ball. Obeying God is not always fun. However, it is important to honor the Lord and stop "messing around."

I think a very important step is to make a vow with God. For some reason, writing it down before the temptation comes really helps. Without that commitment, there can be no help. For Jesus said: "If you love me, keep my commandments."

The vow I made with God is as follows:

Now, therefore, fear the Lord and serve Him in sincerity and truth; and put away the gods which your fathers served beyond the River and in Egypt, and serve the Lord.

And if it is disagreeable in your sight to serve the Lord, choose for yourselves today whom you will serve, but as for me and my house we will serve the Lord (Joshua 24:14-15 [NASB]).

In the inner man I desire a life pleasing to God in every aspect. However, yielding to my greatest temptation is devastating to that life. Satan is behind the system that promotes the very thing my flesh wants. This evil system's objective is to blind me in the idolatry of pleasure. Aggressive methods are used to persuade me to sin. However, nothing more than momentary satisfaction ever occurs from yielding to temptation. The promises made by Satan are lies.

Because of the Word of God and from my personal experiences, I know that there is true satisfaction and lasting peace in a life absolutely committed to the truth. That truth is the revelation of God's love through the living and written Word. Graciously, the Living Word has come that we might have abundant life. That life will abound in peace and satisfaction. My every need will be met, for God does not lie.

I recognize that many opposing philosophies, some under the guise of Christianity, will pursue my enlistment. Consistency through discipline is required to maintain my loyalty. In my own strength I am doomed to fail, but I can do all things through Christ.

Therefore, in the presence of God, I declare that I am putting this old, sinful way of life behind me. As a solemn decision, I promise that I will not actively pursue the sinful style of life that so easily attracts me. I promise to not be passively indifferent when confronted with the temptation. I promise to willfully resist and flee from that temptation when I recognize its presence.

MY PRAYER

Father, I have made this vow to help free myself from what has been the greatest hindrance to my Christian walk. The most difficult thing I've ever had to do is to whole-heartedly agree with your unchanging standards of excellence. Coming to this point has painfully broken my spirit. I am weak and miserably helpless. Apart from Your strength, I am nothing. I entrust the keeping of this vow to Your faithfulness.

Please help me, Father, to immediately dismiss pursuing any desires of the old life when they confront me. Guard my mind from the subtle trap of passive indifference and always make me aware of the seriousness of all sin. Be my strength to flee from temptation each time it calls. Put this vow ever before me. Remind me how satisfying Your excellent way is. Make me know the joy of Thy salvation. Amen.

QUESTION: CAN ONE BE A PRACTICING HOMOSEXUAL AND A
CHRISTIAN?

DAVE: Yes, but not a Spirit-filled one. I guess you need to define
what you mean by *practicing*. Do you mean, having a relationship in the
mind, one every two weeks, two months, or so on? Where do you draw
the line?

I believe if one is truly a Christian, there will be a sense of guilt for the
behavior of homosexuality (or any other sin for that matter). Open defi-
ance, on the other hand, and enjoying the homosexual life-style without
any sense of guilt may be an indication that one is not saved. In the final
analysis, however, God is the judge, not me or anyone else.

I have been a Christian since I was eleven. It took me until my twen-
ties to realize that my behavior was a result of fulfilling the desires of the
flesh.

One question I have had concerns those evangelicals who "practice"
gluttony. The Bible speaks of gluttony as a sin. What about the person
who is a glutton? Because he is a "practicing" sinner in the area of eating, does that mean he is not a Christian?

QUESTION: ARE HOMOSEXUAL TEMPTATIONS WRONG?

DAVE: Absolutely not. As was mentioned previously, it is not a sin to
be tempted; only to yield to the temptation. I have read some Christian
books that have considered temptation a sin, but that position cannot be
substantiated in Scripture. The book of James talks about being carried
away by our own lusts. But sin is not conceived until we have made a
decision to act on it in our minds and enjoy it.

QUESTION: WHEN COUNSELING, HOW DO YOU HELP ONE WITH ONLY
THE TENDENCY OF HOMOSEXUALITY AS COMPARED TO ONE WHO IS
ACTUALLY INVOLVED IN THE ACT OF HOMOSEXUALITY?

DAVE: For the one who already has been involved in homosexual sin,
again I would start with the obedience issue. For those with only the
tendencies, I would help them direct their lives toward healthy heterosexual relationships. I also believe that a person who says he or she has a
homosexual problem should be made to deal with it accordingly, instead
of ignoring the reality of it, as I was advised to do in my life.

QUESTION: HOW SHOULD THE EVANGELICAL COMMUNITY RESPOND
TO THE HOMOSEXUAL PROBLEM?

DAVE: Let me suggest some ways:

1. Address the problem when it appears within the church, and do not deny its reality when it exists.
2. Pastors should be more informed and able to counsel those with the problem.
3. The church should exhort and help the homosexual within the framework of love.
4. The church ought to treat homosexuality as a sin.
5. The church ought to be a place where one with a homosexuality (or any other) problem can go to for real help.
6. The church should realize that changed behavior cannot always be shared in public. The effects of gossip can ruin future ministry.
7. The church ought to teach that all immorality (either homosexual or heterosexual) is sin and that glamorizing such a sin (at testimony meetings, etc.) might produce more harm than good.
8. The church needs to realize that homosexuals are not outcasts, but affirm that homosexuality is a weakness of the flesh. The results of this sin, as is the case with others, is pain and guilt.
9. The church should not make light of the tendencies toward homosexual behavior but should be able to assist a person in the early stages of the problem.

QUESTION: DO YOU HAVE ANY OTHER INSIGHTS TO SHARE?

DAVE: Yes. I would like to describe how I finally got help. Several years ago on a vacation trip to California I visited a Sunday service at an evangelical church. During the Sunday school hour, the teacher was analyzing the Christian duty of counseling those in need. The example he used was in working with the homosexual. What that teacher said really struck me. For the first time ever, I heard that there was hope for the homosexual and that God could help me with my problem. That may seem strange, but after all my years in evangelical churches and Bible college, that was the first time I heard that hope and homosexuality went together.

After the lesson, I asked the teacher if I could write him. Over the course of that year, he counseled me on the telephone and by mail. And as I previously mentioned, the first thing he demanded from me was obedience to God. I knew victory was on the way at last!

In trying to figure out why that teacher had such an influence on me, I concluded it was because of one factor—he loved me as a Christian brother—nothing special—but as any other Christian brother. He did not have to understand my temptation to help me. What he had to understand was that I was tempted as he was tempted (in whatever different ways), and that whenever he or I sinned, guilt and pain resulted.

I took a leave of absence from my job and moved to California. I lived there until I got married.

I guess my opinion of most psychologists (Christian and non-Christian) is not good, as I had so many negative experiences with them. I found going to Christian psychologists to be a dead-end street for me. When I lived in California, I saw a Christian psychologist on a regular basis for several months. And every time, I came away totally frustrated, angry, and uptight for days. Looking back, I discovered two reasons why I felt that way: (1) those psychologists did their Christian duty, they did their job, but they *did not love me!*; and (2) they continually dwelt on the past. That made me more depressed. The apostle Paul said to forget those things that are behind and press on toward the mark, which is Christ Jesus.

Real help came when I finally began to dwell on the victories.

I would like to conclude by saying that God is the great Counselor! In counseling, it is my goal to lead people to be dependent on Him, for in doing so, success will come. My friend the teacher would not let me depend on him, even though I wanted to do so at first. He would let me lean on him just long enough for him to push me right back on the Lord. God understands us perfectly—more than any human can. And when I sin, God still loves and keeps me. Romans 8 still rings out loud and clear: Nothing can separate me from the love of God.

Let me conclude by restating the importance of the vow I made with God. In my life it was imperative for me to place the vow where I could see it every day. That way, I had to acknowledge that commitment to myself. I am married now and have two children. My desires are now shifted toward having a good and happy family. God has given me new areas of fulfillment, including the relationship with my wife. We love each other more every day.

*   *   *

We also interviewed Ed, a psychologist who worked with Dave.

QUESTION: HOW DOES A PERSON BECOME A HOMOSEXUAL?

ED: Basically, there are two ways one becomes trapped in the homosexual life-style. The first is the traditional way we hear about most—the aggressive mother, passive father, family hostility, and so on. However, what I am seeing more and more are individuals getting trapped into the homosexual life-style because the media and society have elevated homosexuality to a state of acceptability. In fact, most homosexuals I have counseled come from good and loving homes, and many from fine Christian homes. We must face the fact that in our society, it is now the "in" thing to do. And as is the case with drugs, people are not prepared to deal with the long-term effects of their actions.

QUESTION: HOW WOULD YOU CHARACTERIZE A HOMOSEXUAL?

ED: As Dave said, I agree with the premise that a major by-product of the problem of homosexuality is a poor self-image. I have yet to counsel a homosexual who possessed a high degree of self-confidence and self-worth. I would like to add one additional thought to Dave's response. The homosexual's life is so characterized by failure that he has developed an inability to make decisions, even small ones. For example, I am constantly receiving calls by those I am counseling asking whether they should go to a certain football game or buy a certain suit. I have found in my counseling that vacillation is a source of frustration for most homosexuals.

QUESTION: WHAT ABOUT THE ARGUMENT THAT "I WAS BORN THAT WAY"?

ED: In my counseling I have heard that line only from those who want to continue in their homosexual life-style. That reasoning is used as a means to rationalize behavior. However, when one realizes something is wrong and consequently seeks help, almost without exception that rationalization is identified as such by the individual. In addition, the research I have conducted has convinced me that there is no correlation between homosexuality and genetics.

QUESTION: WHAT PROCESS DO YOU FOLLOW IN COUNSELING A HOMOSEXUAL?

ED: I wish there were a set formula to follow, but because everyone is so different, the patterns change. For example, counseling a practicing homosexual is far different than counseling one with gay tendencies. The one with the tendencies may never have committed a homosexual act but will label himself as a homosexual. That mind-set will probably lead to the act later on. So, in that instance, we work on changing a thought life, dealing with self-image and self-identity.

When I am dealing with a practicing homosexual, however, the starting point is the client's admission that the basis of homosexual behavior is plain sin. If that point is not acknowledged, therapy is useless.

I stress with the counselee the final goal of victory over the problem.

The problem is so immense that it will take an average of two years to overcome. For that reason I realize that for every two steps forward, the probability of going one step backward in the process is a likelihood. That realization will aid the client in overcoming the guilt and frustration that occurs when failure comes.

As a counselor it is important for me to keep up on the counselee and make him accountable for his behavior, for if he does fail on the road to victory, there will be need for spiritual and psychological support. Another important aspect of therapy to keep in mind is to have the client ask God to reveal what specific stimulus activates the drive or desire for homosexual behavior. That is accomplished by a thorough retracing of the client's steps of the previous 18-24 months, seeking clues that will aid in discovering various items that will reveal the specific stimulus.

Once the stimulus has been identified, the next assignment is to have that individual begin the process of fleeing from it (realizing that if something is taken out of a life, the resulting void must be replaced with something else to prevent psychological chaos from occurring). For example, I counseled two wrestlers recently who became involved with each other sexually. I found that the wrestling turned into fondling, and fondling into the sex act. Both said they "fell" into the situation, however, the stimulus of touching while wrestling led to the act some days later. So I told them if they were intent on changing, they would have to quit wrestling. That they did and replaced the void by participating in another sport. Eventually, both found victory.

In counseling the homosexual, I feel I must be very directive. That is probably a result of the indecisive mind of the homosexual. However, Paul in the book of Galatians said we are to "restore one in a spirit of meekness (or gentleness)." Gentleness does not imply passivity, but firmness bathed in love. Almost without exception, the passage I use with a homosexual is James 1:12-22. It is important for the client to see the progression of his sin, and what will happen if he does not change. As the book of Proverbs puts it, "The fear of the Lord is the beginning of wisdom."

QUESTION: IF A PARENT LEARNS HIS TEENAGER IS INVOLVED IN HOMOSEXUAL BEHAVIOR, WHAT SHOULD HE OR SHE DO?

ED: First, be rational and not emotional. A problem of this magnitude should be handled once the anger has subsided. Then think things through first before dealing with the situation. Ask God for guidance and seek professional help before deciding on a course of action.

A common reaction by parents, especially Christian parents, is one of guilt: "What did I do wrong?" A parent should not self-inflict undue guilt. What has been done is done. At this point, there may be areas in the teenager's life that need to be developed spiritually, which is where the parents should now direct their attention. The parents may have made some mistakes, but once God forgives them (1 John 1:9), they should keep their eyes on Christ Jesus for strength.

Finally, parents should not isolate themselves from their teenager, but rather, continue to show love. They should show through their actions that they love their teen, while at the same time abhorring the problem.

QUESTION: WHAT IS THE EVANGELICAL CHURCH'S RESPONSIBILITY TO THE HOMOSEXUAL?

ED: If a homosexual comes for help admitting that his or her behavior is a sin and wants victory over that sin, then the church has the obligation to assist him on the road to recovery. Unfortunately, what I have seen is that a church may be willing to help, but if the individual falls back into his sin, it is likely he may be abandoned. In my counseling, two or three "falls" can be expected before victory is found. So the key here is a sincere desire to change in order for the church to assist. Thus, if a homosexual is found in the church and refuses to admit that his problem is a sin, then we have no choice but to employ church discipline. As the apostle Paul said, "Do not even dine with that person." Keeping that command in perspective, however, we must note that it applies to anyone engaged in a sin in which a willingness to change is not apparent.

Finally, there is an interesting item I have found in dealing with homosexual therapy. In all my years of counseling, in only one case has God totally removed the desire of homosexuality. What I have seen God do is help one manage that drive as he or she begins a life of heterosexuality. The more one manages that drive, the less frequent he is plagued with it. The bottom line is that sin causes scars. And the scar of homosexuality goes very, very deep. God can provide victory, but the effects may linger for a long period of time.

Admittedly, the track record for rehabilitating homosexuals is not good. That may be because Christians are uninformed, frightened, or prefer (like Dave's church) to bury their heads in the sand rather than confront the sin. This forces the homosexual to stay in the closet. Unfortunately, the result is that the homosexual is usually driven out of the church and into the life-style of the world where homosexuality is accepted and practiced. That only compounds the frustration and indignation. It enables the homosexual to justify his disobedience and sin. His guilt, conscious or unconscious, drives him further away from a healthy self-concept and those who are straight. It often leads to a volatile temperament and even violence. From that twisted mind-set it is difficult for the homosexual to be drawn back into right relationship with the Lord. Nor is he likely to be restored into fellowship with the church.

The best solution is prevention or dealing with the sin in its early stages. The worst solution is to ignore the symptoms or to cut off the offender before he has been lovingly confronted and consistently followed up. The Christian must be informed about homosexuality and know how to deal scripturally with the sin.

The last segment of this book will give some practical suggestions for dealing with the problem of homosexuality.

QUESTIONS TO PONDER

1. If a parent realizes his child is exhibiting early stages of homosexual development, what should that parent's response be?
2. How did most of the authority figures in Dave's life respond to his homosexuality?
3. How might his life's path have been changed had any one of those authority figures responded differently?
4. Give the main steps involved in the rehabilitation of a homosexual.
5. What are the two main causes for the current homosexual revolution?
6. What is the Christian's (or church's) responsibility to a brother or sister who is dealing with homosexuality?

Part Four _____
A Christian Response

The preceding segments of this book have elaborated on the psychological, sociological, and biblical framework needed to deal with feminism, abortion, and homosexuality. It has been established that those issues need to be confronted. But how are we as Christians to go about sorting out secular humanism, integrating God's Word, and loving the brother or sister who is bearing one of those burdens, while at the same time taking a stand against the sin at the root of those issues?

We must accept the responsibility of being accountable for ourselves and for being our brother's keeper. We must roll up our sleeves and face those issues squarely for what they are, and, practically speaking, put our knowledge and love to work to solve the problems that face the church in an ever-increasing intensity.

In this chapter, we will deal with a practical, holistic (whole—all parts relate to each other) confrontation concept of bearing our own burdens, and one another's burdens without being overbearing. We will present some case studies, as well as try to offer some resources for the counselor or lay person confronted with feminism, abortion, or homosexuality.

To begin, consider the two necessary dimensions to counseling: the dynamics of a problem, and after-the-fact counseling. The former sets the foundational basis for counseling. The latter deals with what we are to do and how we are to react (emotionally and spiritually) when a friend, relative, or even we ourselves have committed a sin resulting in deep consequences and scars.

Here we must face two unalterable facts: (1) what has been done is *sin*, and (2) there is no way to undo what has been done. We then ask what is needed to turn a bad situation toward a God-honoring conclusion. That is perhaps the most important question to ask. What is the responsibility of the church as a body to those trapped in sin?

Many evangelical books deal with the results of sin in our lives, but few describe the right pattern of behavior once sin has occurred. Do the high-sounding precepts learned in earlier years hold up at that point, or do we begin to rationalize? Is the church willing to "get its hands dirty" and come to grips with the problems at hand? *Preventative counseling* in most churches is minimal. Fewer churches, however, take the necessary steps in providing *restoration counseling* to those in need.

Why is that the pattern or norm for many evangelicals? The realistic answer is that most seem to feel embarrassed, confused, or hostile toward believers in such predicaments. To change that perspective let us look at a step-by-step approach that can be applied in counseling.

STEP 1: OUR STARTING POINT

We begin by asserting that as Christians we are new creatures in Christ (2 Cor. 5:17), having been recreated by God and indwelt by His Holy Spirit. We necessarily ought to view every aspect of our world and our life with respect to our relationship with our Savior. We know that there will be a day when all men will stand before Christ, and those who have rejected His grace will be judged accordingly and be eternally damned. But those of us who have joyfully heard His voice and received the gospel will live in joy with our Savior for all eternity. The *agape* love that we have received can only come from God, who has offered it freely to all who will believe in His Son, Jesus. Moreover, as we give ourselves to His Holy Spirit, we have the capacity for being filled with His wisdom and power. That then is our ministry in all counseling: to point out the sin of the believer in the light of God's Word; to pray that the Holy Spirit will convince him of his sin; to offer the total forgiveness of God through Christ's suffering in his stead; and to help him reach out for the Holy Spirit's power to deal with that sin.

STEP 2: A LOOK AT THE PROBLEM

As mentioned above, once certain sins have been committed, there is no way to undo what has been done. As Christians, how should we view such a situation? For example, let us consider the circumstances that occur when one goes against God's commands in relation to the value of human life. Here we need to go from the theoretical to the practical in the quest for solutions.

From the theoretical side, we as evangelical Christians should evaluate any problem in terms of a *cause and effect* relationship. Most nonevangelicals do not and, therefore, would not acknowledge sin as the cause of a problem, but would rather identify the source to be the result of observable circumstances only. That directly bypasses the true root: sin.

NON-CHRISTIAN PERSPECTIVE

The problem: abortion
The cause: (1) unwanted child
        (2) rape
        (3) interference with future plans
        (4) others

CHRISTIAN PERSPECTIVE

The problem: an attitude and value structure that is in opposition to God's Word (i.e., selfishness, "me first" philosophy)
The cause: sin
The effect: abortion

An analogy might be appropriate here. A man under a lot of tension and pressure at work develops a skin rash. A wise and perceptive physician, realizing that a variety of things need to be considered in the diagnosis, would look at more than just the outward circumstances. Instead of giving the man only a prescription for skin salve, he would attempt to find the root or real cause of the problem, which possibly could be the patient's mental and emotional condition.

There is a holistic principle here. For that man, the *cause* of the problem was probably due to stress factors, and the *effect* of that stress became visible in the form of a skin rash. So it is with the problems we confront. The stress represents sin as the cause, and the effect of sin thus yields the particular symptoms that need to be dealt with, that is, the rash.

Jesus also argued the cause-and-effect principle to the Jewish scribes in healing the man sick with the palsy. Mark 2:5-12 reads:

> And Jesus seeing their faith said to the paralytic, "My son, your sins are forgiven." But there were some of the scribes sitting there and reasoning in their hearts, "Why does this man speak that way? He is blaspheming; who can forgive sins but God alone?" And immediately Jesus, aware in His spirit that they were reasoning that way within themselves, said to them, "Why are you reasoning about these things in your hearts? Which is easier, to say to the paralytic, 'Your sins are forgiven'; or to say, 'Arise, and take your pallet and walk?' But in order that you may know that the Son of Man has authority on earth to forgive sins"—He said to the paralytic—"I say to you, rise, take up your pallet and go home." And he rose and immediately took up the pallet and went out in the sight of all; so that they were all amazed and were glorifying God, saying, "We have never seen anything like this."

Therefore, it is our presupposition that apart from sin there would be an absence of all problems. That is not to say that every malady has a particular sin, nor are we asserting that the closer we are to God, the fewer problems we will have. However, because Adam did sin and passed on that fallen nature to all mankind and even to the natural world, we must now deal with the consequences in every area of life.

In our mortal bodies we are still sinners. Although saved by grace, the "cancer" of sin will continue to eat away at us and all nature until Christ returns and gives us our glorified bodies. On this subject Paul states in Romans 8:22-23:

> For we know that the whole creation groans and suffers the pains of child-birth together until now. And not only this, but also we ourselves, having the first fruits of the Spirit, even we ourselves groan within ourselves, waiting eagerly for our adoption as sons, the redemption of our body [NASB].

In dealing with an issue, whether it is our own problem or the problem of a brother or sister in the Lord, we must look at the whole picture. We must discern beyond the visible and hidden effects to the root cause—sin. Sin always occurs before (sometimes long before) the act in question. Being aware of that can only help identify not only the root problem, but can often prevent the act from occurring and complicating the life of the sinner and the lives of those around him.

12

Putting Your Own House in Order

Modern American humanism has taught us that coping with our problems is not only unnecessary but outmoded. Having a personal psychiatrist is as prestigious as owning two cars or a videotape recorder. The respect America once held for the work ethic and the discipline of "pulling yourself up by your own bootstraps" is waning. It is no longer popular to be strong, principled, or accountable for oneself.

That is often true of Christians in particular. Prayer and share times in the church can become group therapy or pity parties that replace honest requests for the wisdom and discipline needed to be a doer and not just a hearer. Christians who neglect the Word of God can, because of frustration, indefinitely delay dealing with their own conviction of sin. By casting their particular sin dramatically to the church they avoid dealing with it. It can be a misuse of the local body to cry, "But my problems are just too big; I need outside help!" How important it is to keep in mind that because God has the power to save those who are dead in sin, how much easier it is for Him to rescue His own children when they need to solve a particular problem. Paul elaborated on that point in Romans 8:32: "Since God did not spare even His own Son for us but gave Him up for us all, won't He also surely give us everything else—including help for our problems?"

No problem is too big for Jesus Christ to handle. And even though our problems seem to be getting more difficult in our complex society, the solutions presented in the Word of God have never changed!

If that is true, why is the Christian counseling profession proliferating so rapidly? Because many are willing to settle for a quick second best. They are like the Israelites of old who pleaded to God for a king to lead them; who settled for "second best." Had they searched the Scriptures diligently, many of the heartaches that followed would not have occurred.

From the positive side, if a counselor is true to God's Word, he can act as God's ambassador to an individual in need, steering him back to the one who can solve his problem—the author and finisher of our faith, Jesus Christ.

To some, finding a biblical approach to solving a particular problem is difficult. The following format has proved helpful to some. Please note that this plan is for born-again believers. A nonbeliever is under the control of his master, Satan (John 8:44). Thus he is obligated to fulfill the "lust of his father." Counseling then, for the nonbeliever, is related to a modification of self in a cultural framework. (We know, however, that any change other than salvation through Christ is ultimately nothing more than "filthy rags" in the eyes of God.)

A Self-Guide for Biblical Counseling

1. Meditate on the following Scriptures. These and other verses will put you in touch with the One who can *best* counsel and aid you through any difficult situation or problem.

Psalm 9:9. "All who are oppressed may come to Him. He is a refuge for them in their times of trouble."
Psalm 23:6. "For You are close beside me, guarding, guiding all the way. . . . Your goodness and unfailing kindness shall be with me."
Psalm 46:1. "God is our refuge and strength, a tested help in time of trouble."
Psalm 91:3-4. "For He rescues you from every trap, and protects you from the fatal plague. He will shield you with His wings!"
Proverbs 3:5-6. "Trust the Lord completely; don't ever trust yourself. In everything you do, put God first, and He will direct you."
Proverbs 9:10. "For the reverence and fear of God are basic to all wisdom. Knowing God results in every other kind of understanding."
Proverbs 14:26-27. "Reverence for God gives a man deep strength; His children have a place of refuge and security. Reverence for the Lord is a fountain of life."
1 Corinthians 2:11-15. "No one can really know what anyone else is thinking, or what he is really like, except that person himself. And no one can know God's thoughts except God's own Spirit. And God has actually given us His Spirit to tell us about the wonderful free gifts of grace and blessing that God has given us. . . . But the spiritual man has

insight into everything, and that bothers and baffles the man of the world."

1 Corinthians 10:13. "You can trust God to keep the temptation from becoming so strong that you can't stand up against it, for He has promised this and will do what He says."

Philippians 4:19. "God will supply all your needs from His riches in glory, because of what Christ Jesus has done for us."

Colossians 2:3. "In Him lie hidden all the mighty, untapped treasures of wisdom and knowledge."

2 Peter 2:9. "So also the Lord can rescue you and me from the temptations that surround us, and continue to punish the ungodly until the day of final judgment comes."

2. After meditating on the above verses, begin a notebook for use in the problem-solving process that is to follow. The first item in your notebook should be an accurate description of the problem (as precise as possible). Next, define the causes behind the problem. Analyze the problem from as many angles as you can. Then, on a scale of 1-10 (1 = a small amount of time; 10 = all day) indicate how much of your day is spent dealing with that particular problem. By doing that, you are forced to evaluate the extent of the problem.

As you understand your problem, on a scale of 1-10 (1 = total societal conviction; 10 = total biblical conviction), do you feel it is one of a societal or biblical confrontation or a mixture of both?

We can use the example of divorce. Twenty years ago, divorce was a much greater taboo than it is today. With our society relaxing its standards on the issue, we find more and more Christians getting divorced. Unfortunately, that seems to indicate that, at least in today's world and perhaps all along, society has exerted more influence on Christians than has the Word of God. The important idea here is that we must identify which nature is being affected, our new nature via the Holy Spirit or our old nature via our surrounding culture.

Another example involves the common problem of overeating. Do we diet simply because the world says thin is beautiful, or do we control our appetites because we are daily seeking the fruit of temperance (self-control)?

3. Reread what you have entered thus far in your notebook. Then, again using a scale of 1-10 (1 = there is no rush to get this problem solved; 10 = this problem must get solved), indicate how committed you are to alleviating that problem *now*. Unless you mark 8 or higher

on the scale, it does not pay to continue this counseling process, because total commitment is essential to problem-solving.

4. The following steps should be used in tackling your specific problem. Your real work begins here.

In Galatians, Paul indicated that it is natural to follow our old nature. In one form or another, it is the source of all our problems. The cause-and-effect relationship exists here. The cause of our problems is sin (in the absence of sin, there are no problems). And the effect of sin yields the problem itself.

In chapter 5, Paul pointed out that the more the Holy Spirit controls our lives, the fewer problems we will have. Problems here do not mean an absence of tribulation, trial, or conflict, but rather the extent to which we allow those problems to affect us.

It also must be pointed out that to be effective, the problem-solving process must be worked out through the power of Christ in us. The key verses are Galatians 5:16-17, 19, 22-24:

> I advise you to obey only the Holy Spirit's instructions. He will tell you where to go and what to do.
> For we naturally love to do evil things that are just opposite from the things that the Holy Spirit tells us to do. But when the Holy Spirit controls our lives, He will produce this kind of fruit in us; love, joy, peace, patience, kindness, goodness, faithfulness, and self-control.
> Those who belong to Christ have nailed their natural evil desires to His cross and crucified them there. [TLB*]

WHAT EACH "FRUIT" MEANS

Love. This is one of God's attributes (1 John 4:16). It is produced in the heart of the yielded believer by the Holy Spirit (Rom. 5:5; Gal. 5:22). Its chief ingredient is self-sacrifice for the benefit of the one loved (John 3:16). Its elements are listed in 1 Corinthians 13.

Joy. This is a state of being, an attitude (1 Thess. 1:6).

Peace. This is tranquility of mind based on the consciousness of a right relation to God.

Patience. Includes the idea of forbearance; that is, patient endurance of wrong under ill-treatment without anger or thought of revenge.

Kindness. A quality of sympathy, gentleness, and affection that should pervade and penetrate the whole nature.

Goodness. Refers to that quality in a man who is ruled by and aims at

* *The Living Bible.*

what is good, namely the quality of moral worth (Rom. 15:14; Eph. 5:9; 2 Thess. 1:11).

Faithfulness. An element of loyalty and trustworthiness produced by the Holy Spirit in the life of the yielded Christian.

Gentleness. Refers to the quality of mildness in dealing with others.

Self-control. This involves having mastery or possessing power to control one's desires and impulses.

The real solution or formula for any of our problems is given in these verses. We must let the Holy Spirit control our lives to produce spiritual fruit. Every problem we have—from depression and loneliness to anger and hostility—directly or indirectly reflects the amount of spiritual fruit in our lives. In solving our problems, then, each fruit must be analyzed to pinpoint our areas of deficiency.

On the scale of 1-10 that follows, indicate where you believe you presently stand on each item listed. The development of spiritual characteristics is a hard and tedious process. We are never static in our spiritual development, for we are either progressing or regressing.

Thus the solving of a problem takes time and a lot of hard work. It is accomplished by reading God's Word, praying, and acting on God's promises by faith.

Growth Index

	"little fruit"		"much fruit"
LOVE	1	5	10
JOY	1	5	10
PEACE	1	5	10
PATIENCE	1	5	10
KINDNESS	1	5	10
GOODNESS	1	5	10
FAITHFULNESS	1	5	10
SELF-CONTROL	1	5	10

Figure 12.1

Once we have diagnosed each aspect of the fruit of the Holy Spirit on the scale, we can more readily see the extent of the problem. The following table may be used for this analysis.

1—4. *Critical area.* The problem is too great for you; God needs to *take it off* your shoulders" (Ps. 81:6).

4—6. *Alert area.* The problem is difficult. However, you *are* able to *roll* it onto the Lord (Ps. 37:5; *commit* means "roll").

6—8. *Annoyance area.* The problem is such that you are able to quickly *cast* your problem onto the Lord (1 Pet. 5:7).

9—10. *Victory area.* Analyzing the situation in this category indicates you have achieved a degree of control with the help of the Holy Spirit. It should be noted, however, that if complacency sets in, a recession will occur.

By analyzing each fruit of the Spirit, specific goals can be attained. In that way, you know what to pray for and what to study in the Word of God concerning each problem. For example, if you are overweight, pray, "Lord, I'm in the critical area of self-control and need Your help!" Or if you are depressed, pray, "Lord, I'm in the alert stage of peace and joy and need Your help to increase this fruit in my life."

5. After much prayer, begin making goals for yourself. Be specific. The overweight Christian might ask, "Lord, today help me not to eat that second helping." Or a Christian who needs special work in the area of patience might pray, "Lord, today help me to be calm in voice and spirit as I face this situation." Remember, you cannot reach a 9 or 10 in one week.

6. In addition to keeping a record of weekly goals, you need to do a biblical study on the fruit in which you are deficient. Let us take self-control as an example. What specific passages address that topic? Which Bible characters had problems in that area? How did they learn to overcome it?

7. Summarize and evaluate your progress. This should be done each week. In this step, state what you have learned about your problem from the biblical research completed. Determine what factors contributed to your progression or regression. What biblical truths did you learn concerning your problems? With God's help, what goals will you set for yourself for the coming week?

In the solving of our problems, we must keep our eyes on the mark, Jesus Christ. Keeping our eyes on the mark means we have turned 180 degrees from our past, allowing Christ to guide us in all aspects of our lives. The apostle Peter was able to walk on water as long as he looked at

Jesus, the "mark." Once his eyes strayed from Him, however, he began to sink.

So it is with our problems. We need to be committed to deep and personal communion with God through prayer as well as habitual and practical study and application of His Word in our lives. As we continue in this dynamic life-style, we will see spiritual fruit growing in our lives and become aware that our sovereign and loving Lord is in control of each of our problems.

13 _____

Taking a Stand

BEARING ONE ANOTHER'S BURDENS

Problems that plague believers today seem to be getting more and more complicated. To whom should the Christian turn? a counselor? a friend?

Although seeking advice from others is not forbidden in Scripture, such mortal help is of secondary value. Many believers, in trying to eliminate a problem, lack the patience to allow God to "do His good pleasure" in their lives. Instead, they turn to the first sympathetic ear they find, hoping to find a quick solution. A fast "cure" often acts as a salve on a boil. It makes the boil feel better, but it does not heal the root of the problem.

A verse often used to justify the role of the counselor is Galatians 6:2: "Bear one another's burdens, and thus fulfill the law of Christ" (NASB). It is interesting to note who goes to whom in that passage. Does the one with the problem go to another for help? No, the reverse is true. Because we are members of the Body of Christ, when one member suffers, the rest of the Body also suffers. Therefore, the one who is not initially afflicted goes to the aid of the one who has the problem to get the Body healthy again.

For the Christian then, the counselor's role should be to clarify God's Word and to help the individual spiritually in the loving environment of the Body of Christ. In this passage in Galatians, "to bear another's burdens" refers to the "responsibility each saint should feel for the spiritual welfare of his fellow-saints, especially when they have sinned."

If you become aware of sin in your church, what are the options available to you? If, for example, an abortion occurs, how is the church to react? That and other vital right-to-life questions must be answered every day by many Christians. If it becomes known that a member of your church body is involved in homosexuality, what should be done? When a family deteriorates before your eyes, what should be your response?

ROCKING THE BOAT

The common initial response to sin in the church is fear followed by a reluctance to get involved. Some attitudes are "After all, nobody's perfect and I don't want to be judgmental"; or "I don't want to make waves, I might offend someone"; or "It could destroy the unity of the church."

Let us take a close look at the real cause of conflict and disunity within the Body.

Many Christians, recalling a tense congregational meeting, shudder and quickly turn away from the mere possibility of conflict. They might set their jaws firmly and declare that unity among the brethren must be maintained—at all costs!

We have been concerned about such terms as *conflict* and *unity* in our Christian circles. We have seen where they have been misused and misunderstood, and we have concluded that this "villain" conflict can be the source and motivator for healthy church growth and development, whereas its supposed counterpart, unity, can be the mask for something more lethal. Some of the following conclusions may surprise you.

When it comes to conflict, one of the first misconceptions Christians have is that conflict in itself is evil. Instead, it must be recognized that conflict is an inescapable part of life. True, it can be defined as a barrier to a desired goal, but by itself it is neither good nor bad; conflict only becomes beneficial or harmful when placed into a particular context.

James 4:1 tells us the source for all harmful conflicts: "What causes fights among you? Don't they come from your desires that battle within you?" Recognizing those desires is a beginning step to resolution, but there are other telltale signs.

Usually, when a harmful conflict occurs, the tension level is such that even the air seems charged. Those disagreeing eventually withdraw or angrily explode; the focus becomes people's emotions rather than the job of dealing with a specific issue. Then there are clear we-they distinctions rather than a sense that "we jointly" have a problem. Instead of defining a problem in terms of mutual needs, each person sees the issue only from his or her point of view and begins to develop an "I must win—I must not lose" kind of attitude. Of course, competition thrives in such an atmosphere and cooperation is snuffed out. The saddest result is that usually both sides lose in many ways.

Such is the case in many marital conflicts. We recall a counseling session in which a husband and wife argued over the husband's neglect to pick up his clothes. Within a few minutes voices were raised, verbal punches and counterpunches were thrown, and tension increased. When they were halted, they were asked to restate precisely what was said in the previous five minutes. Oddly enough, except for vague generalities, the core of the conflict was forgotten. The situation had altered their perspectives from the rational to the irrational, with each side seeking to "beef up" his or her debate without the least bit of interest in listening to the other person.

Frightening? Yes, but every day many such marriages end in divorce over less important issues. "I must win" has become the motto of many Christians who even carry that philosophy to church. With that as the basis, it is clear to see how Satan plans to create the same kind of destructive conflicts in the local church!

But just as there are harmful conflicts that become destructive agents in our lives, there are conflicts that, when handled in a right way, become beneficial to us. Psychologists argue that it is in the midst of conflict that people can draw closer together and values be solidified. That is, as pressure becomes a barrier or conflict, the drive for unity among group members increases.

We see that historically as well as scripturally. History has shown that when a major threat plagues a country, it is then that the people solidify. The American response to hostage crises has been a good example of that. Biblically, in Acts we read how the church grew in numbers in the face of adversity and even extreme persecution.

Occasionally there are times when we must question a brother or sister in Christ who is headed in a direction we feel is biblically unwise. But such a disagreement *can* become a positive and beneficial conflict in assisting a person to redirect goals or ways of thinking. The reverse is also true; God can use other people in that way to redirect our lives when necessary.

This can be seen in Galatians 2 where Peter reportedly withdrew from eating with uncircumcised Gentile believers when pressured by some Hebrew Christians. It was a move on his part to "keep peace" with his Hebrew friends. Paul, however, turned the situation into a confrontation when he admonished Peter concerning his error. By his being the barrier or conflict in that situation, Paul was able to redirect Peter's thinking into an alignment with God's intention.

In addition to being a unifying agent in disguise and an authentic challenger of church goals, conflict can create a necessary backdoor revival in a church. When one of the authors was young, his family attended a large, denominational church. At one point his father learned that the choir director was having an affair with a woman on the church staff. When direct confrontation did not produce any change, his father took the matter before the church at a business meeting and demanded that disciplinary measures be taken. Up to that point, those familiar with the situation had turned their heads from what was happening. When the church body became aware of the incident and took definitive action against that man and woman, a parallel to Acts 5:11, 14 took place. We witnessed a fear that came over the whole church. Without the presence of a conflict in that case, God's work would have been crippled. A conflict there was mandated by Scripture; the end result was edification and growth.

As mentioned earlier, the word *unity* also is misused and misunderstood in Christian circles today. That often-uplifted quality, sometimes achieved through negative means, can ultimately nullify the creativity of a group. The results can destroy vibrant, interpersonal relationships between group members.

Basically, unity achieved through negative means is derived from one of two variables. First, it can be an outgrowth of a leader's desire to manipulate the group in a totally authoritarian manner. "Total authoritarianism" is an attempt to turn group members into puppets or carbon copies of the leader or leaders. In a church structure, we have seen cases in which a dynamic pastor, trying to fulfill his role as an overseer has, in effect, molded his flock into patterning their lives after his wishes and prejudices. As a result, the church many times begins to follow a man rather than the Christ of Scripture, the church's true leader.

A second situation in which unity can cause negative effects is when church leadership places guilt on a group member for going against "church norms." In many churches we can observe that pressures to conform to a set social order (church norm) can be so intense that it is almost impossible for one to function unless the status quo is kept. This attempt at suppressing individual differences advocates unity through external pressure and guilt. A common rationalization might be: "For the good of the church and for the unity of our church body, you need to follow our leading." This statement is true to a point, in that we should be submissive one to another; however, people who raise legitimate questions or challenge the validity of existing social norms should not be stifled, nor should social guilt be used as a means of control.

True unity based on positive means ultimately can build and edify the whole group, providing it with purpose and direction. The vital key is a homogeneous message. Because the message is then the pivotal point of unity, a doctrinal compromise cannot be made. And with a strong doctrinal basis, everyone is able to understand his role in relation to the whole body.

For unity to exist, all parties of the church must first acknowledge each other as equal brothers and sisters in Christ (James 2:2-9), and then acknowledge that God's absolutes must guide the internal structure of the church.

It must be an accepted fact, however, that even with a homogeneous message comes a heterogeneous application of that message. The message sets the ground rules; the application expresses a concern for individual differences and particular needs. In that context, group leaders can have strong and dominant personalities, but they must recognize and accept the need for individual expression and creativity in the group. First Corinthians 12:12-31 addresses that issue. There Paul implies that diversity may result from the variety of spiritual gifts (which is an indication of a healthy group). That variety may lead one believer to have more discernment on a particular matter (even a social issue) than another member. And, as Paul points out, those diverse gifts are given to us by God so "that there be no divisions in the body." Of course it is the following chapter (1 Cor. 13) that elaborates that love provides the protective boundary where differences can be expressed.

In achieving unity through conflict, we would like to make some final suggestions in conjunction with Acts 15. That chapter describes a dispute between not only Paul and Barnabas, but with an undisclosed number of men over the issue of circumcision (v. 1). As you recall, Acts outlines the transition from Judaism to Christianity, and in that process, many conflicts needed immediate attention if the message was to remain "pure." Here the main disagreement was over transferring Jewish laws to Gentile believers.

Solving that issue provides us with insight on how to achieve unity through existing conflict. First, all conflicts are not bad. Nowhere in this passage was the disagreement considered sinful. Second, unity is achieved through conflict when the goal is "win-win" and mutual respect among the believers is practiced. Such a foundation encourages active participation and different points of view.

Third, we need to realize that all members have particular as well as interdependent needs. Putting everyone into a mold tends to be counterproductive. In Acts 15 we see the emergence of individual personalities resulting in a genuine attempt to solidify the Body of Christ as a unit.

Fourth, any conflict should be expressed in a nonemotional and rational manner in which all parties involved respect the others' contributions. That includes good listening. In Acts 15, when the conflict occurred, emotions were undoubtedly high. The men, however, waited until they could debate the issue rationally in Jerusalem. Verse 12 supports that: "All the multitude kept silence and gave audience to Barnabas and Paul."

Fifth, to solidify unity after a conflict is resolved, the local body needs to express confidence in the decision reached. To insure that confidence, follow-up sessions and written agreements need to be made. That was the procedure followed by the Jerusalem council.

And last, we must decide not to use a past conflict as ammunition for future conflicts. Once a conflict is solved we must go on with the business of the church. That will result in confirmed direction and peace of mind for those involved (vv. 31, 33).

We cannot rest on the successes or unity gained as a result of conflict resolution; for apart from the Holy Spirit's continual leadership we can fall back into destructive rather than constructive conflicts. God will ultimately work out even those situations in accordance with His sovereign, perfect will.

DISCIPLINING IN THE CHURCH—BIBLICAL BOUNDARIES

We can see then that fear and noninvolvement not only prolong the problem but may even deepen it. Pretending problems do not exist will not make the ailment vanish. We must be willing to act and rock the boat if need be. Just how do we confront the sin and the sinner? We must define operating biblical parameters for church discipline.

Reproof is the first step of discipline, according to Matthew 18:15-19. You are to reprove (confront) a sinning brother or sister in private (v. 15). If he or she will not listen, you are to take one or two more believers with you (v. 16). And if that person still will not listen, the whole church must become involved (v. 17). The only option at this juncture is separation from the body of believers. First Corinthians 5:9-13 states we are not even to associate with a brother who refuses to turn from his wicked ways.

Why is the penalty so harsh? Paul stated the reason earlier in 1 Corinthians 5:7; if believers become accustomed to the presence of sin in their midst, sooner or later, repulsion to sin is minimized and eventually condoned. Every attempt should be made to restore an individual trapped in sin. But if that is not successful, separation from that person is mandatory to keep the righteous from being slowly acclimated to the world's value system.

It is important, however, that the rebuke be done in the spirit of meekness and love, not out of revenge, anger, or pride. There are two biblical truths we ought to keep before us. First, he that thinks he stands must take heed lest he falls. Second, apart from the grace of God, we could very well be in a similar situation.

Another reason for separation from the deliberate, continuing sinner is to show that God cannot tolerate one living in sin. Thus, when true repentance occurs, restoration into the fellowship should also be made. Where would David or Paul have been had they not been forgiven and restored after the murders and inhumane treatment both committed?

In 2 Corinthians 2:5-11, we find part two of the story originated in 1 Corinthians 5. Here we read that restoration to the church was not made (as it should have been) when the offender, repentant of his deed, asked for forgiveness. Paul stated that the church did not act properly by continuing its exclusion of the offender, stating, "You should rather forgive and comfort him now that he has repented, lest somehow such a one be overwhelmed by excessive sorrow. . . . Wherefore I urge you to reaffirm your love for him" (vv. 7-8, NASB).

However, a formal warning must be made. No one can live in a state of sin without expecting to bear the consequences of sin. Whether it be abortion, homosexuality, neglecting the elderly, or whatever, restoration following repentance does not mean that service will not be affected. Sadly, the degree of service one can render will be tainted in some way as a result of the sin. It is much like having an amputation; when an arm is cut off, a person must learn to adjust his life-style. So it is with the Christian walk. Sin may result in a need for an amputation, but once that occurs, life must readjust. Life can be restored and once again productive, but it can never be the same.

It has been said that a problem ceases to be a problem when the individual cannot alter the outcome. At that point it becomes a fact of life. Thus, once sin occurs, and the penalty of that sin is paid, what has been done is done, and the problem no longer exists.

Our heavenly Father looks at our plight in that manner (Ps. 103:12). It can and should be our outlook as well.

14

Restructuring Priorities at Home

Bonnie was twenty-nine years old, married, the mother of a five-year-old boy (Tim), and a professing Christian. While in college (prior to her marriage) she came to the conclusion that the pursuit of a career would exceed or at least carry equal priority to any domestic responsibilities once the marriage took place.

Bonnie and her husband graduated from college (having married between their junior and senior years) with the agreement that after one of them obtained a "good" job, they would both relocate together, and the other would seek a position in that area as best he or she could. As it turned out, Bonnie got the first offer and so the move was made. Bonnie's husband settled for a job out of town, approximately thirty miles from their home.

Their careers became their priorities, and they both excelled. They also enjoyed the standard of living made possible by their joint incomes. Two years into her job, Bonnie became pregnant. However, she determined that motherhood need not interrupt her work, so when Tim came on the scene, he was immediately sent to a surrogate mother for day care.

As Tim developed over the next few years, problems arose. He became unmanageable, constantly getting into mischief or throwing tantrums. Bonnie tried to discipline him, but because of her overtime work, she had to trust her husband to follow through. The husband did his best but often contradicted Bonnie's methods. Even his pleading and rewarding failed to get results.

Finally, a woman in the church took Bonnie aside and asked her to seek help in controlling Tim because he was disrupting the services and causing spats in Sunday school. Bonnie was angry at the exhortation but had to admit that things were out of control, so she came in for counseling.

OBSERVING THE STEPS THAT LED TO THE PROBLEM

Through counseling it was learned that Bonnie's mother possessed a malcontent temperament, a personality that thrived on negativism. Bonnie blamed her father for her mother's outlook on life and vowed she would not fall into the same trap her mother fell into. Thus, Bonnie became so determined to make something of her life, to be her own master, that over a period of years she came to the conclusion that personal fulfillment could be equated only with a prosperous career.

When Bonnie was married, she treated her relationship with her husband in the form of a dichotomy (as oil and water do not mix, neither would her marriage and career). When Tim came on the scene, Bonnie had to somehow justify her dichotomous philosophy. As a result, two things happened. First, Bonnie began to validate her working career by her "need" for maintaining their expected standard of living. She could rationalize letting a day-care mother take care of her child. Second, Bonnie tried to repress the whole value controversy that emerged by stating it was not her problem but the problem of her friends who were making an issue of Tim.

It was also learned that Bonnie's husband enjoyed the dichotomous relationship as well, for within its framework his responsibilities to the family were minimized, allowing him freedom to expand as a person apart from the family unit.

Finally, Tim's tantrums and uncontrollable behavior brought the problem to light. What was initially a simple matter of child discipline turned into something much greater.

OBSERVING THE AFTEREFFECTS OF THE PROBLEM

1. Tim's behavior was in essence a cry for *attention* and *security*; provisions not supplied by parents going in different directions.
2. A drifting-apart of husband and wife in terms of the family as a functioning unit occurred.
3. The overuse of defense mechanisms to combat the problems at hand became apparent.

LOOKING AT THE QUESTIONS RAISED FROM THE SITUATION

1. With an apparent value system that allows a career to take priority over family roles, one might ask how Bonnie came to that conclusion.
2. Was Bonnie's husband asserting his role as directed in Scripture? How did he come to accept Bonnie's views in the first place?
3. Because Bonnie and her husband were seemingly locked into a set standard of living, what could they have done? Should they have scaled down their life-style? That is not easy, for once one becomes accustomed to a high standard of living, it is quite difficult to scale down.
4. What will become of Tim?

THE USE OF MODELS IN THE COUNSELING PROCESS

By graphing Bonnie's interpersonal relationships with her family, it becomes evident that a *dual-archy* marriage existed in which both Bonnie and her husband cohabited in an existential framework (each "doing his or her own thing"). Consequently, Tim was brought up in a framework in which individualism rather than group identity was taught.

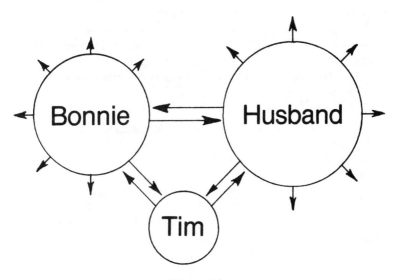

Figure 14.1

As Tim watched his mother, he observed the traditional concept of femininity carefully and deliberately being dismantled. That became the basis then for Tim's insecurity. In addition, that dismantling caused side effects for Tim's parents. It forced them to reevaluate their self-image and marriage roles; it caused a breakdown in terms of a positive role model to Tim; and it created a confusion of sexual expectations in the marriage.

It can be pointed out also from counseling that when a couple decides on a dual-archal kind of marriage, almost without exception, the husband assumes the passive role while the wife takes on the aggressive role of being the dominant force in the relationship. Thus when Christians are involved, some kind of rationalization must be made. The most common rationalization being used today proposes that Scripture passages that deal with role functions in a marriage must be examined only in the context of ancient culture; they are not to be used as a mandate for behavior today.

Bonnie first needed to realize that she was psychologically fighting the distorted perspective of husband-wife roles, a fear that she obviously felt would allow her husband to become a dictator. Second, she needed to realize that, as a Christian, her self-image was not derived from a career, but from how she utilized her gifts within the boundaries set by God (i.e., Romans 13:3ff.). Keep in mind that we are not saying a career is wrong for a mother, but rather that her priorities must be in order. Third, Bonnie needed to learn that roles to be performed within the family directly relate to the theology of Scripture (i.e., the analogy of Christ and the church found in Eph. 5:21-33). And finally, she needed to change her perspective in life from the singular to the plural; that is, from *What I want,* to *What is best for my family.* That change in attitude will provide an impetus for improved behavior in Tim.

BASIC PRINCIPLES FOR COUNSELING

1. Understand the necessity of viewing God's Word as the source of all truth.
2. A proper approach to Scripture must follow this formula:
   a. I have a problem or question
   b. I look at Scripture to see what it has to say about the problem or question
   c. I then base my behavior on those findings
   not:
   a. I have a problem
   b. I decide what behavior I want to take
   c. I then look to Scripture for a supporting passage to back up the decision I have already made.
3. Understand that a wife's priority begins with a commitment to God

and her husband. A husband's priority begins with a commitment to God and his wife. An aspect of priority is the wife's *willful yielding* of her rights over to her husband. Indicate also that an aspect of priority is the husband's *willful loving* of his wife over his own desires or needs.

4. Check the degree of hostility or anger that may be present in the counselee. Many times anger stems from a dislike of self; from the fact that God created and intended the woman to function in a submissive role and the man to function in a leadership role. Many times that anger will result in a woman losing the essence of her femininity or a man losing the essence of his masculinity.

5. Analyze why the counselee's obsessive drive for a career is so important. More often than not it stems from a poor self-image, an over-aggressive temperament, or materialistic desires.

6. Check to see how much time is spent each day in prayer and in reading God's Word.

7. Project into the future. Consider what life will be like ten or twenty years from now for the counselee if the current path is continued. A good exercise is to have an individual write his own obituary.

RESOURCES FOR COUNSELING

Stephen B. Clark. *Man and Woman in Christ.* Ann Arbor, Mich.: Servant Books, 1980.

Susan Foh. *Women and the Word of God.* Nutley, N.J.: Presbyterian and Reformed, 1979.

James B. Hurley. *Man and Woman in Biblical Perspective.* Grand Rapids: Zondervan, 1981.

George W. Knight III. *The New Testament Teaching on the Role Relationship of Men and Women.* Grand Rapids: Baker, 1977.

15

Restoring Dignity
to Human Life

Based on the framework of chapters 12 and 13, we move on to the practical by zeroing in on the following case studies.

SITUATION ONE

Sue, a Christian and active in her local church, let her defenses down little by little. Her boyfriend began to take first place in her life, and she found herself involved in a premarital sexual relationship. As a result, a child was conceived. In a state of panic and not wanting to bring shame on her family, church, or herself, this eighteen-year-old high school senior went to a neighboring town and had an abortion. At first, nobody but her boyfriend and the doctor were aware of what had happened. Following the abortion Sue returned to a "normal" life, although a bit more reserved and withdrawn. Her friends and parents were not alarmed over her withdrawal and felt she was just moody, a stage of life she was going through. Two months later she sought counseling.

SITUATION TWO

Mr. Garrison, a 65-year-old man, refused nursing home care. Although he was still able to function at a moderate pace, he "imposed" on his only son, Bob, to take care of him. Bob was a professing Christian and attended church approximately six to eight times per month. Bob, having plans for marriage, began to get anxious and impatient over the situation. That impatience began to leak out to his friends and to those at his church. Over a period of six months, the problem grew worse and neglect in the care of the father became apparent. Mr. and Mrs. Cooney, elderly church members and friends of Bob and his father, gladly went to Bob to offer some help. Bob gladly accepted and "washed his hands" of any further involvement with his father. The Cooneys, however, were elderly and could not handle the responsibility of complete care for Mr. Garrison. Mr. Garrison, although grateful to the Cooneys, was vocal about his hurt and dissatisfaction in what he considered his son's desertion in his time of need. Bob was aware of those problems. It was not long after that that Mr. Garrison died of natural causes, according to medical reports.

Even though the Cooneys did not voice criticism of Bob to other church members, Bob began to feel so guilty over his father's death that he was quite certain that everyone was talking about him. He felt awkward and defensive at church and his attendance dropped. Because he would not repent and turn to God to erase his guilt, bitterness toward the church, which he blamed for his problems, set in. About nine months later he sought counseling.

INTERPRETATIVE COUNSELING

Let us try to decipher the components of the two problems just presented. Keep the following criteria in mind during your evaluation: (1) if a close friend gets involved in a state of sin (has an abortion, gets a divorce, etc.), what attitude and action should I take as an individual? and (2) if the person is a member of a church, what posture should be taken collectively by that church?

In an attempt to evaluate the two situations holistically, the procedure used will consist of: (1) observing the obvious steps that led to the problem; (2) observing the obvious aftereffects of that problem; (3) looking at questions raised from the case; and (4) the use of models and graphs in the counseling process.

Comparisons that show similarities and differences, along with after-the-fact counseling helps, will be presented after each situation has been appraised individually.

SITUATION ONE

Observing the obvious steps that led to the problem. In pinpointing the problem, what was the obvious path taken by Sue that ultimately led to her having an abortion?

1. She let her defenses down

2. That evolved into a sexual act outside of marriage
3. A child was conceived
4. She began to rationalize
5. She took the step and had an abortion in a state of panic
6. Her personality slowly began to change

Observing the obvious aftereffects of the problem. From the brief description given, what obvious aftereffects on Sue's life resulted from having an abortion?

1. She tried to live as if nothing had happened
2. She became more reserved and withdrawn from her family, friends, and church

Looking at the questions raised from the case. What questions might one ask from this brief case study that would aid in the counseling process?

1. Sue was active in her church. Was her commitment and involvement just a mask to cover up her true self?
2. Why did Sue get into a situation in which she allowed her defenses to break down? Could it be totally blamed on peer pressure?
3. What kind of communication existed between Sue and her family, and Sue and her church that prevented her from going to them with what she had done?
4. What percentage, if any, might be blamed on Sue's parents and her church for not teaching the proper values and attitude structure for her to follow? Or was her downfall totally because of her rebellion?
5. What obstacles kept Sue's parents and church from being aware that something was wrong?
6. What made Sue eventually seek counseling?
7. What help should we then give Sue?

The use of models and graphs in the counseling process. Once the initial questions have been asked and the necessary observations made, the problem can then be plotted by the use of models and graphs. This aids the counselor in understanding the various aspects of the problem by enabling him to see the problem visually in an objective form. (To expedite this procedure, additional information derived from other counseling sessions associated with this case was inserted.)

First, we need to construct models that depict the interpersonal relationships Sue is engaged in.

Sue's Interpersonal Relationships Prior to Her Sin

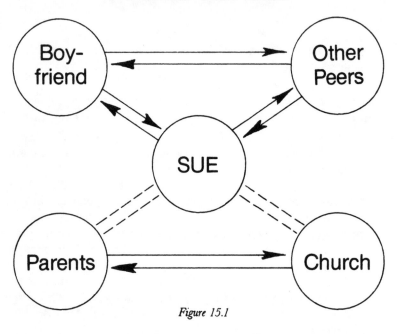

Figure 15.1

From the counseling sessions, it was noted that there was a gap in communication between Sue and her parents and Sue and her church—the two main sources of value learning. Her parents and church, however, were never aware of that problem. Consequently, Sue began to wear a "mask" and never revealed her inner self. Her interpersonal relationships with her parents and church thus became very superficial—hence, the dotted lines.

SUE'S INTERPERSONAL RELATIONSHIPS AT THE TIME OF HER CRISIS

In this model we see that the interpersonal relationship Sue had with her boyfriend was obviously close; the interpersonal relationship with her peers was relatively close (peer pressure on dating habits came into play here, even in an indirect manner); and the interpersonal relationships with her parents and church became somewhat aloof. We also see that more distance had been created between Sue and her parents, and Sue and her church. Finally, notice that the reaction to Sue by both the parents and church did not change, even though Sue's response to them had.

Sue's Interpersonal Relationships at the Time of Her Crisis

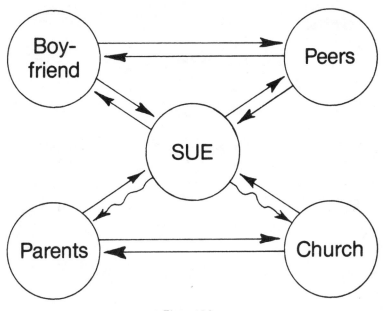

Figure 15.2

Following her abortion, Sue began to develop a barrier around herself. A large part of that was because of guilt; however, because she wore a "mask," she felt trapped. As a result, her relationships became restricted. That was evident in her withdrawal from her significant others (the four groups mentioned above). An analysis from several counseling sessions revealed several reasons for her withdrawal: (1) as mentioned above, guilt over her life-style and the abortion; (2) hostility and anger toward herself and her values for submitting; (3) her boyfriend (for allowing him to "use" her); and (4) her peers, who condoned her life-style, even though they were not actually aware of what had happened.

Sue's Interpersonal Relationships Following the Abortion

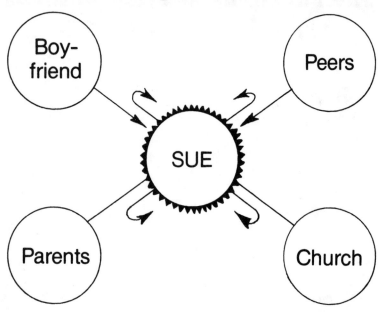

Figure 15.3

ANALYSIS OF POINTS *A-H* (FIG. 15.4)

Point *A* represents the "Christian" path Sue's parents and church set for Sue. We see it as the end of a horizontal line. It was found that Sue's church emphasized the observable components of the Christian walk; that is, the dos and the don'ts. As long as Sue conformed to a particular set of behavioral patterns and the status quo was kept, everyone was assured of her Christian commitment.

Point *B* represents the Christian path found in the Bible. We see it as a gradual, vertical slope. God's path for Christian growth and maturity involves not only actions (the observable) but attitudes as well, which are controlled by the Holy Spirit. In sociology, we refer to this procedure as the *socialization process*. By this process the value system learned becomes *internalized;* that is, a part of the individual. The slope also indicates that stagnation is impossible in the Christian life. An individual is either pressing on "toward the mark," which is Jesus Christ, or he is sliding backward because of a lack of fruit in his life. (It should be noted that this point does not indicate a path toward sinless perfection.)

Point C shows the time when Sue was saved at the age of thirteen (C1). Here she began to "learn the ropes" of Christianity. She began to fit very well into the mold made for her and received peer, church, and parental acceptance for her behavior. However, she quickly learned that acceptance related totally to her overt actions and began to act accordingly (C2). "Learning the ropes" gave Sue a false feeling of assurance.

THE CRITICAL PATH MODEL

The Critical Path taken by Sue in her Christian walk:

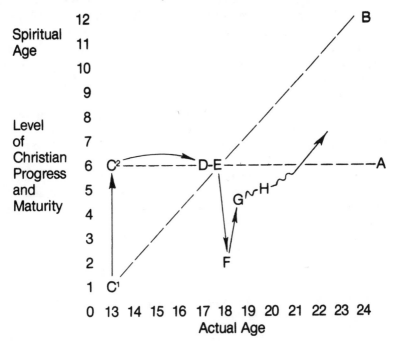

Figure 15.4

Check the distance between Point *A* and Point *B*. In actuality, Sue should still be on the "milk" of the Word, learning the precepts of Scripture.

Point *D* shows Sue at age seventeen. Here we see that the critical paths of points *A* and *B* cross. At that time in Sue's Christian walk, the "excitement" had begun to wear off. We also find that church and parental acceptance for her behavior was not valued as it once had been.

Point *E* is just prior to her act of fornication. Sue became disillusioned with her understanding of Christian commitment. She began to see discrepancies between her expectations and those of the church. Mentally and emotionally she questioned her values. The stage was set for her downfall.

Point *F* plots Sue's emotional and spiritual low following her fornication and abortion. Here the church, and especially Sue's parents, should have been sensitive in noticing the drastic change in her life. That is when we need to "bear one another's burdens" and restore such a one in the spirit of *agape* love.

Point *G*, followed by the use of the wavy line, exemplifies the emotions that resulted from the events in Sue's life. Her withdrawal from her church and parents was because of the guilt, anger, and hostility mentioned earlier. It is interesting to note that the guilt Sue bore was for failing to meet the standards of her church (the horizontal path) rather than biblical standards (the vertical path). Consequently, her depression came about as a result of not meeting the standards outlined in point *A*.

Also notice that the gap is increased between Sue's actual spiritual state and the biblical ideal. Sue found herself slowly getting further and further away from God, even though she seemed to be keeping the status quo set by the church.

Point *H* occurred at the age of nineteen, approximately one and a half years after counseling. A recommitment to God was made in relation to her attitudes as well as her actions. A dramatic step had been taken to "catch up" in her spiritual walk with God.

SITUATION TWO

Observing the obvious steps which led to the problem. In pinpointing this problem, we will visualize the path that ultimately led to Bob's rejection of the church.

1. Bob wanted to make his plans for marriage, but found that his father demanded his total attention and care

2. Because of external pressure (e.g., church, friends), a feeling of guilt compelled Bob to look after his father
3. Bob postponed his marriage plans; frustrations and resentment toward his father developed; Bob verbalized his feelings to church members
4. Bob took out his hostility and bitterness on his father by apparently neglecting to give him the proper care; basically, his sin was more one of attitudinal abuse than physical abuse
5. Mr. Garrison died
6. Bob's guilt made him feel awkward and defensive toward church members
7. Bob's guilt turned to bitterness when he refused to repent
8. Bob left the church and became "hardened" to spiritual things

Observing the obvious aftereffects of the problem. From the brief description given, what obvious aftereffects on Bob's life resulted from this incident?

1. A rejection of biblical values as a guide to conduct and attitudes
2. Insensitivity to others

Looking at the questions raised from the case. What questions might one ask from this brief case study that would aid in the counseling process?

1. Why did Mr. Garrison refuse nursing home care? What was Bob's duty as a Christian to his father?
2. What kind of a father-son relationship preceded this problem?
3. In what ways did Mr. Garrison "impose" on his only son?
4. Define *neglect.* How did Bob mistreat his father?
5. In what ways did the church help Bob and his father?
6. Should this incident have delayed Bob's marriage plans?
7. What help should we give Bob?

The use of models and graphs in the counseling process.

Bob's Interpersonal Relationships Prior to His Problem

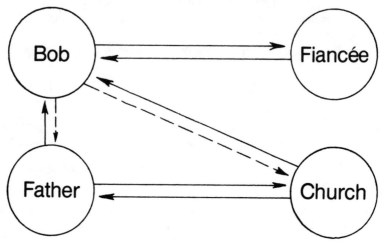

Figure 15.5

Bob's main interpersonal relationship was with his fiancée. The couple had, in effect, isolated themselves from the rest of the church, and especially from Bob's father. When Bob learned of his father's desire to stay with him, he became resentful. Bob was basically a selfish person and was always characterized as having a very strong and stubborn will. He was used to getting his own way and understood little about the meaning of Christian sacrifice. Consequently, any imposition was greeted with discontent because he generally used relational contacts for his own ends. Bob's fiancée was a college sweetheart who resided 150 miles from Bob's home and, from later counseling, it became quite clear that she was unaware of the extent of the problem. Being the selfish person he was, Bob believed the church was obligated to take his problem so he could be free to do as he wished.

Bob's Interpersonal Relationships During His Crisis

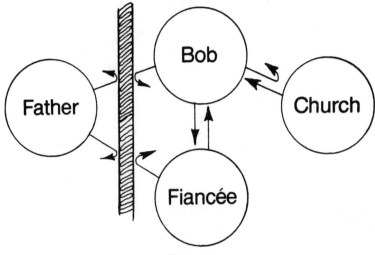

Figure 15.6

Even though Bob was twenty-nine, he still had not lived on his own. The house, utilities, and food were supplied by Bob's father so Bob could save enough money to buy into a local business. About a year after his mother's death, Bob's father had had a stroke that left him semiparalyzed. During that time Bob got engaged, but Mr. Garrison disapproved. Bob then tried to talk his father into moving into a nursing home "where he could get better care." Mr. Garrison refused. That aggravated Bob, and he let his resentment filter out to various friends and church members. The Cooneys, as part of the ministering Body of Christ, attempted to help Bob, but instead, he imposed on their Christian love and left them with the total responsibility for his father. Soon after that, his father died.

Bob's Interpersonal Relationships Following the Death of His Father

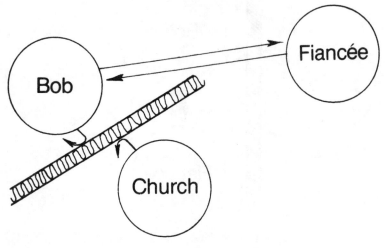

Figure 15.7

Following the death of his father, Bob developed feelings of guilt over his selfishness, but never repented. The outward manifestation of that guilt turned into a defense mechanism: the "I don't care" response. Not long after his father's death, Bob left the church. He again exploded when his fiancée, becoming more aware of his personality problems, said she would not marry him unless he sought counseling.

THE CRITICAL PATH MODEL

The Critical Path taken by Bob in his "Christian" walk:

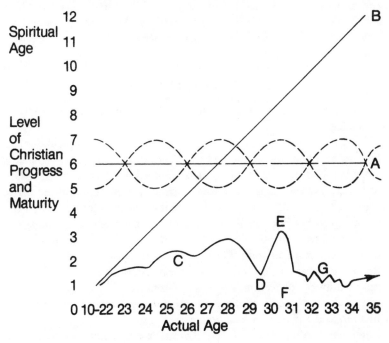

Figure 15.8

AN ANALYSIS OF POINTS *A-G* (FIG. 15.8)

Point *A* represents the "Christian" path set for Bob by his parents and church. The dotted lines show that expected behavior was never clearly defined to Bob in his indulgent upbringing, and therefore, no set guidelines for conduct were enforced.

Point *B* represents the Christian path as found in the Bible (refer to Point *B* in Situation One).

Point *C* graphs Bob's walk as a Christian. The wavy line represents a lack of desire or commitment on Bob's part to walk the Christian path.

Point *D* shows Bob's path after learning of his father's desire to live with him. Depression and hostility had set in.

Point *E* shows elation following the death of his father; for he is then free to marry and live his life as he wishes.

Point *F,* however, indicates the guilt over his father's death and his bitterness toward the church.

Point *G* shows a low after Bob's financeé required him to seek counseling. It was learned then that Bob had never accepted Jesus Christ as Lord and Savior. Any prior commitment Bob had made to Christ had been made to benefit his narcissistic desires. After many counseling sessions, Bob could not force himself to ask God for repentance and eventually quit receiving counsel.

SIZING UP THE TWO SITUATIONS

As we put the two problems side by side, we can see a basic pattern developing.

The crises in both cases came from the same root—love of self. Sue, for example, told herself that she had the abortion so as not to bring shame on her family and church. But a close analysis revealed her real reason was to preserve the "mask" she was wearing, a mask that allowed her to be seen as "spiritual," but one that made it convenient for her to be what *she* wanted to be. Bob, on the other hand, was actually more honest in his interactions with other people, even though it was later discovered that he was not a Christian. For when he was selfish (by not desiring to care for his father), he did not try to hide his selfishness with a mask, but rather exhibited his feelings to his acquaintances.

From those two case studies, several directives can be made for the Christian and the church as a whole.

First, we should not assume an individual is a Christian simply by how he conforms to a prescribed set of rules or norms. Many are lulled into a pseudosecurity through adherence to a social order.

Second, the manner in which sin is dealt with by the evangelical church needs to change drastically. In Sue's church, her ostracism was not for the purpose of eventual "restoration," but rather a corporate desire to keep the status quo. Sue was taught subtly that sin should not be exposed, that it was better to hide sin than confront it.

Third, the evangelical church needs to be sensitive to its people, restoring with a spirit of love and meekness the brother caught in sin. That sensitivity means that we as believers must be so attuned to the Holy Spirit that we will be able to counsel others properly. Galatians 6:2 says, "Bear one another's burdens, and thus fulfill the law of Christ" (NASB).

It is the strong Christian and not the weak brother who initiates the counseling action.[1]

Many of us will be held accountable for not confronting and ultimately restoring a brother who has fallen into sin.

BIBLICAL PRINCIPLES FOR COUNSELING

1. There is a need to observe the presuppositions one has concerning the human life issue (i.e., the uniqueness of man, his origin, his worth).
2. Based on the above understanding, the cause-and-effect relationship between one's philosophy of human life to the application of that philosophy (i.e., in terms of attitude toward specific issues of abortion, euthanasia, etc.) become inseparable. There is no such thing as a "value free" approach to counseling.
3. Realize that in most instances there is a selfish or narcissistic motive in fighting the right-to-life issue.
4. Objectively go through the Scriptures for answers to these issues.
5. Treat with caution what the media and so-called experts say. As Scripture confirms, Satan works in ways that will fool most of the people.

RESOURCES FOR COUNSELING

Harold O. J. Brown. *Death Before Birth.* Nashville: Nelson, 1977.

Millard J. Erickson and Ines E. Bowers. "Euthanasia and Christian Ethics," *Journal of the Evangelical Theological Society,* vol. 19, no. 1 (Winter 1976).

Richard L. Ganz, ed. *Thou Shalt Not Kill: The Christian Case Against Abortion.* New Rochelle, N.Y.: Arlington House, 1978.

C. Everett Koop. *The Right to Live, The Right to Die.* Wheaton, Ill.: Tyndale, 1976.

Bernard N. Nathanson. *Aborting America.* Garden City, N.Y: Doubleday, 1979.

John T. Noonan, Jr. *A Private Choice: Abortion in America in the Seventies.* New York: Free Press (Macmillan), 1979.

1. Alfred M. Freedman and Harold I. Kaplan, ed., *Comprehensive Textbook of Psychiatry* (Baltimore: Williams & Wilkins, 1967), 972-76.

16

Reaching Out to the Homosexual

What can Christians do for their homosexual brothers and sisters? What can parents do for their homosexual child?

We can begin by reasserting that any counseling in this area must be within the boundaries of God's Word. When doing so, however, it is always of deep importance to remember that when dealing with a homosexual, our sole purpose ought to be that of turning a sinner back to God (Gal. 6:1-5) in the spirit of meekness and fear (1 Pet. 3:15).

EARLY WARNING SIGNS OF HOMOSEXUALITY

As with drug-related counseling cases, detecting early warning signals may give the parent, teacher, pastor, or friend clues that can aid in changing the life course of a potential homosexual.

The following are some of the early warning signs in children with homosexual tendencies.

BOYS: AGES 5-10

- They may tend to be afraid of getting hurt
- They may withdraw from contact sports
- They tend to develop a poor self-image
- They may manifest behavior that their peers call "sissy"

GIRLS: AGES 5-10

- They tend to be loners and have doubts about their worth as a person

- As is the case with boys, they exhibit behavior that makes them "different" than other little girls
- They tend to have little or no interest in "little girl" toys, dolls, or dressing up in their mother's clothes

Tomboyishness, however, is not necessarily an indication of homosexual tendencies, for it may merely be an indication of a high energy level.

BOYS: AGES 11-16

- A schism develops even more as these boys are made the target of peer-group hostility
- They will not develop a "crush" on a girl, and may avoid girls completely
- They may be persistent in cross-dressing
- They may use cosmetics
- They may imitate female gestures and roles
- They may express, even subtly, their desire to have been born a girl
- They may appear frail and will not participate in rough, competitive sports
- They may tend to be overpolite, or overanxious to please adults
- They may not have close relationships with male peers
- They may masturbate using female clothing

GIRLS: AGES 11-16

- They may continually show a strong preference for masculine dress and will avoid more typically feminine attire and pursuits
- They may isolate themselves from other girls and consequently make defective peer relationships
- They may develop crushes on other girls or older admired women
- They may avoid contact with boys
- They may adopt masculine gestures and roles
- They may masturbate using male clothing
- They may express a desire to have been born a boy
- They frequently do not like to play "girl games"
- They seem to be more competitive than most girls and tend to have more frequent tantrums (often directed against the mother)

A CASE IN POINT

John, a professing Christian, had a desire to go into the ministry. However, he had a problem in the area of homosexuality. He had had an "experience" with a high school buddy prior to attending college. The memories of that experience still lingered. When John went home on vacation breaks, no matter how hard he tried, the inevitable happened—a sexual experience with his friend. As can be expected, John lived under a cloud of guilt and self-debasement.

Observing the steps to the problem. John did not fit the stereotype of a homosexual. He had loving parents who showed love not only to him but to each other. John's father first learned of his son's problem when he accidentally walked in on John and his friend one evening. Later, John's comment was, "Dad, I have never been comfortable with girls." After some counseling that statement was found to be not entirely true, for John had indeed dated several girls. What John meant was that none of his relationships had developed into a permanent relationship resulting in marriage. Thus he felt it must be a result of his homosexual nature. As a result guilt emerged, and when that guilt was not solved, the problem seemed to torment him continually.

John came to the conclusion that his sexual desire for his high school friend was contrary to God's Word. However, that led him to ask, "God, why am I plagued with this problem?" and, "Why can't I pray to You and get relief?" The reason John did not find the answers at that time was twofold: (1) he did not understand the cycle that kept him from solving the problem; and (2) he did not realize that only in rare circumstances does God provide a miracle of instantaneous healing. Growth is usually slow and the scars of sin linger. Our hope comes in knowing that God is with us and guiding us along on the pathway to recovery.

Not obtaining instantaneous recovery caused more guilt for John. He would dedicate himself to God one night and then be plagued with thoughts of failing God the next. Thus his feeling of guilt was not directly related to a past sin, but was directed toward his *tendency* to that sin, which is quite different.

Observing the aftereffects of the problem. In John's case, several defense mechanisms developed.

1. He began to study harder in college and wanted to be known as "the campus intellectual."
2. It was learned that his Bible major was indirectly related to his problem. It was his thinking that if he majored in Bible, that would compensate or offset his problem and relieve his guilt.
3. When guilt feelings continued, his next reaction was to tell everybody he had the problem. His reasoning was that getting it "off his chest" would help.
4. When that failed, John then tried to cope with his problem by mak-

ing himself believe that his problem was genetic, a situation he could not reverse.

5. Finally, out of desperation, he went from one counselor to another to find one who would provide spiritual direction.

Looking at some of the questions raised from the case.

1. Is there a difference between one having the tendency toward homosexuality and one who is habitually practicing the act of homosexuality?
2. What did John think about himself? Were his defense mechanisms employed to protect his self-image?
3. With John and his friend, what caused the cycle to start? (The answer to this question was very important in the process of helping John.)

The use of models in the counseling process. In John's case, an understanding of the motivational cycle is essential to the explanation of why the fantasy and relationship with his friend continued to exist.

Scripture tells us that the basis for what we do reflects who our master is (either Christ or Satan). Sadly, for the Christian, many times Satan's influence on our lives exceeds God's influence. The result is a struggle, and the *heart* is where that struggle takes place in the individual. The word *heart* is defined in both the Hebrew and Greek as "the thoughts and feelings of the mind." In addition, it is the heart that controls the will, the intellect, and our faculties (hearing, reason, seeing, etc.; Prov. 4:23; Isa. 1:18; Matt. 13:9; 15:8; Mark 7:21; Rev. 22:17).

Christ wants to control the heart, "For as many as are led by the Spirit of God are called the Sons of God." However, for the non-Christian, we must realize that the heart is controlled by Satan (John 8:44). Thus, it was imperative to teach John that his will was subject to the one who controlled his heart.

The motivational cycle is activated by a stimulus. In John's case, going home to old surroundings and a situation that he had not had victory over became that stimulus. Once a drive is started, the rest of the cycle will follow. In John's case, he would seek his high school friend (instrumental behavior) to reach his goal: an experience with that friend. As is the case with alcoholics, once the act has been committed, the need or desire for that act almost becomes compulsive; and for John, it turned into guilt. It is for that reason that the cycle must be stopped prior to the drive state, as 2 Timothy points out: "flee youthful lusts." According to Paul, "Therefore, let him that thinks he stands take heed lest he fall" (1 Cor. 10:12, NASB). No one is so "spiritual" that he can withstand Satan's attacks on his weak areas without the help of the Holy Spirit. In John's case, he should have utilized God's help in keeping away from his high school friend, rather than asking God to bail him out after the cycle began.

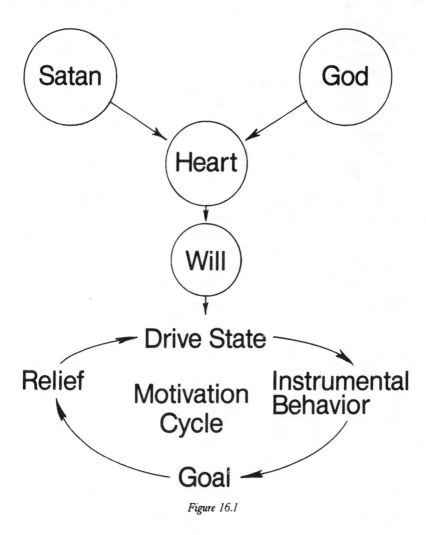

Figure 16.1

The main point is that everyone is capable of fornication, adultery, and even homosexuality. No one is strong enough to flirt with sin and get by with it. Each one of us possesses a weakness, an area, that Satan can use to destroy us if the armor of God is not fully in place. John had asked God to get rid of the symptoms rather than the cause—a heart not fully in tune with God.

BASIC PRINCIPLES FOR COUNSELING

1. Treat homosexuality as a sin. Do not allow the homosexual to rationalize away his or her behavior. Acknowledgement of the sin is essential!
2. Realize that apart from the power of the Holy Spirit, long lasting change cannot be expected.
3. Put love into your counseling.
4. Make sure the converted homosexual breaks all past associations and friendships with other homosexuals. For the homosexual, when confronted or tempted with the problem, the best procedure is to run from it.
5. Help the individual restructure the course of his life (friends, roles, motivation, habits, etc.) to avoid falling into the homosexual trap again.
6. In counseling, deal with the whole person. Realize that homosexuality affects every area of one's life.
7. Realize that homosexual patients often try to anger their counselor to the point of giving up. Being prepared for resistance is important. Be persistent and understand that change is painful.
8. Remember that there is no problem too big for God to handle.

Appendix 1 _____

Structural Development of Genesis 1:26-28

v. 26 Then God said,
"Let us make man in Our image, according to Our likeness;
and let them rule over the fish of the sea
and over the birds of the sky
and over the cattle,
and over all the earth,
and over every creeping thing that creeps on the earth."

v. 27 And God created man in His own image,
in the image of God He created him;
male and female He created them.

v. 28 And God blessed them;
And God said to them,
"Be fruitful and multiply,
and fill the earth, and subdue it;
and rule over the fish of the sea
and over the birds of the sky,
and over every living thing that moves on the earth."

(NASB)

This particular format is suggested in an unpublished paper by Ronald B. Allen, entitled, "Male and Female: the View from Genesis," p. 3, presented at the Seminar on Women in the Ministry, Western Conservative Baptist Seminary, November 1976).

197

Appendix 2 ─────────────

Ephesians 5:21-33

The house-rules in the epistles (Eph. 5:21 — 6:9; Col. 3:18 — 4:1; 1 Pet. 2:18–3:7) should be distinguished from other exhortatory materials (Rom. 13:17; 1 Tim. 2:1-5; 6:1; Titus 2:2-10). None of the latter passages expect reciprocity of submission. As well, those passages of the pastorals, Titus and 1 and 2 Timothy, might better be called *kirchtafeln*, a table of church responsibility.

Certain characteristics are uniform among the tables of Ephesians, Colossians, and 1 Peter:

Col. 3:18	Wives submit yourselves	to your	husbands as it is proper in the Lord	
Eph. 5:22	Wives [submit yourselves]	to your own husbands as		to the Lord
1 Pet. 3:1	Likewise wives submit yourselves	to your own husbands		

Col. 3:19	Husbands love	your wives
Eph. 5:25	Husbands love	your wives
1 Pet. 3:7	Husbands likewise be considerate as you live with your wives	

Col. 3:19	and do not be harsh with them
Eph. 5:25	as Christ loved the church
1 Pet. 3:7	and treat them with respect and as heirs

Many scholars have considered Ephesians 5:21-33 to be very difficult stylistically.[1] The major difficulty is the transition from verse 21 to verse 22; an indication, some believe, that someone endeavored unsuccessfully to bring the portions together.[2] However, one should carefully take into account the judgment of J. Paul Sampley, author of an outstanding

---

1. J. Paul Sampley, ed. Matthew Black, *And The Two Shall Become One Flesh* (Cambridge: Cambridge U., 1971), 4.
2. Winsome Munro, "Col. III.18 – IV.1 and Eph. V.21 – VI.9: Evidence of a Late Literary Stratum?" *New Testament Studies*, 18, 4 (1972): 443. He continues, "We have only to compare this awkward sequence with that which results if we read vi.10ff. directly after v.18-20 to realize how rudely v.21 – vi.10 interrupts the rhythmic flow of the original." Ibid., 443-44.

monograph on Ephesians 5:21-33: "Too often, in complex constructions such as 5:21-33, the interpreter is tempted to express his frustration at the difficulty of understanding by crediting the author of the passage with ineptitude, carelessness or obtuseness."[3]

The problem is that in the Greek text verse 22 does not have a verb, so that the thought of the wives' submission must be understood from verse 21. Because of that, many have considered the *haustafel* to begin with verse 21. Even so, it is probably best to consider the participle in verse 21 as a part of the preceding sentences grammatically (contrast RSV) and so ending a paragraph (United Bible Society and Nestle Greek texts). The connection with verse 22 is one of mood, sense, and rhythm rather than syntax.[4]

Following is a proposed structural arrangement of Ephesians 5:22-33, which will highlight the emphases of the passage:

v. 22	**A**	Wives [submit yourselves] to your husbands as to the Lord	
v. 23		A Because the husband is the head of the wife	(Husband in authority)
		A′ as Christ is the head of the Church	(Christ in authority)
		B He is the Savior of the body	
v. 24		C but as the Church is subject to Christ	(Church in submission)
		C′ Thus also the wives to their husbands in everything	(Wife in submission)
v. 25	**B**	Husbands love your wives	
		A Just as Christ loved the Church and gave Himself for her	
v. 26		B in order that he might sanctify her by cleansing her with washing of the water by the word	
v. 27		C in order that he might present to Himself a glorious Church not having stain or blemish or any such thing	
		B′ But in order that it might be holy and blameless	
v. 28		A′ Thus ought also husbands to love their own wives as their own bodies	
		(The one loving his own wife loves himself,	
v. 29		For no one ever hated his own flesh, but nourishes and cares for it)	
v. 33	**B′**	However each of you must love his own wife as he loves himself	
	A′	And the wife must respect her husband	

---

3. Sampley, 4.

v.18-20 to realize how rudely v.21—vi.10 interrupts the rhythmic flow of the original." Ibid., 443-44.
3. Sampley, 4.
4. The participle should be considered as one of manner or means rather than as an imperative. Note the interesting view of Hendriksen, who says that all the participles in verses 18-21 are best seen as imperatives. William Hendriksen, *Exposition of Ephesians, New Testament Commentary* (Grand Rapids: Baker, 1967), 243, n. 150.

Selected Bibliography

FEMINISM

Christenson, Larry. *The Christian Family*. Minneapolis: Bethany, 1970.

Clark, Stephen B. *Man and Woman in Christ*. Ann Arbor, Mich.: Servant, 1980.

Foh, Susan. *Women and the Word of God: A Response to Biblical Feminism*. Grand Rapids: Baker, 1980.

Hendricks, Howard G. *Heaven Help the Home!* Wheaton: Victor, 1980.

Howe, E. Margaret. *Women and Church Leadership*. Grand Rapids: Zondervan, 1982.

Hurley, James B. *Man and Woman in Biblical Perspective*. Grand Rapids: Zondervan, 1981.

LaHaye, Tim, and Beverly LaHaye. *Spirit-Controlled Family Living*. Old Tappan, N.J.: Revell, 1978.

Mickelsen, Alvera, ed. *Women, Authority and the Bible*. Downers Grove, Ill.: InterVarsity, 1987.

Peterson, Evelyn R., and J. Allan Peterson. *For Women Only: The Fine Art of Being a Woman*. Wheaton: Tyndale, 1974.

Ryrie, Charles C. *The Place of Women in the Church*. Chicago: Moody, 1968.

Strong, Bryan. *The Marriage and Family Experience*. 2d ed. St. Paul: West, 1983.

ABORTION AND EUTHANASIA

Hoffmeier, James K., ed. *Abortion: A Christian Understanding and Response*. Grand Rapids: Baker, 1987.

Koop, C. Everett. *The Right to Live, the Right to Die*. Wheaton: Tyndale, 1976.

Kreeft, Peter. *Unaborted Socrates: A Dramatic Debate on the Issues Surrounding Abortion*. Downers Grove, Ill.: InterVarsity, 1983.

Lammers, Stephen, and Allen Verhey, eds. *On Moral Medicine: Theological Perspectives in Medical Ethics*. Grand Rapids: Eerdmans, 1987.

Lifton, Robert. *The Nazi Doctors: Medical Killing and the Psychology of Genocide*. New York: Basic, 1986.

Noonan, John T., Jr. *A Private Choice: Abortion in America in the Seventies*. New York: Free, 1979.

Spring, Beth, and Ed Larson. *Euthanasia: Spiritual, Medical and Legal Issues.* Portland: Multnomah, 1988.

HOMOSEXUALITY

Antonio, Gene. *The AIDS* Cover-up? The Real and Alarming Facts about AIDS. San Francisco: St. Ignatius, 1986.

Arterburn, Jerry. *How Will I Tell My Mother? A True Story of One Man's Battle with Homosexuality and AIDS.* Nashville: Nelson, 1988.

Bahnsen, Greg. *Homosexuality: A Biblical View.* Grand Rapids: Baker, 1978.

Keysor, Charles, ed. *What You Should Know About Homosexuals.* Grand Rapids: Zondervan, 1979.

Noebel, David, W. Lutton, and Paul Cameron. *AIDS: Guidelines for Containing the Homosexual Venereal Disease.* 2d ed. Manitou Springs, Col.: Summit Research Institute, 1987.

Rueda, Enrique. *The Homosexual Network: Private Lives and Public Policy.* Old Greenwich, Conn.: Devin-Adairn, 1982.

COUNSELING

Adams, Jay E. *The Christian Counselor's Manual.* Nutley, N.J.: Presbyterian and Reformed, 1973.

Benner, David G., ed. *Baker Encyclopedia of Psychology.* Grand Rapids: Baker, 1985.

Downing, Lester N. *Counseling Theories and Techniques.* Chicago: Nelson-Hall, 1975.

Meier, Paul D., Frank B. Minirth, and Frank B. Wichern. *Introduction to Psychology and Counseling: Christian Perspectives and Applications.* Grand Rapids: Baker, 1982.

Narramore, Clyde M. *Encyclopedia of Psychological Problems.* Grand Rapids: Zondervan, 1970.

GENERAL

Kantzer, Kenneth S., ed. *Applying the Scriptures: Papers from the ICBI Summit III.* Grand Rapids: Zondervan, 1987.

Kreeft, Peter. *The Best Things in Life: A Twentieth-Century Socrates Looks at Power, Pleasure, Truth, and the Good Life.* Downers Grove, Ill.: InterVarsity, 1984.

Lasch, Christopher. *The Culture of Narcissism.* New York: Warner, 1979.

Stott, John R. W. *Involvement: Being a Responsible Christian in a Non-Christian Society.* Old Tappan, N.J.: Revell, 1984.

Webber, Robert. *The Church in the World: Opposition, Tension, or Transformation?* Grand Rapids: Zondervan, 1986.

Scripture Index

Genesis
1 — 12, 39
1:22 — 95
1:26-28 — 9, 14, 36, 197
1:28 — 40
1-2 — 19
1-3 — 9, 29
2 — 14, 17, 31, 39, 40, 44,
    45, 133
2:2 — 88
2:7 — 88
2:15 — 40
2:17 — 67
2:18 — 13
2:18-25 — 40
2:24 — 23
3 — 15, 101
3:1-7 — 15
3:16 — 15, 16, 43, 45
4:7 — 16, 17
6:5 — 64
8:21 — 64
19 — 126-27
19:8 — 127
25:25-26 — 85
31:38 — 85
38:28-29 — 85

Exodus
20:13 — 103
21:20-21 — 84
21:22-25 — 82, 83-87
23:26 — 85

Leviticus
9:27 — 129
11:7 — 129
18 — 130
18:22 — 128
20 — 130
20:10 — 129
20:11-13 — 129
20:13 — 128

Joshua
24:14-15 — 141

Judges
17:6 — 61
19 — 126
19:25 — 127

Job
1:21 — 85
3:11 — 85

Psalms
8 — 14, 16, 39
9:9 — 154
19 — 10
23:6 — 154
37:5 — 158
46:1 — 154
51 — 87
51:5 — 64, 87
51:7 — 87
58:3 — 64

81:6 — 158
91:3-4 — 154
103:12 — 167
125:3 — 76
139 — 82
139:13-16 — 82
139:15 — 83
139:16 — 83

Proverbs
3:5-6 — 154
4:23 — 194
6:16 — 64
9:10 — 154
14:12 — 102
14:26-27 — 154
24:11-12 — 79
31 — 12, 51
31:11 — 51
31:15 — 51
31:20 — 51, 54
31:24 — 51

Ecclesiastes
5:15 — 85

Isaiah
1:18 — 194
9:6 — 85
49:1 — 63

Jeremiah
1:5 — 87

11:5 — 85
17:7 — 103
20:18 — 85

Ezekiel
16:49 — 127, 128
16:50 — 127

Hosea
9:14 — 85

Matthew
13:9 — 194
15:8 — 194
18:15-19 — 166
20:26 — 50
22:39 — 77

Mark
2:5-12 — 151
7:21 — 194
10:45 — 43

Luke
1:15 — 63
2:51 — 41

John
3:16 — 156
8:44 — 64, 118, 154, 194
9:1-3 — 83
11:35 — 102
13:13-17 — 43

Acts
5:11 — 164
5:14 — 164
15 — 165, 166
15:1 — 165
15:12 — 165
15:31 — 165
15:33 — 165
17:26 — 88

Romans
1:18-32 — 132
1:24-27 — 130, 132
2:11 — 50
5:5 — 156
5:12-21 — 88
6:17 — 64

8 — 17, 144
8:22-23 — 152
8:32 — 153
12 — 33
12:1-2 — 45
13:3 — 172
13:13 — 41
13:17 — 199
15:14 — 157

1 Corinthians
2:11-15 — 154
5 — 167
5:7 — 166
5:9-13 — 166
6:9-10 — 130-31
6:16 — 132
10:12 — 194
10:13 — 155
11 — 44
11:8-16 — 44
12 — 37
12:12-31 — 165
13 — 31, 156, 165
15:28 — 41
15:55 — 102

2 Corinthians
2:5-11 — 167
5:17 — 150

Galatians
1:15 — 87
2 — 163
3:26-28 — 50
3:28 — 29
5:16-17 — 156
5:19 — 156
5:22-24 — 156
6:1-5 — 191
6:2 — 191

Ephesians
1:3 — 38
1:10 — 37
1:14 — 38
1:22 — 38, 44, 45
2:6 — 38
2:13 — 37
2:19 — 37
4:1 — 37, 39

4:4-6 — 38
4:15 — 37, 45
4:17-24 — 39
4:22-24 — 38
5 — 37-46
5:2 — 38
5:9 — 157
5:15-17 — 45
5:21 — 41, 42
5:21-33 — 18, 172,
　199 – 200
5:21 – 6:9 — 199
5:22 — 41, 199
5:22-33 — 37, 38-46, 95
5:23 — 38, 41
5:24 — 41
5:25 — 23, 49, 199
5:25-28 — 21
5:31 — 45
6:1-4 — 41
6:5-9 — 42

Philippians
2:5-8 — 43
2:26-27 — 43
4:19 — 155

Colossians
1:18 — 44
2:3 — 155
2:10 — 44
2:19 — 44
3:18 — 41
3:18 – 4:1 — 199

1 Thessalonians
1:6 — 156

2 Thessalonians
1:11 — 157

1 Timothy
1:8-11 — 130, 131
2:1-5 — 199
2:13 — 44
5:8 — 50
6:1 — 199

2 Timothy
2:12 — 105
3:12 — 105

Titus
2:1 — 52
2:2-10 — 199
2:4 — 49
2:4-5 — 52
2:5 — 12, 41
2:9 — 41
3:1 — 41

Hebrews
9:27 — 101
12:9 — 41

James
1 — 125

1:12-22 — 146
2:2-9 — 165
4:1 — 162
4:7 — 41

1 Peter
2:13 — 41
2:18 — 41
2:18 — 3:7 — 199
3:1 — 41, 199
3:5 — 141
3:7 — 21, 40, 199
3:15 — 191
5:5 — 41
5:7 — 158

2 Peter
2:9 — 155

1 John
1:9 — 147
2:3 — 102
4:7-11 — 55
4:16 — 156
4:20 — 63

Jude
7 — 127

Revelation
21:4 — 105
22:17 — 194

Subject Index

abomination, defined, 130
abortion, 57, 59, 60, 63-64, 67-100
  and the Bible, 81-87
  and Christianity, 80-87
  Christian consensus on, 77-80
  and the church, 95-96
  church Fathers on, 76-78
  compared to slavery issue, 72-73
  counseling of, 162, 167, 175-82
  and father, 95
  and feminism, 79-80, 98-99
  and Hippocratic Oath, 71
  and humanism, 76
  and mother, 94-95
  in Roman law, 71
  and secularism, 76
  and society, 96-97
  and women's liberation movement, 61,
    63, 102-3
accountability. See personal
  responsibility
active euthanasia, 104-5. See also
  euthanasia
adultery, 130, 132, 195
AIDS (Acquired Immune Deficiency
  Syndrome), 118-19
anger, 157, 179, 182
antislavery movement and women, 3
Athenagoras on abortion, 77
authority, in family, 26-28,
  of husband, 43-44

bestiality, 130

Bible, and abortion, 81-87
  and homosexuality, 125-35
birth control, 68
bitterness, 187

ceremonial law, as part of Levitical laws,
  129-30
children, effect of working mother on,
  7-8, 54
Christ, relationship to church, 42, 45
Christianity and abortion, 80-87
church discipline, 166-67
church Fathers on abortion, 76-78
church, conflict in, 162-66
  and homosexuality, 121-22, 138-39,
    142-43, 147-48
  responsibility on abortion, 94-96
  role in counseling, 149-52, 153-59, 176,
    188
  unity in, 162-66
civil laws, as part of Levitical laws,
  129-30
Clement of Alexandria on abortion,
  77-78
communication, importance of
  in home, 27
  in marriage, 22, 53
counseling, abortion, 175-82
  geriatric care, 175-76, 182-89
  of homosexual, 140-42, 145-47, 191-96
  marital, 162, 169-73
  preventative, 149
  restoration, 149, 153-59

role of church in, 153-59
use of models, 177-88, 194-96
counselor, role of, 161
cultural relativism, 61-62

death with dignity, 101-2. See also
  euthanasia
death. See also euthanasia
  and Jesus, 101-2
  and Paul, 102
defense mechanisms, 186, 193-94
depression, 157
dignity of human life, 175-89
discipline of children, 169, 170
divorce, 30, 155, 163, 176
Dred Scott case of 1857, 72, 76

Equal Rights Amendment, 4
equality in creation, 14
euthanasia, 59, 60, 64, 97, 101-7
Euthanasia Society, 57
existentialism, 22

faithfulness, 157
fall of Adam and Eve, 15, 17, 33
family, authority in, 26-27
  as basic unit of society, 24-25
  biblical principles of, 19-21
  effects of homosexuality on, 117-18
fetus, humanness of, 90-95
forgiveness of God, 149
fornication, 132, 182, 195
fruits of the Spirit, 156-58, 181

gay rights, 109-10
gay. See homosexuality
genetic disorders and
  homosexuality, 113, 116
gentleness, 157
Gibeah, and homosexuality, 126-28
glandular disorders and
  homosexuality, 114
God, fatherhood of, 78
  forgiveness of, 149
  judgment of, 149
goodness, 156-57

headship of husband, 27, 43-46, 50
heart, 194
Holy Spirit, 157, 166, 180, 188, 194, 196
homosexuality, 109-48

causes of, 113-17, 137-39, 144-45
and church, 116, 121-22, 138-39,
  142-43, 147-48
counseling of, 139-40, 142, 145-47
effects on family, 117-18
effects on politics, 120-21
effects on society, 118
in Gibeah, 126
and guilt, 139, 146, 179, 182, 183, 186,
  188, 193, 194
and hostility, 157, 162, 167, 179, 182
and Kingdom of God, 130-31
and learned behavior, 114-15
and Levitical laws, 128-30
medical effects of, 118-19
and New Testament, 130-31
profile of, 111-12, 139, 140, 145,
  191-92
rehabilitation of, 147
in Sodom, 126-27
and Ten Commandments, 128-30
warning signs in children, 191-92
humanism, 61, 62, 63, 64, 75, 89
  and abortion, 76, 149, 153
husband, headship of, 27, 43, 50
  authority of under God, 27, 43

idolatry, 130
infanticide, 59, 60, 62, 77, 78, 79, 96
interpersonal relationship models in
  counseling, 177-88
inversion hypothesis and
  homosexuality, 114
involuntary euthanasia, 104-7. See also
  euthanasia

joy, 156
judgment of God, 149

kindness, 156
Kingdom of God and homosexuality,
  130-31

law of retaliation, 86
learned behavior and homosexuality, 114
lesbian, 111. See also homosexuality
Levitical laws and homosexuality, 128-29
life, beginning of, 62-63, 67, 71, 89-95
  respect for, 59-65
loneliness, 157
love, agape, 43, 49, 54, 55, 149, 156, 182

in marriage, 31-32, 49
phileo, 49, 54

man, created in God's image, 87, 88, 89
  headship over woman, 14
  purpose of God for, 9-12
marital counseling, 163, 169-73
medical effects of homosexuality, 118-19
Minucius Felix on abortion, 77
miscarriage, 84, 86
moral law, as part of Levitical laws,
  129-30
murder, 103
mutual submission, 41-43

narcissism, 24, 79, 114
National Abortion Rights Action League
  (NARAL), 69
New Testament and homosexuality,
  130-31

Old Testament on homosexuality, 125-30
overpopulation, 68

parents, responsibility to child, 92
passive euthanasia, 104-5. See also
  euthanasia
patience, 156
peace, 156
personal responsibility, 149, 153, 189
Plato, view of women, 36
politics, effects of homosexuality on,
  119-20
prayer, 153, 157, 158, 159, 173
premature live birth, 84, 85
preventative counseling, 149

quality of life, 101. See also euthanasia

rebuke, 167
rehabilitation of homosexual, 139-40, 147
relativism, 102-3
repentance, 188
reproof, 166
responsibility
  in home, 26-27
  of parents to child, 92
  personal, 149, 153, 189
restoration counseling, 150, 153-59
right to life, 71, 74-75, 92-93, 102, 162

right to privacy, 71, 74
rights of unborn. See right to life
Roe v. Wade, 70, 71, 72, 76
role, of husband and wife, 29-31,
  33-47, 50
  of women in Greek society, 35-37
  of women in Paul's time, 34-39
  of women in Roman society, 34-35
roles in marriage and feminist
  movement, 30
Rome, respect for life in, 59

scripture. See Bible
secular humanism, 149
secularism and abortion, 76
self-control, 155, 157, 158
self-image, 51, 53, 139, 140, 145, 172,
  173, 191, 194
separation of church and state, 96-97
servanthood in marriage, 41, 43
sexism, defined, 4
sin, 125, 149-52, 153, 179, 188
slavery, compared to abortion, 72-73
society, effects of homosexuality on, 118
soul, creation of, 87-89
stress, 7
submission, 27-28, 34-46
  of wife, 173, 200
subordination, 27-28
suicide, 64, 105
superstition, and value of life, 60

temperance, 155
temptation to sin, 125
Ten Commandments and homosexuality,
  128-30
tension, 7
Tertullian on abortion, 77

unity, in church, 162-66
  of husband and wife, 37
  in submission, 45-46

voluntary euthanasia, 104-5. See also
  euthanasia

wife, as helpmeet, 13
  under authority of husband, 27
  outside employment of, 50-51
  submission of, 173, 200